The media's watching Vault!
Here's a sampling of our coverage.

"For those hoping to climb the ladder of success, [Vault's] insights are priceless."
– *Money magazine*

"The best place on the Web to prepare for a job search."
– *Fortune*

"[Vault guides] make for excellent starting points for job hunters and should be purchased by academic libraries for their career sections [and] university career centers."
– *Library Journal*

"The granddaddy of worker sites."
– *U.S. News & World Report*

"A killer app."
– *The New York Times*

One of Forbes' 33 "Favorite Sites."
– *Forbes*

"To get the unvarnished scoop, check out Vault."
– *Smart Money Magazine*

"Vault has a wealth of information about major employers and job-searching strategies as well as comments from workers about their experiences at specific companies."
– *The Washington Post*

"A key reference for those who want to know what it takes to get hired by a law firm and what to expect once they get there."
– *New York Law Journal*

"Vault [provides] the skinny on working conditions at all kinds of companies from current and former employees."
– *USA Today*

VAULT
> the most trusted name in career information™

VAULT CAREER GUIDE TO

FUNDRAISING & PHILANTHROPY

VAULT CAREER GUIDE TO

FUNDRAISING & PHILANTHROPY

ANNE M. MCCAW
AND THE STAFF OF VAULT

For information about permission to reproduce selections from this book, contact Vault.com
Inc., 150 W. 22nd St., 5th Floor, New York, NY 10011, (212) 366-4212.

Library of Congress CIP Data is available.

ISBN 10: 1-58131-450-7

ISBN 13: 978-1-58131-450-2

Printed in the United States of America

ACKNOWLEDGMENTS

Anne M. McCaw's acknowledgments:

In writing this book, I found myself energized by the dogged determination and unfailing generosity of the professionals and experts who gave me their time and perceptions of the nonprofit world. Each and every person I interviewed made invaluable contributions to the book and continue to provide invaluable service to their communities. So many, many thanks go to Chuck Anderson, Cindy Barrington, Mary Ann Bourbeau, Megan Contakes, Jackie Cook, Mario Diaz, Cameron Dubes, Jessica Fewless, Gardner Flanagan, Tracey Goetchius, Jodie Goldberg, Will Hancock, Andy Johnson, Matt McKean, Steven I. Schneider, Sara Seims, Richard Slutzky, Beth Strachan, Irene Szturo, Lynn Terrill, Meredith Walker, Sally Wells, Doug White, and Bill Wilkins.

I am especially grateful to a close circle of friends and advisors who helped me at every stage of this book—Megan Contakes, Christine Corwin, Jodie Goldberg, Nicole Lungerhausen, Sara Seims, Beth Strachan, Irene Szturo, Sally Wells, Doug White, and Bill Wilkins. I couldn't have asked for a more responsive and insightful group. They carefully read sections of the book in their spare time, introduced me to their friends and colleagues, and provided tremendous moral support.

My editor at Vault, Matt Thornton, also deserves many heartfelt thanks for his guidance and infinite patience as I gathered information for this guide and pounded it into shape. In addition, Sarah DeWeerdt provided sage advice in the final stretch of editing, for which I am deeply grateful.

In addition, I want to thank three women who took the time to mentor me in my own career as a fundraiser—Cathy Card Sterling, Beth Strachan, and Dina Sperling. They went above and beyond the call of duty, and I cannot begin to list all the ways in which they have helped me grow as a person and as a professional.

Finally, I want to thank my family, those present and those who have left us—Ben, Susan, Robert Bruce, Robert Hall, Sally, Peggy, Michelle, Stanley, big James, little James, Calli, and Matthew. They are the enduring influence that spurs me on to make what difference I can in the world.

Vault's acknowledgments:

We are extremely grateful to Vault's entire staff for all their help in the editorial, production and marketing processes. Vault also would like to acknowledge the support of our investors, clients, employees, family and friends. Thank you!

Table of Contents

INTRODUCTION   1

THE SCOOP   3

Chapter 1: History of Fundraising
and Philanthropy   5

The Oldest Profession? 5

Early Thoughts on Charitable Action 8

Origins of Modern American Philanthropy and Fundraising 9

The Booming Business of Fundraising & Philanthropy Today 13

Chapter 2: The Nuts and Bolts of
Fundraising & Philanthropy   17

Philanthropy and the Nonprofit Organization 17

Types of Nonprofit Organizations 19

Where Does the Money Come From? 25

Common Fundraising Jobs 29

Common Philanthropic Giving Jobs 30

Chapter 3: Key Trends   35

Increases in Philanthropic Giving 35

Developments in Fundraising 38

Changes in How We Give Money 40

Fundraising & Philanthropy Highs and Lows 42

The Great Divide between Fundraising and Program Staff 46

Visit Vault at www.vault.com for insider company profiles, expert advice,
career message boards, expert resume reviews, the Vault Job Board and more.

VAULT CAREER LIBRARY   ix

GETTING HIRED 49

Chapter 4: Education and Training 51

Academic Programs 51
Other Classroom Training 52
On-the-Job Training 54

Chapter 5: Resumes and Cover Letters 59

The Winning Resume 59
The Winning Cover Letter 63
Examples of Cover Letters and Resumes 65

Chapter 6: The Interview 77

Interview Process 77
Typical Interview Questions 80
Questions to Ask 83
Negotiating Salary and Benefits 86

Chapter 7: Finding the Right Job 89

Know the Cause 90
Effectiveness of an Organization 91
Choosing the Right Work Environment 95
Transitioning Careers 97

ON THE JOB 103

Chapter 8: Fundamentals of the Field 105

Begging for Money: The Fundamentals of the Job 105
Practical Skills 109
Day-to-Day Activities of a Fundraiser 112
Examples of Effective and Defective Fundraising 117
Day-to-Day Activities of a Philanthropic Giving Professional 121
Examples of Effective and Ineffective Philanthropy 125

Chapter 9: Fundraising and Philanthropic Giving Career Tracks 129

Career Track for Fundraisers 129

Career Track for a Philanthropic Giving Professional 133

The Consulting Path 138

Chapter 10: Fundraising Career Snapshots 143

Institutional Giving/Grant Writer 143

Planned Giving Officer/Specialist 152

Major Gifts Officer 161

Membership/Direct Marketing Specialist 167

Special Events Coordinator 174

Corporate Giving Officer 176

Chapter 11: Philanthropic Giving Career Snapshots 181

Foundation/Program Officer 181

Donor Advisor 189

Social Entrepreneurs and Venture Philanthropists 192

FINAL ANALYSIS 195

APPENDIX 197

Glossary of Terms 199

Key Associations, Web Sites and Resources 207

Selected Bibliography 211

ABOUT THE AUTHOR 215

Visit Vault at **www.vault.com** for insider company profiles, expert advice, career message boards, expert resume reviews, the Vault Job Board and more.

VAULT CAREER LIBRARY

xi

VAULT CAREER GUIDES
GET THE INSIDE SCOOP ON TOP JOBS

"Cliffs Notes for Careers"
– FORBES MAGAZINE

Vault guides and employer profiles have been published since 1997 and are the premier source of insider information on careers.

Each year, Vault surveys and interviews thousands of employees to give readers the inside scoop on industries and specific employers to help them get the jobs they want.

"To get the un-varnished scoop, check out Vault"
– SMARTMONEY MAGAZINE

VAULT

Introduction

Interested in a career in fundraising and/or philanthropy? You are in good company. You are, in fact, entering the ranks of Christian saints and Buddhist monks, the world's greatest thinkers (Plato and Benjamin Franklin, for example), industry giants like Andrew Carnegie, Bill Gates and Warren Buffett, leaders of social change like Booker T. Washington, and celebrities of all sorts, from Robert Redford to Angelina Jolie to Bono.

It is a profession honored throughout time and a practice undertaken by every kind of society and institution—from the Lakota tribe of North America to the villages of Sub-Saharan Africa to the Buddhist temples of Japan to Genghis Khan's Middle Eastern empire. The fundamental principle of the profession —that one should give one's wealth to help the less fortunate and improve the conditions in which we all live—is deeply woven into the fabric of religious doctrine and codified in the earliest laws.

As such, the field of Fundraising & Philanthropy is truly global with opportunity to interact with any and every strata of society. And it is a field that in America alone generates nearly $300 billion a year for social causes and keeps over a million different charitable organizations in America afloat. The role of Fundraising & Philanthropy in American society has never been so prominent, as foundations grow larger, the wealthy grow wealthier, and the nonprofit community grows into an influential sector of the overall economy. In fact, *U.S. News & World Report* recently named fundraising as one of 25 of the best careers to enter.

This guide to Fundraising & Philanthropy covers the wide variety of jobs associated with the business of obtaining and giving money for charitable purposes. We start from the field's noble beginnings and then dive into the down-and-dirty mechanics of securing and distributing funds for social causes. We will also take a look at the people (and their qualifications) charged with bringing in the money for and giving it away to the vast network of charitable groups in the United States.

Notable Quotables

The following poem by Emily Dickinson celebrates the lofty aspirations that characterize the fundraising/philanthropy field, the emotional and spiritual satisfaction of contributing to something greater than ourselves.

Most she touched me by her muteness—

Most she won me by the way

She presented her small figure—

Plea itself—for Charity—

Were a Crumb my whole possession—

Were there famine in the land—

Were it my resource from starving—

Could I such a plea withstand—

Not upon her knee to thank me

Sank this Beggar from the Sky—

But the Crumb partook—departed—

And returned On High—

I supposed—when sudden

Such a Praise began

'Twas as Space sat singing

To herself—and men—

'Twas the Winged Beggar—

Afterward I learned

To her Benefactor

Making Gratitude

There is another apt quote from Aristotle that nicely captures the day-to-day realities of the fundraising professional and the philanthropist:

To give away money is an easy matter in any man's power. But to decide to whom to give it, and how large and when, and for what purpose and how, is neither in every man's power nor an easy matter.

THE SCOOP

Chapter 1: History of Fundraising and Philanthropy

Chapter 2: The Nuts and Bolts of Fundraising and Philanthropy

Chapter 3: Key Trends

History of Fundraising and Philanthropy

Noble as it is, it can be argued that charity has always been a business. Here we describe the evolution of Fundraising & Philanthropy, from early religious doctrine to one of the most dynamic industries in modern day America.

The Oldest Profession?

Organized Fundraising & Philanthropy is in fact as old as civilization itself. The modern terms of philanthropy and charity derive from the Greek and Roman concepts of *philanthropos/philanthropia* (or love of fellow man), *agape* (the Greek term loosely translated as love of others), and *charitas* (the Roman term translated as concern for mankind). Yet centuries before the Greeks established their city-states and the Romans built the Forum, governments, religious institutions and wealthy individuals engaged in what we call philanthropic or charitable activity. One of the earliest references to charitable giving can be found on the tomb walls of an Egyptian nobleman, Harkuf, from the Middle Kingdom chronicling his acts of good will to help the less fortunate more than 4,000 years ago.

Charity and religion

Indeed, the celebration of charitable action is written into the first laws and founding religious texts. The *Book of the Dead* from the Ancient Egyptians (believed to be written in 1500 BCE) decrees that the person who is *maat*— or upright, straight and moral—is one who has helped the unfortunate and needy and will therefore sit with the ruler of the underworld in the Field of Reeds. The concept of *dãna*, loosely translated as giving, is woven into most important Hindu narratives and is described as a basic principle of life and righteous conduct (*dharma*). For the Buddhist, generosity is one of the 10 perfections that one must practice on the path to enlightenment, as written in first compilations of Buddhist teachings, the Tripitaka. For the faithful Jew, the practice of *tzedakah* (sharing what one has with those in need), along with repentance and reflection, is described in the Torah as essential to gaining merit and ensuring good fortune in the coming year. The book of *Corinthians* of the New Testament is largely dedicated to the concept of charity and love of fellow man, which is elevated to the highest of virtues. And the Quran extols the *zakaat*, or alms-giving tax, as one of the five pillars of Islam upon which Muslim life is based.

Visit Vault at **www.vault.com** for insider company profiles, expert advice, career message boards, expert resume reviews, the Vault Job Board and more.

V∧ULT CAREER LIBRARY

5

In keeping with moral precepts, early religious and secular institutions created mechanisms of giving to fulfill this fundamental obligation. Practitioners of Buddhism throughout the Far East received specific instruction on how to provide for monks who would come begging for food. Buddhist temples also undertook fundraising campaigns, known as *kanjin*, to build and maintain orphanages, homes for the elderly, and other public institutions and services. For centuries, a small box or container for donations to charitable causes, known as a *pushke*, has been kept in Jewish households. And long before Christianity emerged as the dominant religion in Europe, church deacons were charged with gathering donations, with each congregation maintaining a treasury of funds to be distributed to the unfortunate. The aristocracy of Iraq, in the days preceding and following the spread of Islam, frequently established family endowments (known as waqfs) to support schools, hospitals and libraries.

Governments intervene

The record of government intervention, often in partnership with wealthy citizens, is equally long and far-reaching. In his code of law inscribed in stone in 2100 BCE, the ruler of ancient Babylon Hammurabi notes that one of his primary purposes in governing is the protection of widows and orphans. Ancient Athenian law required affluent individuals to perform public duties, known as *leitourgia*, usually in the form of donations to theatrical and Olympic events. The ancient Roman with ambitions for public office was expected to sponsor games and theatrical events and to donate funds for the beautification of the city. As is true today, government took a strong philanthropic role in times of war and famine. Athens collected taxes to provide services for widows and veterans of war. Over the course of his reign, Roman Emperor Augustus (63 B.C. to 14 A.D.) provided assistance to 300,000 people in need. In the early centuries of Indian civilization, kings distributed food throughout their provinces when famine struck. Likewise, medieval landowners in China frequently joined locally elected officials in providing assistance to famine-plagued villages. And at the dawn of the settlement of the New World, the Elizabethan Parliament of the early 17th century set the stage for the role that government would play in public welfare by enacting the Statute of Charitable Uses, which officially recognized the responsibility of government to assist the poor and authorized the collection of taxes to provide such assistance.

It all comes down to the individual

It is also important to mention the role that individual religious and secular leaders played in the early practice of Fundraising & Philanthropy. In the third century B.C., one of the greatest rulers of India, Ashoka, fundamentally changed the purpose and function of his government in response to the battle at Kalinga; he and his ministers undertook five-year pilgrimages across the country to spread the word of Buddhism and provide aid to the people. Declaring that benevolence and altruism are innate aspects of human nature, Confucious established the cultural value of philanthropy that Chinese society still adheres to today. For the Western world, the Roman Emperor Constantine, Saint Francis of Assisi and Martin Luther were key players in institutionalizing charitable practices. When declaring Christianity the official religion on the Roman Empire, Constantine also charged the Catholic church with caring for the sick and poor; for the next 1,000 years, the church was the primary welfare institution in Europe, raising money through tithes (or donations of one-tenth of one's income) and other donations. In the 12th century, Saint Francis of Assisi created the first network of laymen (known as Friars) charged with charitable service to the poor, sick and disabled. As part of his battle with the excesses of the Catholic church, Martin Luther established the first formal partnerships between towns and churches to address social problems. His "common chest," which was adopted by communities throughout Europe, formed a central board of citizens (including peasants) to administer and operate charitable efforts, including the collection of donations.

Visit Vault at **www.vault.com** for insider company profiles, expert advice, career message boards, expert resume reviews, the Vault Job Board and more.

VAULT CAREER LIBRARY

7

Early Thoughts on Charitable Action

Hammurabi's Code of Law

That the strong might not injure the weak, in order to protect the widows and orphans ... in order to bespeak justice in the land, to settle all disputes and heal all injuries, [I] set up these my precious words, written upon my memorial stone, before the image of me, as king of righteousness.

Gita (111.13)

He who prepares food for himself [alone], eats nothing but sin ...

King Ashoka of India

Whatever exertion I make, I strive only to discharge the debt that I owe to all living creatures.

Homer, *The Odyssey* (book VI, line 24)

By Jove the stranger and the poor are sent, and what to those we give, to Jove is lent.

Quran 3:86

You will not attain true piety until you voluntarily give of that which you love and whatever you give, God knows of it.

Deuteronomy 15:7-8

If ... there is a needy person among you, do not harden your heart and shut your hand against your needy kinsmen. Rather, you must open your hand and lend him sufficient for whatever he needs.

Lao-Tzu (philosopher and founder of Taoism)

He who obtains has little. He who scatters has much.

2 Corinthians 9:7

God loveth a cheerful giver.

Saint Thomas of Aquinas

Charity is the form, mover, mother and root of all virtues.

Origins of Modern American Philanthropy and Fundraising

Modern philanthropy (or more specifically, philanthropic giving) and fundraising as discussed in this guide is an American product, growing out of the same stalk as the American system of democratic rule. The story begins with the birth of the nation. Initially, the towns that rose out of the first colonies took care of their own, electing an overseer to evaluate the poor and sick and connect the needy with resources that were provided by townspeople. As would seem appropriate from the city of brotherly love, Philadelphia became the center of a new form of philanthropy just a few years before the signing of the Declaration of Independence. Led by Benjamin Franklin, men and women established voluntary associations dedicated to social causes, formalized with written constitutions and governed by a board of officials elected annually. The first association established by Franklin was a kind of support group for mechanics and tradesmen looking to improve themselves through debating, reading circles and other educational activities. While not unique in structure—the first such associations formed in London—these American institutions were the first to be democratic in nature, comprised of tradesmen and their wives rather than the aristocracy. These voluntary associations proliferated, forming the network of charitable organizations that continues to grow and flourish today.

Growth of organized volunteerism

In his seminal chronicle of American life first published in 1835, *Democracy of America*, Alexis de Toqueville took note of the American propensity for forming charitable groups, writing:

"Americans of all ages, all conditions, and all dispositions constantly form … associations of a thousand kinds, religious, moral, serious, futile, general or restricted, enormous and diminutive. The Americans make associations to give entertainments, to found seminaries, to build inns, to construct churches, to diffuse books, to send missionaries to the antipodes; in this manner they found hospitals, prisons and schools. If it is proposed to inculcate some truth or to foster some feeling by the encouragement of a great example, they form a society."

As is true today, these early American associations relied on aggressive fundraising. The strongest and most influential associations attracted support from wealthy individuals and elected officials, who secured a range of

Visit Vault at **www.vault.com** for insider company profiles, expert advice, career message boards, expert resume reviews, the Vault Job Board and more.

V/\ULT CAREER LIBRARY

9

funding from public and private sources. For example, the New York Free School Society was run by the mayor of New York, so it received public funds for overseeing schools for the poor throughout the city. Political influence from association boards and leadership helped many of these groups secure the right to incorporate (which exempted them from taxes and allowed them to obtain property) and to hold fundraising lotteries. Women—especially the wives of politicians, wealthy businessman and religious leaders—played an active role in forming charitable organizations and in fundraising, allowing them to exert political will and promote social change without the right to vote. The first charitable group established and run by women was formed by the Quakers in Philadelphia; the Female Society for the Relief of the Distressed became a model used by other religious groups throughout the country to address the needs of poor women and their children.

Effects of the Civil War

Another significant innovation in the field of Fundraising & Philanthropy emerged after the Civil War, as the South lay in ruins and there was a desperate desire and need to educate newly freed slaves. The federal government established the Freedmen Bureau to empower former slaves, providing them with land, medical care, food and clothing, as well as establishing schools and colleges. However, the agency ultimately could not take on the full range of social services, most importantly education, and soon worked closely with a growing network of volunteers, missionaries, African-American churches and emerging philanthropic foundations to fill in the gaps. Indeed, the first professional foundations (private entities charged with distributing money for social causes) in the United States formed to build educational institutions for African-Americans. Among them were the Peabody Education Fund, established by a banker from Massachusetts, George Peabody, and the John F. Slater Fund, founded by the financier of the same name. Professional administrators and active boards comprised of family members, religious leaders and university presidents ran these foundations, collaborating with education experts and school officials to develop curriculum for emerging schools. A number of African-American educators, the most notable of which was Booker T. Washington, evolved into savvy fundraisers. Washington consulted frequently with the Slater Fund and embarked on a series of speaking tours funded by the foundation to promote mutually agreed upon principles of education. He also aggressively pursued individual donations with written appeals and frequent trips North to meet with wealthy sponsors.

Increasing wealth

The next major evolution of modern Fundraising & Philanthropy was born out of the great wealth amassed by leaders of industry in the late 19th and early 20th centuries. In his essay, *The Gospel to Wealth* published in 1889, Andrew Carnegie dramatically declared that the accumulation of wealth served society as a whole and that the wealthy must make a commitment to curing society's problems. To fulfill his commitment to society, Andrew Carnegie created the Carnegie Corporation as the primary vehicle of his philanthropy, donating an unprecedented $125 million to the venture. *The Gospel of Wealth* became a call to duty that many of his peers heeded. Margaret Olivia Slocum Sage, wife of banker Russell Sage, established the Russell Sage Foundation in 1907 and through it advanced the burgeoning fields of social science and social work. The intention was to carefully study social problems and develop scientifically sound strategies for wiping them out. Similar in approach to the foundations supporting African-American education in the South, these new philanthropic institutions were far more ambitious in scope. John D. Rockefeller Sr.—who had also provided support for the General Education Board, a trust formed in 1902 to assist with the education of African-Americans—created the Rockefeller Foundation in 1913 under the model developed by the Russell Sage Foundation. Today, professionalized foundations still adhere to this approach, carefully assessing social trends and scientific research to target grant giving.

In the first part of the 20th century, Congress enacted laws encouraging a new level of giving among the public at large, further institutionalizing grassroots efforts to raise funds for social causes and institutions. Upon ratification of the 16th Amendment empowering Congress to collect federal taxes without distributing them directly to states, Congress created the first income tax in 1913, and four years later authorized the first tax exemptions for charitable donations.

The community foundation—created with modest individual donations and administered by a board of local bankers, elected officials and other local leaders—also emerged at this time. The first such foundation was founded in 1914 by the president of the Cleveland Trust Company. The mission of the Cleveland Foundation exclusively focused on the well-being of the city's residents and provided a new avenue for prominent local citizens to shape a philanthropic agenda for their community. Over a 15-year period, 21 cities throughout the country formed similar foundations with more than $100,000 in combined assets.

Visit Vault at **www.vault.com** for insider company profiles, expert advice, career message boards, expert resume reviews, the Vault Job Board and more.

VAULT CAREER LIBRARY

11

Over the same period, charitable organizations initiated more and more sophisticated fundraising drives. Looking to the success of a group of Danish postmen in raising funds for charity through the sale of a special stamp at Christmas, Emily Bissell of Wilmington, Delaware, shepherded the first U.S. Christmas seal campaign in 1907, raising $3,000 for a sanitarium caring for tuberculosis patients. The following year, the Christmas seals became a national campaign that continues to this day to support the American Lung Association. Through the efforts of two enterprising volunteers, Charles Sumner Ward and Frank L. Pierce, the YMCA pioneered short-term fundraising campaigns across the country starting in 1903, securing corporate support for advertising and strategic public relations. In 1916, a savvy pastor named Bishop Lawrence worked behind the scenes with the publishers of major New York papers to place stories about the Episcopalian Church's pension fund; the resulting publicity spurred $9 million in donations to the fund. The American Red Cross took fundraising to new level in 1918, when Charles Ward spearheaded a campaign raising $114 million for relief efforts associated with World War I.

Modern philanthropy

In the ensuing decades, the number of charitable groups (known today as nonprofit or not-for-profit organizations) dramatically increased; by 1953, the Internal Revenue Services had registered approximately 50,000 nonprofit groups for tax-exempt status. At the same time, thousands of new private foundations formed; in the early 1960s, more than 1,200 foundations were created each year. And despite the economic hardship brought on by the Great Depression, American wealth and giving grew, especially after World War II; by 1955, giving by individuals, foundations and corporations rose to $7.7 billion. Corporate donations and workplace giving also emerged as important streams of revenue, fueled by the 1934 law allowing corporations a tax deduction for up to 5 percent of their income if donated to charitable causes, the emergence of matching employee gift programs pioneered by General Electric in 1954, and the creation of the combined federal giving campaign in 1961, which provided a mechanism for federal employees to donate some part of their pay check to charitable organizations. In the 1950s, nonprofit organizations hired the first full-time, professional fundraisers, and in 1960, the National Society of Fund Raisers, which eventually became the National Society of Fundraising Executives, and now is the Association of Fundraising Professionals, was founded.

The Booming Business of Fundraising & Philanthropy Today

If ever there was a growth industry, it is the business of serving a cause. The number of charitable organizations has multiplied exponentially in recent decades; since 1989, the number of registered, tax-exempt organizations involved in charitable activities has more than doubled. According to the National Center for Charitable Statistics, nearly 1.5 million such organizations are in operation today—including homeless shelters, performing arts centers, museums, legal aid societies, grant-giving foundations, political advocacy groups and membership organizations (such as trade associations, chambers of commerce and churches), to name just a few. This number does not account for the scores of smaller, informal groups (including many individual church groups and congregations) serving every population, every community and every cause that exists. The National Council of Nonprofit Organizations reports that the expenditures of such organizations total $945 billion in 2003, approximately nine percent of the gross domestic product that year. What is now known as the nonprofit or independent sector has evolved into a vibrant part of American life and its economy, regarded as separate from but in balance with public agencies and private, for-profit businesses.

With such growth, these groups have consistently expanded their staff. For the past 15 years, employment in the sector has increased at an average rate of 2.4 percent, even through the recession in the early 1990s and the more recent economic downturn between 2001 and 2004. This growth is significantly higher than overall employment growth over the same period (1.3 percent) and far outpaced many for-profit industries. The breadth and diversity of the sector has made it difficult to track national employment trends, but the estimate of how many people are currently employed by charitable groups ranges between 8 and 12 million. According to the U.S. Bureau of Labor Statistics and the John Hopkins Center for Civil Society Studies, employment in the independent sector is three times higher than in the entire U.S. agriculture sector, twice as high as that for the transportation industry, and 60 percent higher than either the finance or insurance industries.

Growing pains

Growth also brings many challenges, and the first and foremost on the mind of every leader of a charitable organization is how to raise the necessary money to keep up with increased need and expanding budgets. In a survey of

Visit Vault at **www.vault.com** for insider company profiles, expert advice, career message boards, expert resume reviews, the Vault Job Board and more.

VAULT CAREER LIBRARY   13

more than 700 charitable organizations from across the country conducted by Blackbaud (one of the leading fundraising software companies) in 2006, 65 percent of participating groups reported that their budget increased over the past year, and 72 percent of participants stated that the demand for their services had increased. At the same time, the most pressing concern for these organizations was securing new donations. In 2004, Blackbaud asked more detailed questions about staffing changes and demands. Of the 1,300 organizations that responded, 31 percent said that they were expanding their fundraising staff, and 58 percent stated that they had used a fundraising consultant and will use one in the future.

Recruiters that specialize in finding qualified professionals for charitable organizations—another product of the extraordinary expansion of the sector —confirm that experienced fundraisers are in high demand. One national search firm revealed that more than half of the searches they undertook over a two-year period were for fundraisers. A recent search of one of the most popular job posting sites for charitable organizations, Idealist (www.idealist.org), yielded 933 job openings for full-time fundraisers, approximately one in seven jobs posted on the site and more than any other job category.

It should come as no surprise

The business of fundraising and philanthropic giving is built on Americans' deep commitment to donating money to worthy causes. During the first five years of the 21st Century, we have seen unprecedented philanthropic giving from individuals, foundations, and corporations. According to Giving USA, which publishes an annual report on charitable giving practices, charitable donations in 2005 totaled more than $260 billion, only a fraction of which ($7.4 billion) went to disaster relief efforts for the tsunami in Indonesia, hurricanes in the Gulf Coast, and the earthquake in Pakistan. In 2006, total donations increased to $295 billion. In fact, more than 80 percent of all Americans give to some charitable cause each year, as do more than 70,000 grant-giving foundations, and scores of businesses and corporations. Trends in wealth—especially as the baby boomer generation gets older—only point to more money flowing to charitable causes. By a conservative estimate, $5 trillion will be contributed to charities over the next 50 years through a variety of mechanisms. At current growth rates, there will also be more than 100,000 foundations in operation by 2020.

A maturing field

With so much wealth and so many nonprofit organizations, the field of fundraising and philanthropic giving becomes increasingly diverse, sophisticated and complex. For the fundraiser, the competition for dollars grows ever more intense as wealthy individuals and foundations are bombarded with requests for donations. High-dollar donors also have many different ways to give money. They can hand over funds to a financial advisor who specializes in effective philanthropic giving, set up their own foundation, pool money with other individuals through donor circles, community foundation, or social venture operations, or set up charitable annuities and bequests in order to give steadily over the course of their lifetime. The Internet also adds a new twist to fundraising, as younger generations increasingly conduct all sorts of professional and personal business—including volunteering and charitable giving—from their computer. As a result, there are many different kinds of fundraisers with specialized skills and expertise—from the grant writer who is well versed in crafting a compelling proposal to a foundation to the planned giving officer with in-depth knowledge of the ways in which individuals can give away their wealth over time to the membership specialist focused on the most effective ways to increase the base of supporters who give small amounts each year.

Likewise, there is an ever-widening variety of specialized professionals involved in assisting individuals in giving their money away. At one time, individuals might consult their family lawyer or accountant. Today there are managers of donor-advised funds who manage assets of their clients solely for philanthropic giving—both at community foundations and at the most prominent financial institutions. There are consulting firms focused on creating effective foundations and social venture groups aimed at applying for-profit business practices to building the capacity of nonprofit organizations. There are also organizations (both for-profit and nonprofit) tracking giving trends and researching best practices in giving and nonprofit management. These include associations of grant-makers, university programs, groups like the Foundation Center and Independent Sector, and organizations with extensive web resources like Guidestar.

In short, business is booming for Fundraising & Philanthropy. However, fundraisers and philanthropists need to know far more than how to ask for money or to whom to write a check.

Visit Vault at **www.vault.com** for insider company profiles, expert advice, career message boards, expert resume reviews, the Vault Job Board and more.

VAULT CAREER LIBRARY   15

The Nuts and Bolts of Fundraising & Philanthropy

In the largest sense, philanthropy refers to any activity to improve society—to make communities safer, to shelter the unfortunate, to heal the sick, to give voice to the underserved, to feed the needy, among other important goals. Government agencies—from city-run homeless shelters to state art commissions, to federal welfare programs—play an enormously important philanthropic role. But from the perspective of most Americans today, the wide variety of nonprofit or not-for-profit institutions is the heart of modern philanthropy. This guide focuses almost exclusively on careers associated with these institutions, specifically those having the responsibility of raising the money to keep the organizations going. To avoid confusion, we will use the term *philanthropic giving* from this point forward to describe the work of the professionals who give money away to worthy causes, rather than the more general term of *philanthropy*, which is associated with the good works of nonprofit organizations to address a social problem or cause.

Philanthropy and the Nonprofit Organization

As direct descendents of the associations first created by Benjamin Franklin, modern nonprofit organizations are, in the simplest of terms, entities with some formal structure that do not distribute any profits to its owners or leadership, but rather devote all resources toward a cause. As you can imagine, such a definition covers a staggeringly broad range of organizations—youth clubs, churches, schools, trade associations, free clinics, homeless shelters, hospitals, libraries, museums, advocacy groups, dance and theater troupes, to name just a few. While it is not required, most of these groups incorporate themselves under the laws of the state in which they operate, primarily to prevent lawsuits against individual staff members, volunteers and directors when someone claims negligence or other wrongdoing on the part of the organization itself. Nonprofit groups vary widely in size and shape, but most are required under state law to establish a board of directors ultimately responsible for the policies, practices and overall direction of the organization. The vast majority of these governing boards are comprised of volunteers, as was true in the days of Benjamin Franklin. Similarly, savvy organizations try to recruit board members with political and/or financial clout. Most nonprofits also have a formal leadership structure (an executive director or president at the very least) responsible for overseeing day-to-day operations.

Visit Vault at **www.vault.com** for insider company profiles, expert advice, career message boards, expert resume reviews, the Vault Job Board and more.

VAULT CAREER LIBRARY   17

Tax exemption status

Generally, nonprofit organizations also apply for tax-exempt status under the federal tax code. Such exemptions have been in place since the modern tax code was in enacted, but today's tax-exempt designations emerged in 1954, when Congress approved the first major overhaul of the code. Under current federal law, there are several tax exemption categories for nonprofit groups, depending on their activities. Most groups are public-serving organizations, as outlined in section 501(c)(3) of the Internal Revenue Code. As defined in section 501(c)(3), such as a group must be "a public charity or private foundation, which is established for purposes that are religious, educational, charitable, scientific, literary, testing for public safety, fostering of national or international amateur sports or prevention of cruelty to animals and children." A 501(c)(3) nonprofit organization is not only exempt from federal taxes (and in most cases state taxes as well), but they are also allowed to receive donations that individuals can deduct from their personal income taxes. It is important to note that the 501(c)(3) category covers both charitable organizations that provide services or advocate for a cause and the foundations and other institutions that fund these groups. You should also be aware that there are other tax exempt designations for nonprofit groups; for example, organizations exclusively devoted to lobbying and political activities can apply for tax exempt status under section 501(c)(4) of the Internal Revenue Code. Such groups can also seek donations, but these gifts are not tax deductible.

Types of Nonprofit Organizations

The sheer size and diversity of the nonprofit sector can be daunting to contemplate. With so many different groups taking different approaches to different causes, it's more than a little difficult to talk about the general character or personality of nonprofit organizations.

The IRS, the U.S. Bureau of Labor Statistics and numerous universities and think tanks that study the sector do lump nonprofit organizations into several different categories largely based on approach and purpose. The most common categories used are *health, education, social or human services, religious, civic* and *advocacy, international relief and development, arts and culture* and *funders*. It's a crude kind of taxonomy and definitely not infallible, since many nonprofits fall into more than one category. (The IRS and Bureau of Labor Statistics use a more complicated classification system to capture specific information about the number and kinds of nonprofits; for instance, they try to determine how many community hospitals there are or how many nonprofit theater groups.) But organizations that exemplify one category or another do share with one another characteristics in size, infrastructure, and to some extent, the kinds of people who work there.

What follows is a brief description of each category of nonprofit organizations to provide you with broad sense of how particular nonprofits may operate. Read on with the following disclaimer in mind—you will always find a nonprofit that defies classification.

Health organizations

Health organizations—such as hospitals, clinics, nursing homes, hospice facilities and drug rehabilitation centers—take up the largest piece of the nonprofit pie, in terms of revenue, expenses and the number of people they employ. According to the latest version of the *Nonprofit Almanac* published by the Urban Institute, more than half the revenue earned by or contributed to the entire nonprofit sector goes to organizations providing health services. Perhaps because of their relative wealth, or the demands of physicians, salaries at health organizations (especially hospitals) tend to be among the highest in the nonprofit world. Along with healing the sick, health organizations nurture extensive bureaucracies to deal with stringent state and federal regulations, concerns about patient privacy and the need to navigate complicated health insurance programs—including Medicare and Medicaid—which provide the lion's share of revenue. In some health organizations, politics may go hand in hand with treatment of the sick;

Visit Vault at **www.vault.com** for insider company profiles, expert advice, career message boards, expert resume reviews, the Vault Job Board and more.

V/\ULT CAREER LIBRARY   **19**

hospital associated with universities will have interns, residents and researchers vying for the best residencies, teaching and administrative positions. Different departments at a hospital competing with one another for funding, especially to support clinical research. Facilities focused on community health (including hospice care and community hospitals) are known to have warmer, friendlier environments. It's important to remember that even if you are squirreled away in the administrative offices as a fundraiser, sickness and death will be a part of your everyday existence. For all who work at health organizations—whether in the emergency room or in the back office — sickness and death are a part of everyday existence. Some find it fulfilling, others find it depressing.

Educational institutions

Primarily universities, colleges, and private, independent schools (meaning those that are not part of the system of public schools), educational institutions are the second-largest category based on revenue and employment. For the most part, universities and schools rely heavily on tuitions, as well as funding from individuals, foundations, and state and federal agencies. Schools are also among the oldest American nonprofit institutions; indeed Harvard University, which was founded in 1638, is considered to be the first nonprofit in the U.S. Thus many schools have a strong sense of history which staff and alumni are rather proud of. There is, however, a big difference in the size, infrastructure and organizational culture between a university and an independent school. Universities are large (employing hundreds of people), hierarchical and extremely political places, exacerbated by the fact that professor/scholars tend to have strong personalities. So associate professors jockey for tenure, tenured professors squabble among themselves about their scholarly pursuits and publishing opportunities, and different departments fiercely compete for dollars. Given their size and the myriad demands for resources, universities maintain large fundraising programs with well-paid staff. Independent schools—ranging from Montessori to Catholic to boarding—are considerably smaller. Some mimic universities in style and structure, but most are far less formal. Fundraising teams are also small with as little as two staff. Salaries are also considerable smaller than at universities. Many independent schools have religious affiliations, which employees may be expected to uphold.

Social or human service agencies

This category encompasses a broad array of groups that provide resources and services for the disabled and disenfranchised, including legal aid societies, housing assistance programs and homeless shelters, soup kitchens, job training centers, child welfare groups, day care operations, immigrant assistance organizations, rape crisis centers and mental health counseling facilities, among many, many others. While this class of nonprofits places third in terms of total revenue for the sector, the sheer number of such groups far exceeds any other category. As a result, many scholars in the nonprofit field describe social service agencies as the face of the nonprofit world, the kind of group that most people think of when they hear the word "nonprofit." Most social service operations heavily rely on state and federal funding, either through grants or contracts and are therefore subject to myriad regulations from those for food preparation to client privacy. Social service agencies also wrestle with establishing rigorous and somewhat cumbersome self-evaluation processes, since many government agencies and private foundations award contracts and grants based on performance. Aside from organizations like the Salvation Army, Catholic Charities or the YMCA, most social services groups are small and lean without much of infrastructure beyond what is required of them by state agencies and the federal government. Most are run by clinicians and social workers, a generally caring, compassionate bunch with little experience in the day-to-day management of nonprofit organizations.

The category of religious organizations

Congregations of various religious sects (Christian, Muslim, Jewish, Buddhist, etc.) and any denominations or associations under which congregations may organize constitute the category of religious organizations. There are many hospitals, schools, social services agencies and advocacy groups with religious affiliations (such as the Salvation Army or Catholics for Free Choice), but these organizations fall under the category of the cause that they serve or the assistance they provide. The primary purpose of a congregation is to offer religious guidance and education to the individuals that belong to it, while denominations are regional or national associations that provide additional leadership and support services to individual congregations. It is important to note that a congregation in any given community may be completely independent from a particular denomination. While there are a few large congregations with several paid staff, most are very small and run entirely by volunteers, aside from the priest,

Visit Vault at **www.vault.com** for insider company profiles, expert advice, career message boards, expert resume reviews, the Vault Job Board and more.

V**A**ULT CAREER LIBRARY   **21**

pastors, ministers, rabbis, etc., providing religious instruction. Likewise, any social services that a congregation provides (such as clothes or housing to the needy) are almost entirely volunteer operations. And as you would expect, congregations are almost entirely reliant on donations from its members. As you would expect, the character of congregations and denominations is determined by the structure and culture of the faith, the religious leadership and the individual members.

Civic and advocacy organizations

These organizations comprise a relatively small (in terms of revenue and number of people they employ) category of nonprofits focused on changing policies around a particular issue or problem. Such prominent groups as the Sierra Club, National Organization for Women, American Civil Liberties Union, National Association for the Advancement of Colored People, American Association of Retired People and the Christian Coalition fall into this category, as well as a range of smaller groups focused on specific issues in their communities. Generally these groups engage in four basic activities: (1) educating and organizing people to engage their local policy-makers (county commissioners, state agencies, Members of Congress, etc.); (2) generating interest in an issue with the media; (3) analyzing changes in policy and educating the general public on their impact; and, (4) directly advocating for policy changes with local, state and federal officials. Many of these groups are centered in major metropolitan areas near seats of government. As you would expect, the largest groups have headquarters in Washington, D.C. Advocacy organizations are not political action committees or private lobbying firms, and as public institutions are subject to strict regulations regarding direct lobbying of policy-makers. Most receive very little support from government agencies. Rather the major sources of funding are individuals, corporations and foundations (although foundations have requirements on what kind of advocacy activities they can support). Core staff at advocacy groups is usually comprised of some combination of lawyers, public relations and communications specialists, and organizers who tend to be passionate, driven and somewhat aggressive. The pace at advocacy groups can be more intense, especially when Congress and state legislatures are in session. Some find it energizing, while others quickly burn out.

International relief and development groups

Known abroad as nongovernmental organizations (NGOs), international relief and development groups focus on activities to improve the quality of life for communities outside of the United States, primarily in developing countries. Groups like the American Red Cross and Oxfam provide immediate, direct relief in the wake of war and natural disasters, while other groups devote time and energy to education and building local economies. This category of nonprofits also includes organizations who do not provide direct assistance to communities but peripherally impact quality of life— environmental organizations like The Ocean Conservancy and Conservation International are examples. Most groups also have a dual focus on direct relief activities and advocacy. According to the *Nonprofit Almanac*, more than 5,000 such groups are incorporated in the United States. The majority of the United Nation's and U.S. government's humanitarian relief funds are funneled through these international groups, which usually have headquarters in Washington, D.C., or New York (to connect more directly to the United Nations), as well as field offices in the countries where they work. The rest of the staff at these international groups is usually comprised of policy experts from the U.S. and abroad with field staff who are largely from the country in which they are working. In some countries, field staff are at considerable risk from terrorism and civil strife, and most are used to living without much luxury. With a truly global workforce, cultural difference is a challenge, especially in navigating different communication styles.

"Arts and culture" organizations

These organizations include community and professional theaters, dance companies, nonprofit art galleries and museums, orchestras and symphonies, literary and cultural magazines, as well as a range of arts appreciation groups. While there are almost as many arts groups in the country as there are in health care, the arts community is far less wealthy. Revenue to health care groups is in fact 25 times greater than what goes to the arts. Salaries are therefore considerably smaller at arts organizations. Most revenue comes from ticket sales, so marketing and audience development is an important concern and a constant challenge. Art organizations also tend to work in close partnership with schools to support arts education programs. They also try to foster relationships with corporate interests that see a variety of opportunities to elevate their profile through the arts. Most arts groups struggle to keep qualified and experienced administrative staff because of the lower salaries, long hours (especially when working for a performance group) and the strong temperament of artistic directors and boards. It is not at all unusual for highly public and bitter fights to break out between boards and organizational leadership over the artistic direction of an organization. That

Visit Vault at **www.vault.com** for insider company profiles, expert advice, career message boards, expert resume reviews, the Vault Job Board and more.

VAULT CAREER LIBRARY   23

said, the passion, dedication and talent of artists involved with these organizations is intoxicating.

Funders

Like private foundations and federated charities, grant-giving organizations fall into the "funders" category. These groups generally do not engage in any other activity other than giving away money, although there are exceptions, such as the Pew Charitable Trusts, which provides grants and is also involved in advocacy work. While private foundations like the Ford Foundation are the most commonly known, there are in fact a variety of nonprofit organizations that function as grant givers. Federated charities are organizations that collect donations from individuals and distribute them to a chosen group of nonprofit organizations. Those charities that wish to receive funds usually go through an application process to demonstrate that they are legal and viable nonprofits. Most people are familiar with the United Way, but there are other such groups, such as Jewish federations and societies that raise funds for research and treatment of diseases—an example is the Leukemia and Lymphoma Society. Investment firms can also establish donor-advised funds that are registered as nonprofit organizations. These funds are comprised of donations from wealthy individuals and are managed by a financial advisor who may either follow the instructions of the donor on which charities to support or may make those decisions on their own. Most community foundations also create donor-advised funds to help donors in any given location be effective in their philanthropy. Like other nonprofit organizations, a board of directors (usually known as the board of trustees) oversees the general direction of grant-giving. A professional staff of financial advisors, policy experts and those with expertise in nonprofit management make day-to-day decisions about how to wisely invest the pool of funds and how to distribute grants. Like the rest of the nonprofit sector, there are far more small family foundations and donor-advised funds run by one or two staff than large, professional foundations run by many. The larger foundations and federated charities generally pay well and provide rather generous benefits. As we will discuss later in the guide, jobs at foundations are among the most competitive in the fundraising and philanthropic giving field.

Where Does the Money Come From?

As a fundraiser or philanthropic giving professional working for any given nonprofit organization, it is your job to supply the money needed to allow that nonprofit organization to carry out its mission. Like any successful business, a nonprofit tries to tap as many income streams as possible, for it never makes sense to rely solely on one of a handful of donors. After all, donors die or lose their fortunes, foundations change strategic direction or become disenchanted with an organization. A stable revenue base should be comprised of many kinds of donors giving in many different kinds of ways. Generally, donations (or "contributed revenue") fall into one of the following categories:

Membership gifts

Small-sized donations—usually somewhere between $10 and $999—are referred to as membership gifts, and many (but not all) nonprofit organizations build some kind of membership program focused on expanding the pool of individuals who give a small amount on an annual basis. To recruit new donors, nonprofits launch membership drives at least once a year, including solicitations by mail (also known as direct mail marketing), requests via e-mail and telemarketing. The most well known of these membership or pledge drives are those held by public broadcasting stations either every six months or every quarter. Many nonprofit organizations, like public broadcasting stations, offer awards depending on the size of the gift— mugs, T-shirts, subscriptions to newsletters and magazines, free passes to exhibits and shows, etc. The strategy behind membership programs will be described in more detail in connection to the fundraising professionals who oversee them, but the basic principle is that an organization invests in bringing new members on board; the investment is returned over time when the individual gives year after year after year, and when their small donations increase over time. In the best of all worlds, someone who gives at a modest level at first eventually becomes a major donor (described below).

Membership programs may also be important to advancing the mission, especially if the nonprofit is involved in grassroots organization. It's logical to assume that individuals who give money to an organization care about the issue and are easily tapped to get involved in letter-writing campaigns to public officials, boycotts of corporations, shareholder resolutions, protests and litigation. Many organizations also count employee matching gifts from corporations in this category of contributions. These are where an employee

Visit Vault at **www.vault.com** for insider company profiles, expert advice, career message boards, expert resume reviews, the Vault Job Board and more.

VAULT CAREER LIBRARY   25

gives a modest donation to a group and submits a request to his or her employer to donate the same amount. Likewise, donations through the Combined Federal Campaign—the workplace-giving program managed by the federal government that helps federal employees give donations to designated charities—all into the membership category.

Major donors

An individual who gives a large or major gift to an organization is known as a "major donor." Depending on their size, organizations have different thresholds for major gifts; for a small nonprofit with a budget of less than $1 million, a gift of $100 may put you in the major donor category. Larger organizations generally think of major donors as those that give $1,000 or more. Securing a major gift requires some relationship-building over time with the hope that the individual will increase his or her donations and invest in a number of ways, such as connecting friends and business partners to the organization, endorsing a grant proposal if he or she is on the board of a foundation, donating stock from the public company that he or she owns, or leaving a bequest to the organization in his or her will. A savvy fundraiser will assess an individual's ability and interest to give to the organization and then decide how much of an investment to make in that relationship. For instance, if you know from an initial meeting or phone call that an individual lives on a fixed income and at most will give $1,000 a year, it is probably not worth the time to meet face-to-face more than once a year. An individual with the potential of giving millions of dollars and who has powerful friends is worth engaging in any number of ways, including with an invitation to serve on the organization's board of directors.

Grants

A gift from an institution—such as a foundation, government agency or corporation—is usually called a "grant." In most cases, there is a formal process for requesting and receiving a grant, where an organization seeking support submits a written proposal describing its mission and the activities that a grant would fund. The grant-giving entity then reviews a number of proposals at any given time and decides if and how to fund them. Once a grant is awarded, the grant-giving organization (or grantor) often requires that the nonprofit receiving the grant (or grantee) submit a written report describing the work funded by the grant. The size of grants and grant-giving entities varies widely. There are small family foundations that give no more than $1,000 to any particular nonprofit in a year, and there are large, highly professional and sophisticated foundations that give millions of dollars annually. Under the partnership with Warren Buffett, the Bill & Melinda Gates Foundation is now charged with giving away more than $3 billion each year. The size, shape and structure of foundations will be discussed in more detail later on in this guide.

Events

Nonprofit organizations also secure contributions through public events— conferences, marathons, lecture series, theater productions and dinners— where individuals and corporations pay to participate. Many events are highly visible in specific communities and nationally, such as the Black and White ball held for the San Francisco Symphony and the various AIDS bike rides across the country. Nonprofits hope for high turnout at these events not only to raise money, but also to raise awareness about an issue. Events are also important vehicles for establishing relationships with small businesses and corporations that enjoy the publicity that comes with a successful and high-profile event. To this end, nonprofit organizations encourage donors to sponsor events and offer a variety of ways to recognize and highlight these sponsors. The size of the donation dictates the level of recognition, as well as other perks, such as seats at a dinner table and opportunities to meet with well-known speakers. Naturally, those donors that give the largest gifts receive the most publicity and recognition.

Planned giving

Individuals can also donate cash, property or other assets—including artwork, life insurance policies and retirement funds—either over time or upon their death. Such donations are known as "planned gifts," and they come in a variety of structured arrangements, some of which are relatively simple, like a bequest written into a will, and others that are more complicated. Planned gifts should be arranged by someone with technical expertise (a lawyer is usually involved) and can be of great benefit to both the organization and the individual. Such gifts provide substantial tax breaks both for donors while they are living, as well as for their families upon death. Certain charitable trusts and annuities can also be a source of income for the donor. There are many examples, including a charitable remainder trust, where an individual promises to donate property and/or assets and receives a fixed payment over time until death. After, the property and/or assets are officially turned over to the nonprofit. The largest planned gift in history is the pledge that Warren Buffett has made to donate the bulk of his fortune in the form of company

Visit Vault at **www.vault.com** for insider company profiles, expert advice, career message boards, expert resume reviews, the Vault Job Board and more.

VAULT CAREER LIBRARY   **27**

stock to the Bill and Melinda Gates Foundation. Planned gifts also allow people of modest means to establish a legacy in their community or for a cause with their accumulated assets. For example, a janitor in a small town in Indiana bequeathed more than $200,000 to the elementary school where he worked and to the local community foundation, and a handyman bequeathed more than $1.4 million to New York City after the September 11 terrorist attacks. For a nonprofit organization, planned gifts from charitable remainder trusts and other such vehicles can provide a reliable stream of income over many years. Moreover, a charitable bequest can be the largest gift an organization receives in a given year. In the ideal situation, a sophisticated fundraiser will help her most enthusiastic donors arrange planned gifts in addition to an annual donation of cash or stock.

In-kind gifts

Expertise, volunteer time, office space or supplies are also important contributions known as "in-kind gifts." While these may not have a dollar amount directly attached, many organizations keep track of them like other charitable contributions, and some grant-giving entities require that an organization account for the value of in-kind gifts when generating a budget for a program or project. In-kind gifts of space, food or the waiving of a speaker's fee can be particularly important for fundraising events, and we will discuss later in this guide some of the strategies that event planners use to secure them.

Nonprofit organizations may also derive revenue from services, products or other assets, like a for-profit business. For example, a facility that provides counseling services for women and their families may charge a nominal fee for one-on-one counseling or support groups. Likewise, a nonprofit theater generally charges for admission to performances. Nonprofits may also hold valuable property (such as buildings or land) that can also provide income. Or a nonprofit group may sell products, such as publications. In the past decade, a number of nonprofit organizations have experimented with more creative ways of generating "earned revenue." For example, some have established companion for-profit businesses to support the work of the nonprofit. Some have also developed partnerships with foundations, government agencies, and venture capitalists to pool resources and direct investments toward social causes. The range of social venture enterprises will be described in a later chapter of this guide.

Common Fundraising Jobs

With the demand to raise more money each year and the numerous ways in which donors give, most nonprofit organizations employ a team of fundraisers. At a small nonprofit organization with budgets of less than $1 million, there may be one or two fundraisers—also known as development professionals, which is shorthand for either resource or donor development— who manage all kinds of donors. At these smaller groups, there is usually a "director of development" who oversees all fundraising activities, and a "development associate" who provides support and may manage one particular aspect of fundraising, such as the membership program. Larger organizations employ a team of fundraisers comprised of specialists. There are many different titles that usually refer to the kind of donors that the fundraiser interacts with. A fully staffed team typically includes some combination of the following:

- *Director of development*, who oversees all aspects of fundraising
- *Membership director or coordinator*, who oversees a membership program
- *Major giving officer(s)*, who focuses on major donors
- *Grant writer or institutional relations manager*, who focuses on securing grants
- *Special events coordinator or manager*, who supervises fundraising events for the organization
- *Planned giving officer*, who focuses on arranging planned gifts
- *Development associate or assistant*, who provides administrative support

As you would expect, the largest nonprofit organizations employ a whole department of development professionals focused on each category of donation and even subcategories; for instance, an organization may have one grant writer focused on government agencies and another on private foundations. The following charts below provide examples of different fundraising teams. The makeup and structure will vary depending on size, resources of the nonprofit and salary demands in any given community, conflicts of interest that the nonprofit organization would consider and the nature of the organization's work. For example, an advocacy organization with a focus on changing federal policy is unlikely to have a fundraiser to secure grants from federal agencies because the organization wants to maintain absolute independence from the government. However, that same advocacy group may depend on grassroots organizing and therefore employs both a membership coordinator focused on direct mail appeals and a

Visit Vault at **www.vault.com** for insider company profiles, expert advice, career message boards, expert resume reviews, the Vault Job Board and more.

VAULT CAREER LIBRARY   29

specialist charged with building and maintaining a robust electronic membership program.

It is also important to note that a nonprofit organization's board of directors usually plays a crucial role in fundraising. An organization's board may include the largest donors, corporate executives and even the leadership at private foundations. An executive director and the fundraising team can therefore spend a good deal of time coordinating the fundraising activities of the board, or simply encouraging board members to give.

Common Philanthropic Giving Jobs

On the philanthropic giving front, there are professionals with general expertise, usually lawyers and financial advisors who provide a full range of financial services for individuals and companies. However, the philanthropic giving professionals discussed in this guide are specialists in particular kind of gift giving. While fundraising operations generally follow the team models outlined previously, it is difficult to describe the typical philanthropic giving team, especially as new models for giving (such as social venture enterprises) emerge. So here are just a few examples of philanthropic giving specialists:

- Private foundations usually have an executive director overseeing all grant giving and foundation program officers who focus on a particular part of the foundation's mission. A larger foundation may have many different giving initiatives and therefore employs several program officers. For example, a foundation that gives to the arts, the environment and education may have program officers assigned to each of those areas.

- State and federal government agencies offer a range of grant-giving programs, which are usually supervised by one or more grants administrators.

- Corporations may establish a separate foundation that operates like any other, or may distribute funds through a community development or community affairs department, usually run by a director of community relations.

- There are also financial advisors who specialize in philanthropic giving for wealthy individuals. They assist their clients with establishing foundations and charitable trusts, and often serve as the primary administrators. They also assist with investment strategies to allow these trusts to grow.

• There are other forms of grant-giving organizations that function like other nonprofits, both raising money for their own purposes and also dispersing grants. The most well known of these are United Way organizations that operate across the country, seeking donations from small businesses and corporations in their communities, which are then distributed to various nonprofit organizations that have signed up for the program. Like other nonprofits, they have an executive director (or CEO), as well as fundraising or resource development staff charged with securing donations and in-kind support for the United Way itself. In addition, various program staff provide assistance in distributing donations and in evaluating grant proposals from community groups.

• The social venture enterprise is a rather new invention in the philanthropic world generally defined as a hybrid of nonprofit and for-profit business models focused on social change. There are many different kinds of social venture enterprises, from for-profit businesses focused on social causes (such as reforming public education) to partnerships between investors, foundations and investment firms to expand resources directed at a social issue (such as employment in low-income neighborhoods). The social venture model is still in an experimental phase, so it is difficult to characterize in general terms the kinds of social venture professionals. Later we will provide some examples of these professionals, such as entrepreneurs who establish for-profit businesses with a mission to financial specialists who design financing schemes for directing money toward a cause.

In addition, there is an ever-growing pool of consultants with expertise in every aspect of fundraising and philanthropic giving, from overall strategic planning to database management to development of membership programs to grant proposal writing to independent financial advisors. Consulting can be quite lucrative, and many seasoned professionals turn to freelancing as an alternative to full-time employment at a nonprofit organization, corporation or foundation.

Visit Vault at **www.vault.com** for insider company profiles, expert advice, career message boards, expert resume reviews, the Vault Job Board and more.

VAULT CAREER LIBRARY   31

Examples of Fundraising or Development Teams

Team for a Small Nonprofit Organization (budget of $750,000)

Executive Director (spends 50 percent of his/her time meeting with donors and coordinating fundraising activities of the board of directors)

Director of Development (coordinates overall fundraising strategy, supervises development associate, and undertakes cultivation of major donors and fundations)

Development Associate (provides administrative support and oversees the membership program)

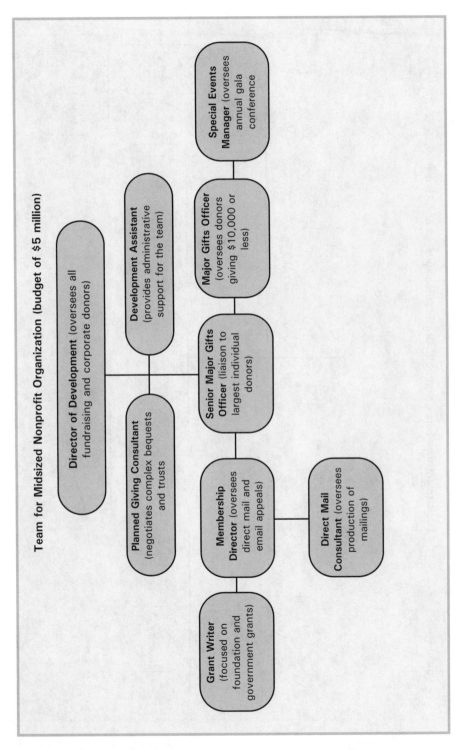

Team for Midsized Nonprofit Organization (budget of $5 million)

Director of Development (oversees all fundraising and corporate donors)

Development Assistant (provides administrative support for the team)

Special Events Manager (oversees annual gala conference)

Major Gifts Officer (oversees donors giving $10,000 or less)

Senior Major Gifts Officer (liaison to largest individual donors)

Planned Giving Consultant (negotiates complex bequests and trusts)

Membership Director (oversees direct mail and email appeals)

Direct Mail Consultant (oversees production of mailings)

Grant Writer (focused on foundation and government grants)

Visit Vault at **www.vault.com** for insider company profiles, expert advice, career message boards, expert resume reviews, the Vault Job Board and more.

V∧ULT CAREER LIBRARY   33

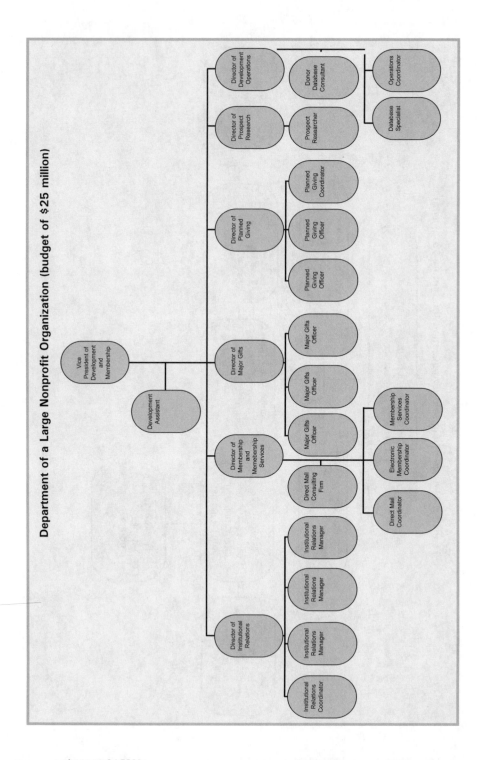

Department of a Large Nonprofit Organization (budget of $25 million)

Key Trends

While the history of fundraising and philanthropic giving in America is long, the field has only recently evolved into a sophisticated profession and practice. Fundraising and philanthropic giving professionals now have a lot to keep up with—from emerging technologies to attract donors to new scrutiny brought to bear by legislators concerned about the high-profile scandals. The following is a general discussion of major trends that impact the everyday lives of these professionals. It is also important to note that there are trends related to particular fields of giving—education, arts, conservation, voter education, communications and media. These trends are not discussed in this guide, but warrant further research on your part as you learn more about the field.

Increases in Philanthropic Giving

Nearly $300 billion was donated to charities in 2006, a new record that dwarfs charitable giving from before the dot-com boom. As part of this giving trend, foundations continue to proliferate, as does the amount of money they distribute to worthy causes. But the upward trend in giving isn't the whole story.

More money, more competition for dollars

In fact, the rapid growth of the nonprofit sector has made fundraising and philanthropic giving all the more difficult. Moreover, public funding for nonprofit organizations from federal, state and local government agencies continues in a downward trend. While many larger organizations flourish, most nonprofit groups are working harder than ever at fundraising, and many midsized and smaller groups have great difficulty raising money to maintain skeletal staff. One United Way in the middle of the country was able to increase its donations in 2006, but not enough to pay for all the staff it needed to raise that money and keep the organization going.

Both fundraisers and philanthropic giving professionals find themselves feeling the pressure—the pressure from executive directors to obtain resources from what often seems like a limited pool, especially for smaller groups who do not have access to the wealthiest donors. Thoughtful planning in cultivating relationships and mapping organizational growth is a requirement in a world of increasing competition, where fundraisers try to distinguish their group from the pack and philanthropic giving professionals try to make strategic decisions when they have more requests for funding than they can possibly fulfill.

Deeper investment, greater control

Foundation officers have long seen themselves as much more than administrators of grant-giving programs, but rather leaders in social change. Now many wealthy individuals are taking on a similar role, wishing to exert more control over the organizations for which they have become patrons. More and more, foundations and wealthy donors require sophisticated and lengthy proposals describing how their money will make a positive impact. Donors of all sorts are also trying to facilitate new ways of thinking about age-old social problems. Large foundations and community foundations especially are engaged in the actual strategy of social change, from hosting planning sessions with different interest groups to defining advocacy, communications and outreach strategies themselves. The risk for nonprofit organizations is that they allow their donors to define the direction of work, rather than investigate and evaluate their own strategies and activities. Fundraisers are often caught in the middle of such situations, wanting to make their fundraising goal but understanding that program staff need to distinguish between work that the foundations think is necessary and work that fulfills the mission of a nonprofit. The philanthropic giving professional needs to make careful decisions of when and when not to intervene with grantees.

Emphasis on partnerships

The growth of the nonprofit sector and greater competition for donations has also led many philanthropic giving entities, especially foundations, to strongly encourage (or even require) partnerships among nonprofits that work on similar issues or provide similar services. Given that many donors are deeply invested in issues and communities, they have a good sense of where there might be duplication of effort. For the fundraiser, it is important to understand a nonprofit's unique role around an issue or within a community and to be familiar with the range of partner groups with which the nonprofit is affiliated. Often, the fundraiser reminds her colleagues engaged in the work of a nonprofit of other nonprofits that perform similar work and can help identify the services and expertise they provide that complements communitywide efforts to affect change. Philanthropic giving professionals should spend a great deal of time studying the mechanics of partnerships to understand how to strengthen and replicate them. They should also understand when a partnership should dissolve, including those between funders.

Scrutiny on nonprofits

From The Nature Conservancy's questionable loans to board members to embezzlement at the United Way to disgraced lobbyist Jack Abramoff's use of a nonprofit foundation to direct money toward lobbying trips, a number of scandals have turned the spotlight on nonprofits, grant-giving organizations, and their financial and administrative practices. Over the past several years, there have been a number of Congressional hearings focused on many different aspects of charitable giving and nonprofit accountability. Members of Congress—led by Iowa Senator Chuck Grassley—and the Internal Revenue Service have proposed policies to tighten oversight, from changing tax law to limit deductions on certain kinds of contributions to greater disclosure by donor-advised funds and corporate giving programs to an overhaul of the 990 form, the key document submitted to the IRS outlining the financial state and practices of foundations and nonprofits. The direct impact on fundraising and philanthropic giving is that donors, especially foundations, require more information from nonprofits on their financial status than ever before, and are turning greater attention to the management of donations. Ethical business practices should always be the norm, but it is critically important in this climate that nonprofit organizations and grant-giving institutions are scrupulous in their dealings with one another.

Measuring impact

For all the reasons discussed in this section, donors (and grant-makers in particular) are requiring nonprofit organizations to evaluate the effectiveness of their work and to provide qualitative and quantitative measures of impact. For service organizations—such as hospitals, schools and counseling centers—this may be a relatively easy exercise; they can measure the number of people they serve and track the health and progress of patients, students and clients over time. Evaluating impact is more difficult for advocacy groups and arts organizations, where change can take decades or where the final product is somewhat ephemeral (such as a theatrical or dance performance). It is important for fundraisers, particularly grant writers, to be familiar with the particular evaluation tools that a nonprofit uses, or should use, to assess impact. There are also various program planning models that can assist nonprofits in identifying measures of success. A popular tool used

Visit Vault at **www.vault.com** for insider company profiles, expert advice, career message boards, expert resume reviews, the Vault Job Board and more.

VAULT CAREER LIBRARY   37

by the foundation community is the program logic model, a system of diagrams to identify and describe relationships between different program components defined as inputs, outputs, indicators and outcomes. Do these terms sound fuzzy? They sure are, and philanthropic giving professionals themselves struggle to define what they mean.

Developments in Fundraising

For the fundraiser, greater wealth and stiff competition have led to innovation and creative thinking. More than ever before, fundraisers take advantage of new technologies and invent new ways to market their organizations.

Technology as a tool for fundraising

The rise of the Internet has had a profound impact on fundraising, and now a whole new industry has evolved around consultants and agencies helping nonprofit organizations reach donors through their computer. Just as political candidates use YouTube and MySpace to generate buzz, so are nonprofit organizations creating online videos, social networks, blogs and targeted e-mail appeals to raise awareness about social problems and generate donations. Beyond a link to an organization's donation page, there are a host of new tools for making donations quickly and securely, as well as web sites that help donors determine which organizations are worthy of support. Nonprofit organizations also help their existing donors become fundraisers in of themselves, providing tools that allow donors to solicit gifts from personal web pages. The tools for gathering information from existing donors have also become more sophisticated, from customized online databases to screening mechanisms to identify donors for more personalized cultivation to a variety of survey instruments. While the basic philosophy of fundraising hasn't changed—that direct engagement with donors leads to larger gifts—the methods of engagement are entirely new and largely untested. The Internet does infuse a new creative energy into fundraising, which many of the X and Y generation find appealing.

The perpetual major gifts campaign

There comes a turning point for most nonprofit organizations when the leadership realizes that a major investment in resources is needed to take the organization's work to an entirely new level. That moment is quite clear for schools, performing arts organizations and churches that rely on their surroundings to do their work—there's a moment in time when they must upgrade their facilities. Leadership then decide to embark on what is known as a capital or major gifts campaign—an intensive fundraising effort over a specific time line focused on securing the funds to build, purchase, or renovate a building. In the past, these campaigns tended to be long-term—over a five- or 10-year period—and were thought of as a one-time event (or at least one that wouldn't happen for another 20 years or so).

Over the last 10 years, the philosophy of the major gifts campaign has changed. They have become perpetual efforts for all sorts of organizations trying to significantly raise their operating budgets. Organizations not only raise millions of new dollars for their physical surroundings, they raise it for new staff and new program. And once one 10-year major gifts campaign ends, the planning for the next campaign begins. As a result, a whole new specialty in fundraising has evolved, one focused on helping organizations plan and implement successful major gifts campaigns. Consultants and in-house specialists assist organizations in various aspects of these campaigns—from conducting a study with current and prospective donors to determine the feasibility of such a campaign to writing the promotional materials. Almost any fundraising professional entering the field will be involved in a major gifts campaign in one way or another. And the line between fundraising for yearly operations and these campaigns is often quite blurry; it often seems like a major gifts campaign is merely a gimmick for getting your existing donors to significant increase their yearly gifts or secure a commitment for multiyear support.

The creation of the nonprofit brand

As part of the effort to distinguish themselves from the dozens of other organizations involved in similar work, many nonprofit organizations have adopted the marketing concept of branding. In the same way that corporations market themselves and their major products, nonprofits try to build a recognizable and consistent look and language that conveys the organization's unique values and mission. Many nonprofits go no further than developing a sexy, new logo and clever tagline for their web site and brochures. However, a true branding campaign will go beyond the creation of new visuals to disseminate a consistent story and emotional feel through everything that the nonprofit does. Those nonprofits that can afford it will bring on branding consultants to help the organization rethink its mission, articulate values and redesign logo. Nonprofits will also hire in-house branding specialists charged with ensuring that everything publication, press release and public statement represents "the brand." It may be the next fad in

Visit Vault at **www.vault.com** for insider company profiles, expert advice, career message boards, expert resume reviews, the Vault Job Board and more.

VAULT CAREER LIBRARY   **39**

modern marketing, but large nonprofit organizations are investing hundreds of thousands of dollars in these efforts. The most successful are the largest nonprofit groups that have that kind of money. The World Wildlife Fund is perhaps one of the most effective in branding; almost anyone will recognize their signature panda logo—which is splashed over every publication, public services advertisement and web page—and the average person knows immediately that the organization's work focuses on protecting endangered animals across the globe.

Fundraising efforts are often enhanced by these branding efforts, largely because branding exercises force a nonprofit organization to describe in detail how it is different from other groups. Branding can also be a selling point for certain donors, especially corporations, who view the process as an important part of sophisticated marketing and communications.

Changes in How We Give Money

Fundraisers don't have the corner on innovation. As nonprofits develop new ways to obtain funding, so do philanthropic giving professionals devise new ways to leverage donations to get the most bang for their buck.

Emergence of community foundations

While large foundations, like the Ford Foundation, the Lucille and David Packard Foundation and the various Rockefeller funds, are perhaps the most visible grant-giving institutions, most foundations are much smaller. Community foundations—formed to serve specific regions, counties and cities—are usually relatively small, but are increasingly seen as powerful agents of social change. The assets of community foundations are comprised of contributions from numerous donors at the discretion of a governing board made up of community leaders. According to the Foundation Center, there are more than 700 community foundations in existence today, and in 2005, community foundations increased their grant-making by more than 10 percent, nearly double the increase in giving for any other kind of foundation. Moreover, many community foundations invest in social change in myriad ways—from bringing together different interest groups to advising and shaping public policy initiatives to training nonprofits in fundraising. As a fundraiser, it is important to understand the role of community foundations in your region and to build relationships with governing members of foundations, as well as donors that contribute to them. Philanthropic giving professionals, especially financial advisors, need to investigate community foundations as an efficient means to serve clients' philanthropic endeavors.

Giving circles and funder networks

While the wealthiest foundations and individuals receive widespread attention for their philanthropic activities, most Americans give to charitable organizations in one way or another. And many individuals look for ways to leverage their modest donations. As a result, new mechanisms have emerged, where groups of like-minded individuals pool donations and initiate their own grant-making effort. Most of these so-called giving circles focus on a cause (such as helping children or the homeless) and/or an affiliation (many African-American, Latino and Asian American groups have formed). Women in particular have taken the lead in creating giving circles, but it's also a popular funding mechanism for a younger generation who may not have significant resources but want to make a contribution to their communities. The Forum of Regional Grant-makers, which followed the emergence of giving circles, has compiled a database of more than 400 giving circles across the country. Most have formed since 2000 and vary in size and structure. Some giving circles raise funds through annual events, while others establish nonprofit organizations and initiate sophisticated fundraising campaigns. Community foundations play a major role in facilitating giving circles, helping them create donor-advised funds. Most donations go to local nonprofits, although giving circles are also a popular mechanism for immigrants to send donations back to their communities of origin.

Foundations of all sizes have taken similar approach, developing funder networks that pool grant-making funds to address a particular issue or population, from promoting diversity in philanthropy (a focus of Hispanics in Philanthropy) to urban planning (the priority of the Funders Network for Smart Growth and Livable Communities). For both fundraisers and philanthropic giving professionals, these collaborations offer exciting new opportunities to connect with new donors, especially from communities of color.

Venture philanthropy

As discussed throughout this guide, foundations and many individual philanthropists are exploring a number of new ways to invest in nonprofits beyond awarding a grant. Program-related investments—loans to nonprofits at below-market rates—and recoverable grants where nonprofits return funds

Visit Vault at **www.vault.com** for insider company profiles, expert advice, career message boards, expert resume reviews, the Vault Job Board and more.

VAULT CAREER LIBRARY   41

with no interest payments are two such examples. The third kind of experiment, ventures to establish an earned income base for nonprofits, has received more attention in the press than other forms, especially as a number of high-profile business leaders adopt this model for their charitable giving. Certain foundations are keenly interested in this kind of approach. Nonprofit leaders are finding that if an organization wants to pursue a social venture enterprise, there needs to be a serious discussion among board members and senior management to determine if a profit-making model will substantially increase a nonprofit's capacity to do its work—such a decision should not be based on potential grant revenue alone. In fact, continuing evaluation of startup social venture operations reveal that many fail to bring in any substantial new revenue for nonprofits.

Fundraising & Philanthropy Highs and Lows

Now that you are inspired to raise and/or give money for your favorite cause, it's important to understand some of the primary challenges you are likely to face. So before turning the page to tips on getting hired, here are a few words of caution to keep in mind.

Fundraising

In many ways, times can't get much better for the fundraising professional. Nonprofit organizations of all sizes are in perpetual need of smart, experienced fundraisers, and they rarely fire one. After all, the organization's operating revenue is on the line. Fundraisers today largely have their pick of opportunities, even with just a few years of experience. They are in fact some of the highest paid in the nonprofit sector and can often negotiate for more, including flexible work hours, telecommuting and additional vacation time.

That said, the pressure on fundraising professionals is intense. After all, they are responsible for bringing in the money that keeps the doors of the nonprofit open. Deadlines for submitting proposals and meeting fundraising goals never go away, and it can feel like a never-ending grind with little time to enjoy the rewards. Unfortunately, fundraisers are often victims of their own success, especially at organizations that grow quickly without addressing the need to build infrastructure for that growth. Fundraising goals may increase year to year and the number of staff to handle requests for information, membership mailings, proposal submissions and donor visits does not. The result is long hours, frustration and burnout for many fundraisers. Turnover in the field is high; the average length of stay for a fundraising is only two years.

Philanthropic giving

What could be better? You are working to give money away to worthy causes. You regularly interact with the pillars of the nonprofit community, as well as academics, politicians and the very wealthy. And you are paid well, in most cases far better than you would be if you worked for those nonprofit organizations. What's more, there are new and exciting opportunities in philanthropic giving, including social venture philanthropy, giving circles and funder collaborations. Land a job at the right institution, and you can be working at the cutting edge of the field.

And there's the challenge—getting that job. It's actually a small field of players. The vast majority of foundations do not employ professional staff. And while growing in numbers, social venture groups are a tiny piece of the larger philanthropic picture. Those philanthropic giving institutions that maintain a staff, employ the best and brightest with extensive training and experience. As a director at one of the top foundations in the country advises, "you don't wake up one day and have a career in philanthropy." For the largest and most prestigious foundations, you will most likely need a doctorate in a particular field of interest and at least five years work for nonprofit organizations. The training and experience needed for other philanthropic jobs is equally rigorous. As one giving advisor managing endowment funds for nonprofit organizations puts it, "Would you give your $20 million endowment to a 24-year-old?" A job as a philanthropic giving professional is a long-term goal, and one that will take a lot of work to achieve.

The cause

On the one hand, you are working for a cause. On the other hand, you are working for a cause. Most fundraisers and philanthropic giving professionals will tell you that there is immense satisfaction to be found in their work, for everyone has a story of success about an initiative that they helped fund that made a difference. For one fundraiser, nothing beats the high of a donor responding to a thank you for a gift with, "no, thank *you* for all the wonderful work you do and for helping make the world a better place for all of us."

Visit Vault at **www.vault.com** for insider company profiles, expert advice, career message boards, expert resume reviews, the Vault Job Board and more.

V/\ULT CAREER LIBRARY   **43**

But keep in mind that social change is slow, steady work fraught with conflict and disappointment. As Martin Luther King Jr. once said, "All progress is precarious, and the solution of one problem brings us face to face with another problem." There are always people in need. There is always another damaging piece of legislation or an unsatisfactory compromise among policy makers. And there are always people who will disagree with what you are doing; it's not unheard of for fundraisers to receive death threats when an organization is engaged in a particularly controversial issue.

The front line of social change is therefore rewarding and draining. Some decide that they don't ultimately have the stamina for it, especially given the pay, as well as a general lack of infrastructure to support the work.

The function and dysfunction of nonprofits organizations

Every organization is different, but there are some unique characteristics of the nonprofit world that some people love and some hate. Those drawn to the nonprofit sector tend to be passionate, opinionated and determined—all wonderful qualities that inspire fundraisers and giving professionals. Unfortunately, passion and commitment does not necessarily translate into professional behavior or effective business practices. Some nonprofit leaders are openly resistant to professionalizing their nonprofit organization, believing that focus on administrative and organizational matters takes time and resources away from the cause. The result can be disastrous—low pay and stingy benefits, high turnover, poor management and unethical practices. Most fundraisers complain about unprofessional attitudes at nonprofit organizations. As one fundraiser put it, "The amount of time spent navigating or fighting through issues (from better internal controls to major ethical violations) takes far too much time away from direct fundraising activities." Moreover, planning for the future often takes a backseat to the crisis of the moment, and that's a real problem for a fundraiser attempting to secure long-term commitments from donors.

Another perk (or drawback) can be the more relaxed atmosphere at nonprofit organizations, especially for those who come from a corporate environment. The dress code is usually loose (environment groups are notorious for the shorts-and-sandals look in the office), and there may be more flexibility in setting your work schedule. Yet this is largely a result of the fact that staff are paid less than they would be in the for-profit sector and there simply aren't enough resources for fancy offices and up-to-date equipment. And be aware that a large, national nonprofit group may operate more like its corporate counterparts. You are likely to be better paid and have your own office, but there may be a dress code and you may work longer hours.

Please bear in mind that these are generalities. Many nonprofits today adopt the business practices of the for-profit world, including long-term strategic planning and management training for supervisors. Moreover, nonprofit managers increasingly recognize that adequate compensation and benefits are critical to retaining staff. As previously noted, most executive directors believe it is especially important to recruit and retain experienced fundraising professionals, and salaries reflect demand. While you will never become a millionaire, you can work your way up to a six-figure salary as an experienced fundraiser and/or consultant. Large, private foundations tend to pay their employees extremely well (in fact, there's been some concern from Members of Congress about compensation for foundation staff at the largest foundations). And those on the for-profit side of the philanthropic giving business (financial advisors and community development officers) have all the compensation benefits of working for a corporation or investment firm.

You can avoid some of the unpleasant aspects of the fundraising and philanthropic giving business by carefully researching the nonprofit organization or giving institution where you wish to work. In the next section, some of the key resources for your research will be described, as well as some of the probing questions that you should ask at any interview.

The Great Divide Between Fundraising and Program Staff

While united in mission, staff at a nonprofit quickly discover that lines are drawn between the different operating functions of the organization. These divisions are less distinct at small nonprofits, where a general lack of resources means that everyone is sharing administrative and fundraising duties. However, once an organization is large enough (and stable enough) to hire its first fundraiser to focus exclusively on increasing revenue, and/or an administrator to cut checks, the trench is dug. Two camps emerge, with the fundraisers and administrative staff that keep the organization awash in cash, do the taxes and file the paperwork on one side of the trench, and those that go out into the world and do the good work to fulfill the nonprofit's purpose, known as program staff, on the other.

This not to say that every nonprofit with more than 10 staff is a battleground, with frequent fights across deep trenches in a "fundraising versus program" environment. As is the case for any business, the culture of a nonprofit is defined by many factors, not the least of which is the leadership coming from the executive director or president (does he/she recognize everyone's important role or favor one staff person over another?).

Most fundraisers will tell you that the principle inspiration for their efforts is the commitment of program staff; likewise a good program person appreciates the fundraiser who brings in the cash to make program activities possible. Yet it is also not unusual for fundraisers to feel cut off from "the action" of the nonprofit or feel invisible when the executive director neglects to thank the fundraiser's role in a major victory. Likewise, program staff can view fundraising as a mysterious process in which that they have little say or stake.

An effective leader at a well-run nonprofit makes it clear that fundraising is everyone's responsibility, and he/she fosters strong communication and information-sharing between fundraising and program staff. Such a nonprofit will be extraordinarily effective in fundraising because it is collaborative—program staff and major donor officers make joint presentations to important donors, grant writers have close relationships with program staff in developing proposals and both fundraisers and program staff are strongly motivated by each other's enthusiasm. Without such collaboration, the fundraising process breaks down in many ways, tensions rise and the financial stability of the organization can be put in jeopardy. The following are just a few of the nightmare scenarios that can occur.

- A grant writer is never able to reach a program person to finalize a grant proposal. The deadline approaches, and the proposal is submitted without the program person signing off on it. The foundation officer reviewing the proposal realizes there is a major factual error in the introduction. He calls the program person directly to discuss. The program person never returns the phone call, and the proposal is rejected.

- A major donor officer lands a $100,000 gift for a new publication; unfortunately, program staff hadn't decided if this publication was really a good idea and had planned to table it for another year or two.

- A nonprofit lands a $200,000, two-year grant for a new advocacy campaign; program staff are thrilled until they read the grant for the first time and realize they need to oversee a major polling effort that they hadn't discussed in order to fulfill the foundation's evaluation requirements.

- In discussions with finance staff and the executive director about next year's budget, a program director is told that he must cut at least one staff person from his team because there isn't enough dedicated funding to cover everyone's salaries and benefits. This is the first time that the program director has heard there was a funding gap. He accuses the executive director and fundraising staff of collusion and incompetence, storms out of the meeting and starts looking for another job.

Visit Vault at **www.vault.com** for insider company profiles, expert advice, career message boards, expert resume reviews, the Vault Job Board and more.

V/\ULT CAREER LIBRARY   **47**

GETTING HIRED

Chapter 4: Education and Training

Chapter 5: Resumes and Cover Letters

Chapter 6: The Interview

Chapter 7: Finding the Right Job

Education and Training

The advent of college courses and training programs specifically geared toward fundraising and philanthropic giving is a very recent occurrence. Most in the field learn on the job and are somewhat suspicious of skills taught in the classroom. That said, universities and trade associations are putting more and more resources into creating sophisticated curricula to prepare undergraduates and graduate students for entry into the field. A combination of course work, workshops and real-life experience puts you in the best position to get your first meaningful job in the profession.

Academic Programs

Undergraduate options

Most major universities offer courses in nonprofit management that will expose you to all aspects of nonprofits, from financial operations to strategic planning to fundraising. Many classes are offered through adult education programs. Likewise, many community colleges offer classes in nonprofit management, including those in fundraising.

Smaller liberal arts colleges may not offer the breadth of courses specifically focused on nonprofit management and fundraising. However, a range of coursework that is traditionally a part of a liberal arts education will provide you with fundamental skills and knowledge easily transferable to a career in fundraising and/or philanthropic giving. Fundraising professionals strongly suggest that undergraduates interested in the field take classes that emphasize writing, so enroll in classes that require term papers. Technical writing classes of any kind are beneficial (the author took a class in science writing at a small liberal arts school which provided the best training she received for her career as a grant writer). Classes that introduce you to basic marketing principles are also extremely helpful, especially if you are interested in direct response fundraising or e-philanthropy. It's also important you keep up your math skills, since budgeting and financial analysis will be an integral part of your life as a fundraising or philanthropic giving professional. One fundraiser suggests that undergraduates take a statistics class, especially if you are interested in grant writing. Course work in accounting and finance can also help prepare you for your first job in the field.

Visit Vault at **www.vault.com** for insider company profiles, expert advice, career message boards, expert resume reviews, the Vault Job Board and more.

VAULT CAREER LIBRARY   51

Graduate programs

While a graduate education is not a prerequisite for a job in fundraising, a master's degree in nonprofit management can help you make a leap to leadership; someone with a combination of experience in fundraising and education in nonprofit management makes a strong candidate for executive director. You can learn more about the elements of the nonprofit management degree and the schools that offer them from the Nonprofit Management Academic Center Council (www.naccouncil.org). The council lists 44 member universities with centers on nonprofit management.

A Master in Business Administration is another option for higher education in the field, especially since nonprofit management, social entrepreneurship and socially responsible business practices have become major focuses for many graduate business school programs. To learn more about MBA programs with an emphasis in social change and nonprofit management, there are two good resources. NETimpact (www.netimpact.org) is a network for business student groups dedicated to incorporating social responsibility into business education. The group recently published a guide on business schools offering courses and other resources in social responsibility. Beyond Pinstripes (www.beyondpinstripes.org) is a project of World Resources Institute that periodically ranks business schools by how well they integrate social and environmental responsibility into their curriculum.

Finally, there are doctorate programs in philanthropy focused on research and scholarship in nonprofit management, fundraising and philanthropic giving. The most well-known program is at the Center for Philanthropy at the University of Indiana.

Other Classroom Training

While the mantra of the field is learn on the job, fundraising and philanthropic giving professionals do return to the classroom from time to time to build their expertise. There are in fact innumerable workshops, lectures and online tutorials on various aspects of fundraising. What's more, you can stock at least one floor of a library with books that have been written about the field; a recent search of Amazon.com yielded more than 17,000 different books and articles on the subject of fundraising and philanthropy.

These training resources are important and it's worth your time and a little of your money to enroll in a class. There's even a certification program for fundraisers offered by the primary trade group, the Association of

Fundraising Professionals (although this program is mainly for those who have been in the field for a number of years). It's just important to remember that most prospective employers value real world experience over classroom training. And many in the field are downright skeptical about the certification program; as one consultant states, "many feel that someone who is spending their time getting the certification is not out there raising money."

So here are some suggested training resources. Keep in mind this list is only a starting place. There's plenty more out there.

Workshops and tutorials

- The Association of Fundraising Professionals holds all sorts of trainings throughout the country; all you need to do is call your local chapter. They also offer online tutorials. You may need to purchase a membership to take these courses, although you can often get someone who is already a member to sponsor you.

- If you know you want to pursue a specialty within fundraising or philanthropy, there are other trade groups to join, including the Association of Planned Giving Professionals, Council for the Advancement and Support of Education (CASE) and the American Grant Writers Association. Most hold conferences and workshops where there are training opportunities.

- Local governments and community foundations offer workshops and classes in fundraising; this may be the most cost effective form of classroom training. See if local agencies sponsor adult education or career training workshops. Local art councils also hold fundraising workshops.

- Grant-making associations, which are member groups for foundations, frequently hold workshops related to grantsmanship. There are many such associations usually comprised of foundations within a particular region, such as the Northern Californian Grantmakers' Association. Some are based on interest, such as the Environmental Grantmakers Association. You may need to demonstrate that you are affiliated with a member foundation to participate in any training opportunities.

- There are several local and national nonprofit organizations with missions to strengthen the operation of other nonprofit organizations. Two of the most visible are The Foundation Center (www.foundationcenter.org) and CompassPoint Nonprofit Services (www.compasspoint.org), but others include CompuMentor (focused on helping the nonprofit community use technology) and the Social Action and Leadership School for Activists in

Visit Vault at **www.vault.com** for insider company profiles, expert advice, career message boards, expert resume reviews, the Vault Job Board and more.

V/\ULT CAREER LIBRARY   **53**

Washington, D.C. (www.hotsalsa.org). Most offer both online tutorials and workshops in fundraising.

- The University of Indiana offers coursework through its School of Fundraising, and classes are held throughout the country, primarily in Chicago, Indianapolis, and San Francisco. The classes are more expensive (ranging from $700 to $1200 per class), but they do offer scholarships. The university has also created a series of audio and online courses.

- Many fundraising consultants hold workshops and online training sessions, largely as part of their marketing efforts. There's always the danger that these consultants are scam artists, so check in with local nonprofits or other groups to confirm that a consultant really worked for them and provided valuable advice.

On-the-Job Training

Swimming in the deep end

"In this field, you're dropped into the deep end." That's how one fundraiser describes the way in which most people learn the nitty-gritty of fundraising and philanthropy. While a plethora of workshops, online tutorials and classes have sprung up in the last decade (as described above), most nonprofit leaders believe there's no substitute for hands-on experience.

But this is not an impossible, catch-22 situation for you. Luckily, that on-the-job training is available in a vast array of volunteering and internship opportunities, as well as temporary job assignments through staffing agencies.

Volunteering

According to the Corporation for National and Community Service, between 61 and 65 million Americans volunteer annually, which is more than a quarter of the population. For the lean and mean nonprofit organization with limited manpower, volunteers are an important and highly valued part of their workforce. What's more, the second most popular volunteer activity (behind coaching, tutoring or mentoring) is fundraising. So nonprofits recognize that volunteers not only provide free services, but are often a financial windfall. The business of attracting volunteers has therefore become rather sophisticated. Many nonprofit organizations employ full-time volunteer coordinators charged with training and placing volunteers so that both the nonprofit and the volunteer get the most out of the experience.

To dip their feet into nonprofit waters, many people volunteer to participate in fundraising events. There are all sorts of ways to get involved with a fundraiser—you can man the registration table, deal cards at casino night or run the marathon. Fundraisers are a great way to get to know an organization and a cause. It's particularly useful for someone in the corporate world who is interested in philanthropic giving to help out with fundraisers for nonprofit organizations that their employer already sponsors.

While any volunteer experience helps, you ultimately need to make a longer term commitment where there are opportunities to observe fundraising staff in action, get some training or simply learn more about the range of strategies the nonprofit community engages in to tackle an issue. And nothing beats taking some time to volunteer in the development office. You may start off with some rudimentary administrative work—such as entering information into the database—but the interactions with the staff are invaluable. If you show initiative and enthusiasm, there are a range of projects that staff may ask you to help out with, such as writing articles for the organization's newsletter, researching potential grant funders or finding vendors for the next fundraising event. In most cases, staff will provide you with informal training so that you can help out with these more meaty projects.

For the best long-term volunteer experience, make sure that the organization has a structured volunteer program run by a coordinator. As a former volunteer coordinator put it, "a volunteer position should feel as much like a job as possible." One of the best resources for finding volunteer opportunities is www.volunteermatch.org. The site requires nonprofit organizations to register and submit a detailed description of the tasks that they need volunteers to take on. The search engine on the site allows you to pick those opportunities that best meet your schedule and the kinds of projects you want to take on.

Another important volunteer activity—especially for those interested in philanthropic giving—is serving on the board of a nonprofit organization. Board members provide critical leadership and oversight to help an organization thrive and grow, so board membership can give you an opportunity to demonstrate leadership and commitment. Serving on a board also lets you apply skills and experience that you already have while learning from your fellow board members and the staff of the organization. You are also likely to get to know leaders in the nonprofit community and major donors—two groups that often sit on nonprofit boards. If you are going to get

Visit Vault at **www.vault.com** for insider company profiles, expert advice, career message boards, expert resume reviews, the Vault Job Board and more.

V/\ULT CAREER LIBRARY   55

anything out of the experience, however, it's important that you make a serious commitment to the board beyond showing up for meetings. For more information on what it takes to be an effective board member, check out BoardSource (www.boardsource.org), a nonprofit organization dedicated to creating effective boards. There are many, many opportunities to join nonprofit boards, even if you don't have a great deal of experience in the nonprofit world. A good resource that links nonprofits with board members is www.boardnetusa.org. Nonprofits may also advertise for board members on www.volunteermatch.org.

Volunteering at a nonprofit organization may be the most effective way for you to find a job. If you volunteer for any length of time, you will not only learn about job openings (in many cases before they are posted), but will also gain allies who will recommend you to their colleagues.

Internships

Many nonprofit organizations offer internships—usually for college students, graduate students and those who have recently graduated—that are structured to provide a meaningful work experience with direct supervision from an experienced professional. Like volunteers, interns are highly valued; as one planning giving director describes them, "Interns are the jewels of our organization." Beyond taking on activities and projects that over-stretched staff don't have time for, boards and executive directors see interns as the next generation of nonprofit leaders. This transition in leadership has become an important issue of late as many executive directors—who are for the most part in their 50s and 60s—plan to retire.

While most internships in the nonprofit world are unpaid, there are some that provide a modest stipend. Universities usually have an internship placement program, a good place to start to research internship opportunities, especially those where you can also receive course credits. Many study abroad programs incorporate internships into their course curriculum. In addition, universities across the country (including Georgetown, University of California-Irvine, Harvard and New York University, to name just a few) have internships programs linked to curriculum in fundraising and nonprofit management. And many foundations offer internships and fellowships.

As is true for volunteering, you'll get the most out of a structured, established program where intern positions look a lot like full-time jobs. Many internships—especially the paid positions at the largest and most prestigious nonprofit organizations—are competitive. It's important that you do your research and follow application guidelines. As you would for a paid position, you want to highlight any work experience, volunteering or academic projects that relate to the issue that the nonprofit organization to which you are applying addresses, or any activities that demonstrate you have knack for fundraising. For more information on those specific skills and experiences, refer to the "The Winning Resume" chapter of this guide.

Temporary positions

Not everyone has the luxury of devoting themselves to a nonprofit organization for little or no pay. If that's true for you, you can also build your resume or get your foot in the door through a staffing agency. Many established nonprofit organizations use staffing agencies to fill entry-level positions, such as development coordinators, usually on a temp-to-perm basis. There are in fact staffing firms that focus exclusively on nonprofit organizations, like Professionals for Nonprofits, which is headquartered in New York City but also has an office in Washington, D.C. The temp-to-perm arrangement is often ideal for you and the nonprofit; you both can get to know each other before making a commitment. And if you are working full time for a period of months, the agency may offer you health benefits as if you were a full-time employee for the organization. It's important to remember that the positions that agencies are trying to fill are administrative; you will be filing, faxing, copying and typing. That said, most nonprofits welcome enthusiasm and initiative, and you may soon be taking on more substantive projects.

Visit Vault at **www.vault.com** for insider company profiles, expert advice, career message boards, expert resume reviews, the Vault Job Board and more.

VAULT CAREER LIBRARY   57

Resumes and Cover Letters

CHAPTER 5

In this chapter, we provide tips on writing the winning resume and cover letter. The advice here applies both to college undergraduates fresh out of school and those seasoned professionals looking to transition into a new career.

The Winning Resume

When seeking a job in fundraising or philanthropic giving, all the fundamental principles for crafting a powerful resume apply. Your resume should distill and summarize the experience that is most relevant to the position you are applying for, and you should customize your resume to demonstrate how you would transfer the skills and experience you have gained thus far to the specific job at hand. The resume should be easy to read with concise (and mostly bulleted) statements about your specific work experiences. You should use active verbs to describe you duties, responsibilities and achievements. And most importantly, you should emphasize where you have demonstrated leadership and describe your distinct role in realizing organizational goals and successes.

Any direct experience in either fundraising or philanthropic giving is important to a prospective employer. But it is important to remember that most nonprofit employers give equal weight to your volunteer or internship experience as they would paid employment, especially when you are first starting out. "Nonprofits take volunteering very seriously," says one recruiter who fills positions for nonprofit groups. Nonprofit employers understand that volunteering is one of the primary ways to get experience in the field. Moreover, they want to see that you have made a commitment to making the world a better place. You should therefore have a separate section of your resume dedicated to your volunteer activities, where you describe any experience you have had with fundraising or philanthropic giving. Don't forget to include any charity fundraisers that you might have been involved with, especially those that require you to raise money, such as triathlons, marathons or bike rides. And if you haven't participated in a fundraising event before, nonprofit recruiters recommend that you do so.

If you participated in an internship program, you can either list the position in the work experience section of your resume or create a new section dedicated to internships. Be careful not to mislead prospective employers about how much work experience you have. As a general rule, if you were paid for the internship, it's perfectly fine to include it in your work summary. If it was a volunteer position or it was directly related to your academic work in college, it should be included in your volunteering section or as a separate educational internships section. The sample resumes on the following pages provide you with a couple of different models for incorporating both volunteer and intern experiences.

Questions to ask yourself

In outlining your fundraising or philanthropic giving experiences, you should carefully describe the specific work that you did and make sure to highlight any contributions you made to building the infrastructure or capacity of a nonprofit organization. You might want to ask yourself these questions to help you write about your fundraising/philanthropic giving experience.

- How did you help make a fundraising event successful? Did you design invitations? Recruit participants? Write a letter requesting sponsorships? Secure items for a silent auction? Fundraisers for college activities — student dance or theater productions, field trips, sporting events or equipment — do count. You should also state how many people attended, how much money was raised, and make note if you helped bring in any corporate sponsors.

- Have you participated in a bike ride, marathon, or hike for a charity? How much money did you raise and how many people donated?

- If you wrote materials for an organization (invitations, letters of inquiry, grant proposals, case statements, etc), what was the result? How many people gave? If you wrote a letter of inquiry, did the foundation request a full proposal or fund the project?

If you are trying to transition from the for-profit world, think about how you've engaged with nonprofit organizations in your current position. For instance, you might ask yourself the following:

- Did you convince leadership at your company to participate in any fundraising activities? How much did they give? Have you helped your company become more involved with any one charitable organization?

- Did you convince your fellow employees to participate in your company's matching gift program? How much money was raised as a result of your efforts?

- Have you provided any other expertise or services (such as help producing a brochure or designing a public relations or direct response campaign) to help with fundraising activities? Keep in mind that assisting a nonprofit with public relations can indirectly impact fundraising, since the organization's profile is raised within the community. If you did such work for a group, ask the development department if they saw any increase in giving as a result of your work.

- If you took a leadership role at your company in your philanthropy, how much money was given out and how many charities did you assist?

While it's important to list any direct experience you may have had in fundraising or philanthropic giving, recruiters warn that you must be specific and clear about your role. "We know that this work is team oriented." explains a recruiter, "so it's important to know what you did as a member of a team, what you took a lead role in and what you did as an individual."

What employers are looking for

Beyond direct experience in fundraising and philanthropic giving, there is a range of other skills that demonstrate you have an interest in and knack for the field. Nonprofit employers will certainly look for the following:

- **Experience and ability to build relationships**—In the fundraising and philanthropic giving field, you will always be interacting with people with different backgrounds, interests and communication styles. So any kind of work with customers, clients, consultants or vendors is extremely relevant. As a special events coordinator, for example, you will work with all sorts of vendors and volunteers. You may also want to highlight any experience you have had in dealing with difficult clients; as a fundraiser, you will certainly be in a position where you must answer to a disgruntled or difficult donor.

- **Experience in conflict resolution and negotiation**—Comfort and ability in finding common ground among many different interests is particularly important as a philanthropic giving professional. At a foundation, a program officer is often tasked with forming a coalition of nonprofit groups to build a common strategy around an issue. For example, a foundation may bring landowners, conservation groups, timber companies and land managers to the table to discuss ways to support sustainable forestry and protection of wildlife habitat. As a financial advisor, you may be helping feuding family members to devise a giving strategy or set up a foundation. And as a fundraiser, negotiation skills come in handy when dealing with a donor who has strong ideas about how his or her money should be spent.

Visit Vault at **www.vault.com** for insider company profiles, expert advice, career message boards, expert resume reviews, the Vault Job Board and more.

V/\ULT CAREER LIBRARY   61

- **Ability to write and communicate about complicated ideas related to the cause of the organization**—From thank-you notes to grant proposals to briefings to the board of trustees, fundraisers and philanthropic giving professionals spend a significant portion of their time writing. Any experience with writing about complicated concepts is important to highlight in your resume. Theses and research papers count. In most cases, prospective employers will ask for a writing sample along with a resume and cover letter.

- **Experience and comfort with relational databases**—As discussed earlier in this section, sophisticated fundraising teams are absolutely reliant on the donor relations database that store all kinds of information about past, current and prospective donors—from where they live to when they last gave to when a major donor officer last paid a visit. Most prospective employers would like you to have some sort of working knowledge of the donor relations databases—Raiser's Edge, Team Approach or Donor Perfect, among others—but any experience with a relational database should be noted on your resume. Also make note if you have ever customized a database in either Oracle or Access. Most donor relations databases are based on these two basic database platforms.

- **Comfort with budgets and basic accounting principles**—Very few fundraisers or philanthropic giving professionals have extensive backgrounds in accounting, but they are comfortable with number crunching and are expected to assist in building organizational budgets. They may also be involved in analyzing cash flow. So make a note in your resume of any experience you have had in building or adhering to a budget (again, experiences in college, such as meeting budget constraints to pull off a theatrical production, are relevant). Also note any course work you have had in accounting or finance.

- **Ability to research, compile, and analyze information**—Most activities in fundraising and philanthropic giving require some form of research. You may be reviewing 990 tax forms of foundations to find out what organizations they give to, culling press releases to learn more about a potential donor or reviewing position papers to better understand the latest policy arguments on a particular issue. Provide information on various forms of research you have undertaken for college papers (especially your thesis) or as part of an internship. And make a note of any specialized databases or information services you may have used, such as FoundationSearch, LexisNexis, or Guidestar.

- **Relationships with existing or potential donors**—The old adage that it's important who you know certainly applies to fundraising and philanthropic giving. Familiarity with a major donor, corporate sponsor or foundation that supports or could support the organization to which you are applying for a job could give you a critical edge over another candidate. But be clear what your interactions with the donor have been; don't lead potential employers into believing that you can deliver funding if you have worked with an donor or corporation in a different capacity or just happen to run into a CEO or executive director of a major foundation at a party.

- **Personal experience with the focal issue for the organization**—Passion is a prerequisite for any job in fundraising and philanthropic giving. So is a working knowledge of the issues that an organization (whether a foundation or a charity) addresses. So make sure to list any and all experience you have related to the cause of the organization to which you are applying for a job. Again, volunteering, internships and academic research count.

Once you have compiled and shaped your work, volunteer and educational experience, you should develop a short summary of your experience and place it at the top of your resume. This summary is the first thing that busy nonprofit professionals will read when reviewing resumes and can be the determining factor for you getting that first interview, especially if you have limited experience. A good summary includes the three to five bullet points describing the skills, work experience and accomplishments that are most relevant to the job you are applying for. Your summary should reflect that you have carefully read the job description and can show how your experience makes you the best candidate for the job. You should therefore tailor the professional summary for the specific job you are applying for. If you are applying for a development coordinator position, for example, make sure to highlight in your professional summary any experience you have with databases and in drafting acknowledgements. The professional summary also provides an opportunity to distinguish yourself from other candidates, so it's not a bad idea to describe your connection or passion for the cause that the organization addresses.

The Winning Cover Letter

Cover letters can be just as important as your resume in showing off your skills and experience. Beyond declaring your interest and summarizing your qualifications, a well-crafted cover letter can demonstrate that you are articulate, professional and thoughtful, and that you have carefully researched

Visit Vault at **www.vault.com** for insider company profiles, expert advice, career message boards, expert resume reviews, the Vault Job Board and more.

V/\ULT CAREER LIBRARY   **63**

the organization to which you are applying. Moreover, most employers use the cover letter as a writing sample.

A cover letter should be short—three or four paragraphs that fit on one page. The letter should explain how you learned about the position, briefly outline your most relevant work experiences and accomplishments and describe the unique contribution that you can make to the organization. You should also describe why this particular organization or cause is so important to you. Again, nonprofit employers want to see your passion and that you have a strong connection to the mission of the organization. So it's important to review the organization's web site and describe why you think the organization and its mission are meaningful to you. A personal story is totally appropriate, although don't reveal anything that you wouldn't tell a stranger at a cocktail party. And make sure you understand what the organization does; don't describe the fulfilling experience you had as a GED tutor for the homeless if you are applying to an organization focused on youth sports.

Details, details

As is true for most employers, nonprofit organizations want their fundraising and/or philanthropic giving professionals to be detailed oriented, and that can be tough to capture in a resume. However, there are ways to provide evidence of your attention to detail. First and foremost, make sure that you or a friend with a good eye carefully proofreads your resume and cover letter. A prospective employer will stop reading your resume as soon as they find a typographical error or misspelling. Also make sure that you have spelled the primary contact person's name correctly in all documents, and make sure you have their correct title. A resume will land in the trash when the prospective employers sees that the cover letter is addressed to the wrong person, especially if the job posting provides clear instructions on who will be reviewing your resume.

Another important way to demonstrate your attention to detail is in tailoring your cover letter and resume to the specific job you are applying for. As stated above, carefully read the job description and review the organization's web site. Try to use the same terminology found in the job description to describe your own work. Ideally, your resume should touch upon the majority, if not all, the duties and skills that are listed in the job description. And your cover letter should provide a concise but complete summary of your work experience as it directly relates to the job description.

These are some hints to give to a prospective employer that can get you in the door. Once you are in the interview, you will be asked more probing questions about your experience to get a sense of your attention to detail. And you are likely to be given some tests as well. We'll discuss these later in describing the interviewing process.

Examples of Cover Letters and Resumes

Annabeth Sampson
3348 Connecticut Avenue, NW, Washington, D.C. 20008
202-429-4537 (home) 202-371-8751 (cell)
annabeths34@gmail.com

February 15, 2008

Katherine Gibney, Associate Vice President of Development
Americans for the Arts
1000 Vermont Avenue NW, 6th Floor
Washington, D.C. 20005

Dear Ms. Gibney:

I am writing to express my interest in the corporate relations coordinator position at Americans for the Arts posted on the Idealist web site. With significant experience assisting with a wide range of development activities—including efforts to cultivate partnerships with corporations—I have the skills and drive to help strengthen the corporate relations work at Americans for the Arts.

As can be seen from my resume, I have worked in the development offices of two prestigious arts organizations, helping with all aspects of fundraising—from researching potential foundation funders to maintaining donor records to drafting proposals and corporate solicitations. Beyond building the key administrative skills needed to keep fundraising campaigns running smoothly, I am a careful researcher with demonstrated success in identifying important new prospects. At the National Museum of Women in the Arts, for example, my research resulted in $15,000 in new support from foundations and $10,000 from new corporate sponsors. I am also an organized and motivated person with a deep commitment to supporting the arts. At Wesleyan University, I served as one of 10 board members of the student theater company that produced 20 productions a semester. To raise funds for the company, I organized a benefit showcase of new plays that far exceeded the fundraising goal. In addition, I completed coursework and an internship in fundraising and philanthropy through the Fund for American Studies' Institute of Philanthropy and Voluntary Service in Washington, D.C.

I have seen time and again how art—theater in particular—builds community. After graduating college, I worked with at-risk children to design and build sets for a summer circus. Children who first seemed sullen and shy quickly made friends when they got to work painting set pieces. It was frustrating for me to see how the organization that ran the circus struggled to find the funds to keep this important program going.

Americans for the Arts serves a critical role in providing the arts community the political power and resources to ensure that the arts continue to catalyze growth, change and connection. I look forward to meeting with you in person to discuss how I can support this important mission.

Sincerely,

Annabeth Sampson

Visit Vault at **www.vault.com** for insider company profiles, expert advice, career message boards, expert resume reviews, the Vault Job Board and more.

V∧ULT CAREER LIBRARY

65

Annabeth Sampson
3348 Connecticut Avenue, NW Washington, D.C. 20008
202-429-4537 (home) 202-371-8751 (cell)
annabeths34@gmail.com

OBJECTIVE

To assist a dynamic development team to cultivate and strengthen relationships with donors at an established and esteemed arts organization

HIGHLIGHTS OF EXPERIENCE AND SKILLS

- Significant experience in drafting most forms of donor communications, including solicitations of sponsorship for special events, letters of inquiry and reports to foundations, and acknowledgements to foundations and major donors
- Significant experience in donor prospect research; helped identify new corporate and foundation funders bringing new revenue to arts organizations
- Significant experience in maintaining donor records, both paper and electronic; familiar with both custom Access databases and Raiser's Edge
- Extensive knowledge of theater and visual arts
- Proficient in Microsoft Word, Access, Front Page, Painter, and familiar with various web-based databases, including FoundationSearch, Guidestar and LexisNexis

DEVELOPMENT AND COMMUNICATIONS EXPERIENCE

Development Intern   September 2007-February 2008

National Museum for Women in the Arts, Washington, D.C.
- Provided support for all aspects of fundraising for the museum, including researching and soliciting foundation prospects, helping draft solicitation for sponsors of upcoming gala dinner, maintaining donor database and drafting acknowledgements to major donors
- Drafted successful letter of inquiry to community foundation to support exhibit on Japanese print artists; museum was asked to submit a full proposal, which was funded for $10,000
- Compiled in-depth research on 20 foundation prospects to approach for upcoming exhibit on Japanese print artists; two foundations were selected for deeper cultivation, ultimately leading to $15,000 in new support for the exhibit
- Compiled profiles of 15 local businesses to approach for sponsorship of annual gala dinner; helped draft invitation for sponsorship, which led to $10,000 in new sponsor funding

Development Intern   May-August 2006

Washington National Opera, Washington, D.C.
through the Institute of Philanthropy and Voluntary Service
- Developed first draft of interim report to major foundation supporter describing accomplishments of outreach program to high school students
- Conducted extensive research on foundation prospects for outreach program to high school students; created custom database in Access to compile prospecting information
- Part of student team that won award for best community service project, one of 10 projects developed as part of philanthropy seminar

Board Member   June 2005-June 2007

'92 Theatre, Wesleyan University, Middletown, CT
- Served as one of 10 board members charged with producing 20 theater productions each year; duties included evaluating production ideas, crafting budgets for each production and assisting with marketing to student body
- Helped organize successful benefit showcase of original short plays that raised $1,500 for student productions
- Wrote articles on upcoming productions for periodic newsletter distributed to theater students

Tour Guide   February 2005-June 2007

Wesleyan University, Middletown, CT
- Conducted weekly tours of campus for prospective students and their families providing a comprehensive overview of history, educational principles, and culture of university; helped train new tour guides

ARTS EXPERIENCE

Assistant Set Designer   June-August 2006

Middletown Children's Summer Circus, Middletown, CT
- Researched concepts for and helped create set design for outdoor summer performance involving children from ages 10 to 13; helped teach volunteers to assist with construction of set pieces

Student Intern   June-August 2005

Hampton Playhouse, Hampton, NH
- One of 20 college students selected to assist with summer series of children's plays; both acted in and helped design sets for weekly productions

EDUCATION

2005 Bachelor of Arts in Theater with honors, Wesleyan University wrote honors thesis on Russian set designers of the early 20th century
2004 Graduate, Institute of Philanthropy and Voluntary Service, Fund For American Studies

Visit Vault at **www.vault.com** for insider company profiles, expert advice, career message boards, expert resume reviews, the Vault Job Board and more.

V/\ULT CAREER LIBRARY   **67**

Peggy Sue Kim
Phone: 415.205.3706
911 O'Farrell Street, Apt 5, San Francisco, CA 94109
E-mail: peggykimsue11@yahoo.com

December 1, 2007

Melissa Moody
Director of Development
The School for Self-Healing
2218 48th Avenue
San Francisco, CA 94116

Dear Ms. Moody:

With great interest and enthusiasm, I am writing to apply for the events planning coordinator position at The School for Self-Healing posted on Craig's List. With my combined experience in customer service, events planning and holistic health, I can design and organize successful events to raise the school's visibility in the community and bring in significant new revenue.

I am a dedicated and creative professional who has spent my entire career in holistic health. My primary focus has been customer relations and event planning, helping foster a greater awareness and understanding of holistic health principles. As the retreat coordinator for the Sacred Space Health Center, I ensured that clients with a range of health issues received the best experience possible at retreats. In many cases, I helped enhance retreat experiences by assisting facilitators in tailoring activities to meet the specific needs of customers, finding the most suitable accommodations and in improving meal quality. At the Bodytonic Health Club and Spa, I organized a number of well-attended events, including a Holistic Health Happy Hour, resulting in greater membership loyalty and participation in the club's programs. I am also a certified yoga instructor and recently designed a unique workout class that combines yogic postures, modern dance and visualization exercises. The class—which has proven quite popular—is similar in approach to programs offered at the School for Self-Healing. The enclosed resume provides a more detailed description of my experience and accomplishments.

I am greatly inspired by the story of The School of Self-Healing's founder Meir Schneider and his triumph over blindness. His philosophy of linking meditation, massage and yogic principles to heal the sick resonates with me. I myself have seen the power of yoga and visualization in working with emotionally disturbed young women. I would greatly appreciate the opportunity to apply my expertise in event planning to help the School of Self-Healing continue to prosper. I look forward to speaking with you soon.

Best,

Peggy Sue Kim

Peggy Sue Kim
Phone: 415.205.3706
911 O'Farrell Street, Apt. 5, San Francisco, CA 94109
E-mail: peggykimsue11@yahoo.com

OVERVIEW

A dedicated, enthusiastic and creative professional with solid experience in customer service and extensive knowledge of holistic health seeking to apply skills and experience to assist a community health organization

- Demonstrated success in fostering strong, long-term relationships with customers with wide ranging needs and personalities
- Experienced and comfortable in negotiating with a variety of vendors to ensure successful events and effective marketing materials within limited budgets
- Detailed oriented and experienced in variety of databases and accounting software, including Microsoft Access and Quickbooks
- Certified yoga instructor who designs unique classes that link yogic principles with modern dance and stress reduction techniques

WORK EXPERIENCE

Bodytonic Health Club and Spa, *San Francisco*   2004-present
Member Services Coordinator/Instructor

- Serve as primary liaison to more than 200 members seeking fitness and health resources and services; assess needs and fitness goals of members and help design individualized fitness and health programs; work with disgruntled members to ensure that complaints are heard and addressed; refine and maintain comprehensive membership database to track billing and informational mailings; succeeded in significantly increasing membership retention
- Collaborate with staff and consultants to produce monthly calendar, event announcements and brochures for members; worked closely with web programmer to expand company web site to include members-only section and create mechanism for regular e-mail announcements
- Supervise variety of vendors and staff to host four to six annual member appreciation events, including orientation parties, workshops and lectures; develop yearly budget for member appreciation activities and track expenses to ensure high-quality events within budget constraints
- Assist staff in assessing quality of personalized workout regimes and classes by surveying members on their experiences and impressions; compile results of informal surveys into periodic reports for management used for refining structure and content of classes and workshops
- Designed and lead innovative and popular workout class that combine yogic postures, modern dance and visualization exercises

Sacred Space Healing Center, *San Francisco*   2002-2004
Receptionist/Retreat Coordinator
- Provided intensive customer support to clients seeking holistic health services; served as primary information resource for customers on the principles of holistic health and assisted in designing individualized course schedules for customers with range of health issues
- Worked with array of vendors (including food services, facilities, graphic designers and printers) to create successful retreats for wide range of customers; tracked fees and expenses to ensure retreats met revenue goals; created comprehensive database to assist in bidding and selection of vendors and organized electronic calendar to more effectively schedule retreats
- Assisted instructors and consultants to design effective agendas for retreats by compiling information on customers needs and goals; designed survey instrument to assist in evaluating success of retreats

VOLUNTEER EXPERIENCE

Youth Yoga Dharma, *San Francisco*   2005-present
Volunteer Instructor
- Guide emotionally disturbed young women in relaxation exercises and basic yoga postures to manage stress and build self-esteem
- Worked with range of vendors to supply health food samples and gift certificates for raffle at annual fundraising event, which raised $20,000

Manifesti-val: Dance Brigade's Festival for Social Change, *San Francisco*   2003
Dancer
- Chosen as part of select ensemble for series of short dance pieces about the politics of immigration

New Moves Student Choreography Showcase, *San Francisco State University*   2001
Dancer/Choreographer
- Choreographed and performed original dance piece adapting the story of *Beauty and the Beast*

EDUCATION

Yoga Tree	Yoga Alliance Level One Certification	2004
San Francisco State University Bachelor of Arts, Dance		2002

ERIC PORTHOUSE
781.612.9745 | 51 COMMONWEALTH AVENUE #4, BOSTON, MA 02116
EPORTHOUSE@GMAIL.COM

March 2, 2007

Janet Cady, President
Children's Hospital Trust
One Autumn Street
Boston, MA 02215

Dear Ms. Cady:

Joe Crafton at Crossmark suggested that I get in touch with you to express my interest in becoming the new director of cause-related marketing and corporate sponsorships at Children's Hospital Trust. As a veteran marketing and public relations professional with considerable experience building alliances between nonprofit organizations and businesses, I have the expertise, talent and creativity to broaden and diversify the hospital's circle of corporate supporters.

For the past five years, I have led a wide range of marketing and communications efforts to help corporations and nonprofits increase their visibility, connect with target audiences and build brand identity. Social responsibility has always been a guiding principle for my work, both as part of the marketing team at Timberland and in advising clients at Red Javelin Communications. Whenever possible, I have looked for opportunities to foster mutually beneficial collaborations between businesses and charities. The following are just a few ways in which I have worked to promote this kind of synergy:

• As a marketing director at Timberland, I built partnerships with community groups in key markets through sponsorship of events, donation of equipment and cause-related marketing. I am particularly proud of the advertising campaign I developed with the YMCA in Vermont, where Timberland customers throughout the state were encouraged to make donations for an outdoor hiking program for at-risk teens. With a matching grant from a community foundation, the YMCA and Timberland arranged a series of hikes into the Green Mountain National Forest.

• At Red Javelin Communications, I created a highly successful public relations efforts to establish the founder of Divorce.net as an expert in the field, resulting in widespread media coverage and a major increase in web site traffic. As part of the initiative, I negotiated an arrangement with counseling centers in critical media markets to allow clients free access to the web site. Both the web site and counseling groups received positive attention from local press around the partnership.

• As a volunteer consultant for the Taproot Foundation, I develop an online recruitment campaign that substantially expanded membership for One Family, a Massachusetts nonprofit advocating for the homeless. I also obtained funding for the campaign from a number of Internet businesses associated with Red Javelin Communications.

I grew up in Boston and know how important Children's Hospital is to the community and for the education of the finest doctors in the country. It would be an honor and privilege to work for you at one of the nation's most prestigious hospitals—and a place that provides so much for Boston's residents. I hope to meet with you soon to talk about how I can help take the hospital's corporate sponsorship program to a new level.

Sincerely,
Eric Porthouse

Visit Vault at **www.vault.com** for insider company profiles, expert advice, career message boards, expert resume reviews, the Vault Job Board and more.

V\ULT CAREER LIBRARY   71

ERIC PORTHOUSE
781.612.9745 | 51 COMMONWEALTH AVENUE #4, BOSTON, MA 02116
EPORTHOUSE@GMAIL.COM

Highlights of Qualifications
Veteran marketing and public relations specialist with more than five years experience leading effective and innovative branding, advertising and direct response campaigns for businesses and charities
• Significant experience in cause-related marketing and building partnerships between charities and business interests
• Demonstrated ability to use technology in innovative ways to engage and motivate target audiences
• Creative, solutions-oriented and motivated working for organizations devoted to social change

PROFESSIONAL EXPERIENCE

Red Javelin Communications, Sudbury, MA | www.redjavelin.com   1.05–present
A boutique communications consulting firm focused on targeted public relations and marketing for emerging technology and consumer companies

Account Director
Provide guidance and leadership to diverse portfolio of clients in order to increase their visibility and market share; assist in establishing and strengthening brand recognition by redesigning marketing pieces, developing innovative advertising campaigns and aggressive public relations efforts; executed range of direct response marketing efforts, including viral e-mail initiatives, banner advertising and development of interactive internet videos; developed and implemented highly successful public relations effort to establish founder of online resource on divorce as expert in the field, resulting in widespread media coverage and major increase in web site traffic; clients include Divorce.net, Tripadvisor.com, and Reef Point Systems.

Timberland, Stratham, NH | www.timberland.com   1.02–11.04
An internationally renowned retail business for footwear and apparel, also widely recognized for its socially responsible business practices and its investment in communities around the world

Marketing Manager   9.03–11.04
Developed and implemented effective marketing plans to expand marketplace for outdoor specialty, running specialty and sporting goods; oversaw two associates and range of consultants to implement marketing efforts that included direct response (both print and electronic), promotions and events at retailers across the country, trade show presentations, print and web advertising, web site development and earned media; managed multimillion-dollar budgets and tracked monthly performance of marketing efforts to regularly exceed strategic goals and targets; conceptualized and implemented range of community relations activities (such as corporate sponsorships of events and donation of equipment) to engage nonprofit partners and retailers in key markets; arranged adventure mountain hike as a silent auction item for national breast cancer survivor group and helped develop cause-related marketing campaign for around outdoor education for regional youth organization.

Marketing Associate   01.02–09.03
Coordinated successful marketing strategies with a focus on outdoor accessories; managed large-scale direct response marketing efforts (both print and electronic), including copywriting and editing, supervising contract writers, graphic designers, printers and mail houses, and in-depth analysis of results; oversaw various print and online advertising campaigns, including creative development and media buys; prepared and presented analyses of marketing efforts to organizational leadership, including presentation on efforts to expand viral marketing strategies; assisted in developing and executing major online promotional campaign to introduce new shoe product resulting in significant surge in sales.

Pirozzola Company, Wellesley, MA | www.pirozzola.com   01.00–10.01
A 20-year-old public relations firm providing a full range of services for technology, international relations, real estate and housing, and institutional investment clients in the United States and Pacific Rim

Copywriter   9.00-10.01
Drafted compelling copy for wide range of marketing materials and campaigns, including direct response pieces (both mail and e-mail), press releases and media alerts, online advertising and web pages; collaborated with public relation consultants to ensure consistency in style and voice across campaigns; chosen by principal consultant to lead effort to develop style guide for trade association operating in Vietnam; served as primary liaison with client's technical and legal staff to ensure copy met all product and legal requirements; researched and compiled analysis of emerging online marketing in China and Vietnam for principal consultants.

Public Relations Intern   01.00–08.00
Provided critical assistance for range of marketing and communications campaigns, including constructing media relations databases, creating and updating press kits, compiling public relations value reports and contacting television advertising representatives; assisted in drafting various marketing materials.

EDUCATION
Bachelor of Arts, English – University of Massachusetts, Amherst   1999
Emphasis in creative and technical writing

EXTRACURRICULAR
Taproot Foundation   2006
Chosen as volunteer marketing consultant to develop online recruitment campaign to expand membership for One Family, a Massachusetts nonprofit advocating for the homeless

Harbor to Bay AIDS Ride   2005
Raised more than $7,000 for AIDS and HIV research and completed 68-mile bicycle ride from Boston to Provincetown

Habitat for Humanity   2004
Served as volunteer to build new homes in the greater Boston area

Visit Vault at **www.vault.com** for insider company profiles, expert advice, career message boards, expert resume reviews, the Vault Job Board and more.

VAULT CAREER LIBRARY   73

Peter Patrick Dunlap
385 East 17th Avenue #4 Oakland, CA 94606
cell: 415-870-8477 / e-mail: ppdunlap@gmail.com

January 26, 2008

Suzanne Frederick
Human Resources Department
William Penn Foundation
Two Logan Square, 11th Floor
100 North 18th Street
Philadelphia, PA 19103-2757

Dear Ms. Frederick:

I write to express my deep interest in serving as the new environment and communities program associate at the William Penn Foundation. To assist the foundation with its strategic philanthropy, I bring to this position extensive knowledge of environmental issues that affect urban communities, considerable experience in conflict resolution and coalition building and an understanding of how to develop effective partnerships between funders and conservation activists.

Throughout my education and career, I have focused my attention and energy toward fostering consensus to drive urban planning and land-use policy. I have conducted extensive research that has facilitated better policy-making, including a critique of collaborative planning around oil and gas development in Alaska's North Slope that was used by the National Congress of American Indians to assist partner groups in places like Otero Mesa, New Mexico. For the past three years, I have led efforts in and around Oakland to engage a diverse group of community and union leaders, public health advocates, foundations and locally elected officials in efforts to reduce air pollution caused by freight transport. In addition to compiling information for a comprehensive report on freight transport, I have been the primary liaison between the coalition and a range of funders, helping secure more than $50,000 for collaborative advocacy and city planning.

As you well know, the need for partnerships with unlikely players is more necessary than ever to move contentious environmental issues. I am impressed with the foundation's willingness to embrace unorthodox collaborations, especially between land protection groups, land trusts, real estate developers and venture capitalists to preserve open space in and around Philadelphia. I look forward to speaking with you and your colleague about how I can use my unique skills set and expertise to help the foundation support other initiatives to ensure that ecological and social integrity of the greater Philadelphia area.

Sincerely,

Peter Patrick Dunlap

Peter Patrick Dunlap
385 East 17th Avenue #4 Oakland, CA 94606
cell: 415-870-8477 / e-mail: ppdunlap@gmail.com

OVERVIEW

Dedicated nonprofit professional with solid background in environmental advocacy and partnership-building seeking to expand expertise in development and philanthropy

• Experienced and comfortable working with foundation officers to build programs; assisted in raising $50,000 to expand environmental advocacy program
• Demonstrated ability to compile statistics and facts to draft comprehensive reports and updates on complex policy questions
• Versed in conflict resolution with considerable experience bringing together a broad array of stakeholders; provided critical leadership to build diverse and active coalition around freight transport issues
• Detailed oriented and focused with an ability to see short-term tasks through while keeping an eye on the long-term vision

WORK HISTORY:

The Pacific Institute, Oakland, CA

2004–present   Program Associate, Community Strategies for Sustainability and Justice Program

  • Serve as primary liaison between Institute, community leaders, and local governments officials on freight transport issues; analyze and translate local, regional, and statewide policies on freight transport for variety of audiences; facilitate communication between community leaders and local and state officials on freight transport issues
  • Conduct research (including review of U.S. Census data, GIS maps, and policy papers) on community health, environmental quality, public safety and related topics for a Neighborhood Indicators project for West Contra Costa County; cultivated relationships with wide range of partners to engage them in research, including grassroots groups, community leaders, chambers of commerce and community foundations; led effort to build new regional coalition on freight transport
  • Develop trainings for local partner organizations on participatory planning, public speaking and grassroots organizing; hosted 15 well-attended and highly regarded workshops to date
  • Collaborate with the Institute's communications staff to prepare range of informational materials on freight transport issues (including those on health concerns and fundamentals of city planning), such as press releases, web page updates, action alerts and fact sheets; with communications staff, developed successful media outreach strategy to encourage participation in city-planning effort, resulting in widespread local coverage and unprecedented attendance at public hearings
  • Assisted in securing $50,000 in new funding for outreach efforts from individual donors and foundations; gave series of presentations on freight transport issues to consortium of foundations; conducted field tours with foundation staff and individual donors; drafted detailed updates and proposals

Visit Vault at **www.vault.com** for insider company profiles, expert advice, career message boards, expert resume reviews, the Vault Job Board and more.

V∧ULT CAREER LIBRARY   **75**

2003-2004 **American Hiking Society, Chattanooga,** TN
Grassroots Organizing Intern

- Recruited member groups of Southeastern Foot Trails Coalition to participate in third annual Southeastern Foot Trails Conference; gave series of presentations to coalition members and fielded questions about conference agenda; succeeded in convincing four key member groups to attend conference
- Provided range of logistical assistance for conference, including distributing agenda and informational materials to conference participants and taking detailed notes on plenary sessions
- Assisted in drafting comprehensive report on conference and its impact for major foundations
- Led trail maintenance effort in Smoky Mountain National Park in collaboration with Park Service staff; recruited team of 12 volunteers to participate in three-day project

EDUCATIONAL INTERNSHIPS

2003   National Congress of American Indians, Land Use Management, Anchorage, AK
Developed case study critiquing collaborative planning between state and federal land management agencies and native communities around oil and gas drilling in the North Slope

2000, 2001   Wilmer, Cutler, Pickering, LLC, Environmental Law, Washington, D.C.,
Conducted extensive research and developed annotated bibliography for book to be written by senior partner on the history of superfund litigation

EDUCATION

2002 – 2003 University of Vermont, Environmental Law Center
South Royalton, VT
Master of Studies in Environmental Law

1999 – 2002 Syracuse University, Maxwell School of Citizenship and Public Affairs
Syracuse, NY
Bachelor of Arts, Conflict Resolution and Public Policy

ADDITIONAL SKILLS AND INTERESTS

- Experience with range of computer programs, including Microsoft Office, Access and Dreamweaver
- Fluent in Spanish
- Avid bicyclist and hiker

The Interview

So you've submitted your cover letter, resume and writing sample for an exciting job at a nonprofit organization that you could fall in love with. A few days later (although don't be surprised if it takes a couple of weeks or more), your cell phone rings and it's someone from the organization (the director of human resources, the director of development's assistant, the head of the foundation, etc.), wanting to schedule an interview. Once the first wave of elation wears off, it's time to get to work preparing for the interview.

Interview Process

Just as there is no typical nonprofit, there is no typical interview process for jobs in fundraising and philanthropic giving. Generally, you'll meet with a number of different people in one or two interview sessions, including your direct supervisor, a few of your work colleagues and the executive director or vice president of the department (depending on the size of the organization). The interview process may stretch over a few days or a couple of weeks, depending on how many people you meet with at the organization and their schedules. While a bit nerve wracking, it's good to interview with as many people as you can (within reason) so you can get a sense of the group's culture, work ethic and the general approach of management. Each interview is also an opportunity to do some detective work on the kinds of challenges you might face.

As is true in the for-profit world, a professional demeanor is essential, even if the executive director is dressed in blue jeans and sits behind a secondhand desk. Every interview counts, whether you are meeting with the vice president of development or the development assistant. Don't be late for interviews, and don't treat your interviewers as your best friends. And buy an interview suit if you don't already have one. Once you're hired, you can come to work in your blue jeans and worn-out sneakers, but only if you aren't meeting with a donor or grantee.

In addition to interviews, you may be asked to take a few tests to gauge your familiarity with fundraising or philanthropic giving, your writing skills and your attention to detail. If writing is a big part of the job (which is certainly true for a grant writer), you could be given a take-home writing assignment.

For example, you may be asked to draft a letter of inquiry to a foundation for one of the organization's programs. If you applied for a coordinator position, you may be given a timed data entry assignment or a copyediting/ proofreading test.

Whatever the interview scenario, be prepared. Be prepared to speak about the breadth of your fundraising or philanthropic giving experience, your understanding of fundraising and philanthropy trends, and your familiarity with the organization. And be prepared to ask questions of your own.

Homework

Before you put on that tie or suit jacket, you should have a working knowledge of the organization for which you are interviewing. Word-for-word memorization of facts and statistics isn't necessary, but you should know and be able to describe the following:

- the mission statement
- the year the organization was founded
- the approach the organization takes to addressing an issue; for example, you should understand and be able to describe the teaching philosophy of a charter school, or the doctrine of a religious institution
- the major activities that the organization undertakes
- the qualifications and history of the organization's executive director; and,
- the organization's operating budget

All of this information should be available on the organization's web site. Generally, you should thoroughly review as much material on the web site as you can absorb. At the very least, look over the "About Us" section where most of the information listed above can be found and read the following documents:

- **The organization's Form 990**. The Form 990 is the federal tax form that every nonprofit registered for federal tax-exempt status must file with the Internal Revenue Service. It is also a public document that nonprofit organizations are required to make available to anyone who asks for it. If it isn't on the organization's web site, 990 forms for many nonprofits can be found through Guidstar (www.guidestar.org).

It's a difficult document to follow, but the IRS is currently in the process of completely revising the form 990 to be more user-friendly. It's worth a read in any case because it is full of important information for fundraisers, including the amount of revenue raised that year, a list of major funders and the salaries of top employees (a very useful piece of information when negotiating your own salary). 990 forms for foundations also include a complete list of all their grantees in a given year.

- **The organization's most recent annual report.** Like publicly traded, for-profit corporations, most established nonprofit groups publish a report each year that provides a description of major activities and accomplishments, as well as a summary of financial information (including a breakdown of income raised from each major revenue source). The report often includes a list of donors as well. The annual report is the best document for gaining a basic understanding of the size and scope of an organization.

- **The organization's strategic plan.** While the organization's overall approach is outlined in the annual report, the strategic plan provides much more detail on the organization's next steps. It's also a great resource for understanding the context in which the organization works, for it usually describes past accomplishments, current and future challenges, as well as the unique niche that the organization fills in the nonprofit community.

- **Press releases and news clippings.** Press materials give you a good sense of the specific issues and activities that the organization is focused on at the moment and how the organization talks about them. For example, a more radical advocacy group is likely to take an aggressive, slanted stance on any given issue in a press release. Pay close attention to the language used in these materials and compile a list of key concepts and phrases that might be useful in the interview.

Beyond the organization's web site, it's worth investing some time in a wider Internet search on the organization. It's important to know how the media, policy-makers, and the nonprofit community view the organization and its work. It's also important to know if the organization is or has been involved in any major controversy and/or scandal. A search on Wikipedia can be useful; because anyone is allowed to edit and revise articles, you can find out a lot about what others say about a given organization, especially if it is involved in a controversial issue.

Finally, make sure to read up on the issue that the organization is trying to address. Usually, nonprofits post fact sheets, position papers and other informational materials on their web sites. Make sure to read a few news articles as well. An organization may have a strong stance on an issue, especially an advocacy group, when there are likely to be many different perspectives.

Visit Vault at **www.vault.com** for insider company profiles, expert advice, career message boards, expert resume reviews, the Vault Job Board and more.

V/\ULT CAREER·
LIBRARY

79

Again, no one expects you to have a photographic memory, so it's fine to take notes and bring them to the interview. In fact, you are likely to impress the person conducting the interview by demonstrating that you have done your homework.

Typical Interview Questions

Interviewers will likely take one of two tacks. The formal approach is what most of us think of as a typical interview. The interviewer has a list of questions that they ask each candidate, and the interviewer tries to keep the format and content of the interview as structured as possible so that they can easily compare candidates. The other approach is much less formal and structured, where the interviewer initiates a directed conversation, where each shares information about themselves and their perspectives on the organization. In general, either kind of interviewer will touch upon the following questions:

What do you know about the organization?

Don't underestimate how important your answer to this question is; this is a test to see how thorough you are in your homework. The last thing you want to say is that you don't know a thing about the group. Such an answer implies that either you are lazy or you don't care about working there. At the very least you should be able to describe in your own words the organization's mission, the year it was founded, its approach and activities, the name of the executive director and the most recent accomplishments as published on the web site.

What do you know about the issue that the organization addresses?

While no one will expects you to be an expert (with the exception of when you are applying for a high-level position at a foundation), as a liaison to donors you will be asked to describe how important an issue is and why the organization plays an important role. On the philanthropic giving side, you need to understand different strategies for approaching an issue so you can help shape giving priorities. This question is therefore an opportunity to show how you would formulate a pitch to either a donor or board member. So as part of your homework, take some time to shape and practice your pitch. Take notes on the major points you would want a donor to know about the issue and the organization's role in addressing it. Make sure you have an answer that hits all those points but is as succinct as possible. Rambling on without direction is just as bad as not answering the question at all. If you are interviewing for a job at an advocacy organization, the interviewer may want to know how familiar you are with the fundamentals of government policy-making and the specific decision-making bodies that the organization interacts with on a regular basis. For example, if you are interviewing at an organization that works on shaping environmental policy in California, you should know that the state has established its own Environmental Protection Agency independent from the federal agency.

Describe your experience in fundraising and philanthropy.

Your answer in response should not be a recitation of every single activity outlined in your resume. Rather, you should demonstrate a working knowledge of the organization's key funders (foundations, corporations, membership, major donors, etc.) and how you can apply your particular skill set to strengthening relationships with those donors. Likewise, if you are applying for a position in philanthropic giving, you should describe how your skills and experience will help you interact with the particular kind of grantees that the foundation or corporation gives to, or the individuals who will be asking for your assistance in managing their giving. The job description is an important resource for answering this question; if the major responsibilities focus on cultivating partnerships with corporations, for example, make sure that you can talk about how your particular experience applies to working with corporate donors. If the position description is more general, such as one for a development associate, information from the annual report and Form 990 is critical to formulating your answer. You should be able to discern the major funding streams (or grantees) from these two documents. Be as specific as you can by providing examples of your work in the past and at least one success story where you played a role in managing a donor or grantee. Try to describe your role in as much detail as possible from the start of a process to its conclusion. This gives the interviewer a good sense of how much you understand the time and attention it takes to engage a donor or grantee. But don't exaggerate your role. The interviewer is likely to ask probing, follow-up questions to fully understand what you did and did not do in a fundraising or philanthropic giving success. Remember the comments from recruiters cited earlier in this chapter; fundraising and philanthropic giving are inherently collaborative, so interviewers understand that many people will be involved in any particular success.

Visit Vault at **www.vault.com** for insider company profiles, expert advice, career message boards, expert resume reviews, the Vault Job Board and more.

VAULT CAREER LIBRARY   81

Describe how you have interacted with donors (or grantees).

While similar to the previous question about your fundraising or philanthropic giving experience, the objective of this question is different. Beyond getting a handle on your actual experience, the interviewer is trying to discern your personal approach with donors and/or grantees. There are many variations to this question. Are you aggressive or passive with donors? Do you prefer to do a lot of research and carefully craft of a pitch before meeting with a donor, or do you wait until you are in front of the donor to decide which tack to take? Do you have a strong opinion about how a foundation should work with grantees? These are just a few ways the question may be phrased. It's important to remember that there are no right answers. Rather, you want to be honest about your level of involvement. If you have not had a lot of face time with donors or grantees, say so, but describe how you have prepared others for such interactions. And be thoughtful about your own philosophy on working with donors and/or grantees. Describe the approach of a development or giving professional that you have worked with and admire. And don't assume that the interviewer is looking for one particular kind of fundraiser or giving professional. In fact, most experienced fundraisers and philanthropic giving professionals adjust their style depending on the person or group they are working with at the time. If you have worked with donors that have funded the organization or with grantees that the organization funds, make sure to mention them by name and describe at least one interaction with them.

Why do you want to work here?

This is a critically important question, so spend some time thinking about your answer before the interview. You response is in fact another way for the interviewer to gauge how you will interact with donors or grantees. Your personal connection to and passion for an organization is a critical factor for most donors; your enthusiasm can be the deciding factor for whether or not a gift is made. Moreover, the more articulate and thoughtful you can be in describing your personal reasons for supporting an organization, the more successful you are likely to be in the field. So in answering the question, be specific and thoughtful. "I just love the arts, and I think you are all are really effective," is not a good answer. Relate the question to your personal experiences and to your research on the organization. A better answer might be the following:

"My parents had season tickets to the local orchestra, and I grew up playing the violin. I even played in a youth concert in the local symphony hall. I think back to that experience often when I doubt myself, remembering the rush of self-confidence I felt when the audience applauded. I am impressed with the emphasis that your organization places on engaging young people in music appreciation. Like your executive director, I believe that exposure to all sorts of music can help broaden a child's horizons as it did for me. I would very much like to help you expand these programs."

Don't be afraid to describe your professional goals as well and what you think you can learn from the organization's fundraising or philanthropic giving team.

Questions to Ask

Whether structured or conversational, an interview is an important information-gathering tool for you as well, so make sure to have a list of questions of your own. Try to find out as much as possible about the challenges you may face at the organization. Most interviewers are delighted and impressed by tough questions. You once again demonstrate your familiarity with the field, as well as your level of thoughtfulness and thoroughness. Here are a few questions you might want to ask:

What is the organization's strategic planning process?

What are the organization's plans for growth? This question helps you discern how forward thinking and strategic the organization's leadership is. An effective fundraising or philanthropic giving team considers a strategic plan to be a critical tool for their work. Without it, the team is at a serious disadvantage in engaging sophisticated donors and in prioritizing activities. (The next chapter on finding the right job dives into this issue in more detail.)

Can you describe the process for developing the organization's annual fundraising plan?

Or, can you describe the process for determine the organization's giving priorities? This is another question to help you determine how much planning and analysis goes into the organization's fundraising or philanthropic giving efforts. Beware of an organization that does not have some kind of written plan or formal planning process.

How active is the executive director in fundraising or setting giving priorities?

Ideally, the executive director at a nonprofit organization plays an active role in fundraising, since he/she is the face and voice of the organization; if the executive director is disinterested or intimidated by fundraising, the organization is at a major disadvantage. Likewise, the executive director or president at a foundation should provide leadership in setting priorities for grantmaking. On the other hand, an executive director can be too engaged in fundraising and/or grantmaking and may micromanage the fundraising or philanthropic giving team. Try to ask this question of as many people as possible, especially staff who will be your peers. Your supervisor, the person most likely to conduct the primary interview, may be reluctant to share his/her own difficulties with the executive director, but others may be more forthright.

How active is the board in decision-making, fundraising and/or philanthropic giving?

Board members are important ambassadors for any nonprofit organization or philanthropic giving institution. They therefore should be major players in fundraising or giving activities. Ask this question of both your immediate supervisor and upper management, if you get the chance to meet with the vice president of development or the executive director. Ideally, the board provides critical support to the fundraising or philanthropic giving team without micromanaging staff or undermining the authority of the executive director.

What is your management style?

An effective fundraising or philanthropic-giving team functions collaboratively, so your supervisor should foster an environment of open communication. Planning is also critical to successful fundraising, and your supervisor should be engaged and encouraging planning efforts. In addition, your supervisor should provide training and mentoring. Finally, your supervisor should be supportive of balancing work and personal life, especially since your salary is likely to be lower than what you might earn in more high pressure, for-profit industries. Ask your potential supervisor to address these issues as they discuss their management style. Also ask your potential peers about the supervisor. Many supervisors would describe themselves as collaborative or committed to work/life balance, but their employees would say otherwise.

What is the performance review process for employees?

No matter what the size, a nonprofit or philanthropic giving institution should have a formal and rigorous process for reviewing the performance of employees. The organization should also have a policy of awarding cost-of-living raises each year and/or bonuses, even if they are small. Startup organizations, or those that are poorly managed, will not have thought through these kinds of personnel issues. You probably don't want to work for these places.

What is level of commitment from the leadership to the giving program (for those seeking a job at a business/corporation with a giving or community development program)?

There's always the danger that a for-profit organization professing a commitment to giving back to the community does not follow up on that promise. If you are looking for a job with a corporate giving program, make sure that the company provides the necessary staff and resources. Such a program will always have more requests for donations that it can possibly accommodate; however, you don't want to put yourself in the frustrating position of always saying no, or of spending long hours reviewing hundreds of requests because you are the only one assigned to the task.

How do program staff participate in fundraising (for those seeking a fundraising job)?

It is important that program staff be aware and supportive of fundraising efforts; in many cases, donors would rather speak with program staff with direct knowledge of the organization's activities. On the other hand, it's also important that the fundraising team be the lead in engaging donors. In other words, you want to make sure that fundraising is a collaborative and coordinated effort across the organization.

Visit Vault at **www.vault.com** for insider company profiles, expert advice, career message boards, expert resume reviews, the Vault Job Board and more.

VAULT CAREER LIBRARY   85

Negotiating Salary and Benefits

Now you've made it through a round of interviews and you're more excited than ever about the organization. You're especially enthusiastic about your potential new boss, a sharp and funny woman who was delighted that you asked detailed questions about the long-term growth of the organization. You're about to walk out the door to meet with your friends for a drink when your cell phone rings. It's her and she says the magic words: "We'd really like to hire you."

Before committing to a start date, it's important to have an in-depth conversation with your new boss about salary and benefits. While compensation levels in the nonprofit world have increased substantially in recent years, especially for those involved in fundraising, you won't be making nearly as much as your friends working for for-profit enterprises. And benefits may not be much more than health care coverage—but that doesn't mean there isn't room for negotiation. First and foremost, make sure that you understand what your compensation will be, the schedule for annual reviews and the full plate of benefits that you will receive, including the health care plan, annual leave policy and retirement plan options. Here are few other tips for getting the most you can from the organization:

• **Research average salaries in your area.** Several salary surveys that focus in part or exclusively on the nonprofit sector are now readily available. *Nonprofit Times* publishes an annual survey, which breaks down nonprofit salaries by position and by region. Use this information in your negotiation. Be clear that you have done your research and that your salary should meet or exceed the region's average.

• **Explore different pay structures.** Unfortunately, many small nonprofit organizations will not budge on their initial salary offer simply because they don't have the resources to pay you more. But they might be amenable to providing you some kind of bonus, either up front or some time during the year based on performance. They may also be willing to revisit salary negotiations in six months. If you can't get your new boss to move beyond the initial offer, ask about these other options.

• **Negotiate for more paid leave.** Some organizations may be willing to give you an extra week of paid leave to compensate for a lower salary. Time can be more important than money, so discuss such an option with your boss.

• **Negotiate a flexible schedule.** Understanding that they are underpaying their employees, many nonprofits offer flexible schedules, from telecommuting to shorter workweeks. If you want more time to spend with your friends and family, if you want to take a class, or if you need a second job, push for flexible hours.

- **Get a commitment to review your salary in 12 months.** As described above, smaller nonprofit organizations may not have established performance review schedules. If you are still interested in working for such an organization, demand that your boss conduct a review no later than 12 months after you have started. And make sure your boss commits to a salary discussion as part of the review.

Visit Vault at **www.vault.com** for insider company profiles, expert advice, career message boards, expert resume reviews, the Vault Job Board and more.

V/\ULT CAREER LIBRARY   **87**

Finding the Right Job

Wherever you are in the United States, you are surrounded by opportunities that can lead to a meaningful and rewarding career in fundraising and philanthropic giving. The real challenge is finding the right one for you.

In all likelihood, you live within miles of a nonprofit hospital or medical center, a church group assisting the homeless, a local community theater, a museum, a private school or university, a tutoring program for at-risk students—most of which are looking for enthusiastic fundraisers. Likewise, there is a foundation, small business, corporate affiliate or the United Way leading efforts to fund charities in your community. Yet the size, shape and culture of these organizations (both on the giving and receiving side) are as varied as the species of flowering plants in a rainforest. More importantly, the effectiveness and professionalism of these organizations wildly varies. For every nonprofit with strong leadership that fills an important niche in the community, there is another that duplicates efforts of another group, that is territorial and resistant to change, ruled by personality and politics and is struggling to keep its doors open. As Doug White (a consultant and author of the recently published *Charities on Trial*) puts it, "In my own view, if you lost a third of the fundraising charities in the United States, the world wouldn't be that worse off."

So how do you navigate the jungle to get the training and experience you need? First you have to know what you are looking for. Then you have to go out and find it. In this chapter, we will discuss what makes an effective nonprofit organization and how you can look for the telltale signs of dysfunction either to avoid or at least be aware of when looking for a job.

Let's be clear—there is no perfect nonprofit, just as there is no perfect business or family. But as someone just starting a career in fundraising and philanthropy, you should be choosy. It's not unlike buying a house or a car—there are many, many choices out there and you should have in mind the features that are most important to you. And when shopping for your first nonprofit or philanthropic institution, the following features (described in more detail below) are essential:

- An organization doing work or addressing an issue that you care about
- An effective organization with dynamic leadership
- A team environment
- A mentor

Visit Vault at **www.vault.com** for insider company profiles, expert advice, career message boards, expert resume reviews, the Vault Job Board and more.

V/\ULT CAREER LIBRARY 89

Know the Cause

Most fundraising professionals will tell you that the most successful in the field are people who are passionate about a cause. Likewise, those involved in philanthropic giving have deep feelings about the issues they promote and the various groups that they help fund. And while a consultant may advise a variety of organizations, their eyes will shine when talking one particular organization that they themselves are passionate about.

Have passion

So some level of passion and enthusiasm for the mission and activities of an organization is a requirement.

But that passion can come in many forms. Many fundraisers and philanthropic giving professionals have some personal connection to a cause. They remember the hospice nurse that provided such tender care to their ailing grandmother. Their aunt died of breast cancer. They used to go fly-fishing with their dad until a favorite fishing hole was destroyed by the construction of a new gated community.

Others in the field take a broader view, hoping to advance a range of issues or causes. One fundraiser, for example, may feel strongly about progressive policies—from reproductive choice to stronger labor laws; another may care about promoting a conservative Christian ethic. So the decision on where to work is less about one issue but the perspective of the people that they work with and fundraise for.

Still others feel strongly about how a group approaches an issue. One fundraiser may feel that civil disobedience is a crucial tactic to raising awareness about an issue, while another passionately believes that protest movements are a waste of time. Another may think it's morally wrong to partner with corporations to address an issue like land protection or climate change; another may feel it's essential.

Know yourself and the cause

Whatever your perspective, it's worth taking the time to do a little soul searching. What do you care about? What kind of organization would you be willing to work for? Are there perspectives that make you uncomfortable? Are there positions on issues that you feel are unreasonable?

As part of your soul search, do your homework. If you are concerned about the growing number of homeless people you see on the street, read your local weekly paper and find out what your local politicians are doing about it. Scope out the web sites of local shelters and policy groups to see what services they provide. Skim through a position paper from a national think tank devoted to urban issues.

It's a worthwhile exercise for yourself personally and professionally, for the donors that you will meet later on will not only expect you to be passionate, but also knowledgeable. In conversations with donors, foundations or other colleagues, you will be asked about the local bond initiative, a controversial feature story or news article or debates in Congress or the state legislature. They will want you to have a broad perspective on why you think a gift to a particular organization is important both to the organization and the larger cause.

Effectiveness of an Organization

Any charity in the country will have dedicated staff with noble aims. But is that organization truly effective? Consultants and advisors in the field of fundraising and philanthropy are concerned that many charities are not. As a lawyer who advises charitable organizations puts it, "there is a tendency to start new nonprofits that are not necessary."

It may be difficult to determine how effective an organization is until you are working for it. But there are characteristics you can look for from the outside looking in.

Transparency

By law, nonprofit organizations are public institutions, which means that their financial status and decision-making processes should be readily apparent to anyone. For example, the tax form that 501(c)(3) nonprofit organizations are required to file each year (known as Form 990) must be made available to the public. Likewise, board meetings are supposed to be open at least to the staff of the organization, and proceedings for each meeting should be published. So when researching a charitable organization or foundation, check out their web site to make sure you can readily access documents such as Form 990, the annual report, the list of the board of directors and minutes from board meetings. If you can't easily find at least some of these documents, there's a good chance that the organization's leadership is secretive, perhaps with

Visit Vault at **www.vault.com** for insider company profiles, expert advice, career message boards, expert resume reviews, the Vault Job Board and more.

VAULT CAREER LIBRARY   91

something to hide. It could also mean that the organization is not aware of its legal obligations or has lost sight of key aspect of its mission, which is to serve the public.

A strong strategic plan and mission statement

While strategic planning has long been embraced by for-profit businesses, the nonprofit community has been slow to adopt formal processes for assessing effectiveness and planning for the future. Only in the past 10 years has strategic planning and the development of a planning document become a widely accepted business practice for nonprofits, and most groups are not very good at it. Likewise, all groups have formalized a mission statement describing what they hope to achieve in the long term, but they are often vague and confusing to the person off the street. A group that promises too much is unlikely to deliver on that promise and may often waste resources on too many different activities. In many cases, an organization can do one thing very well but offers a range of services that are mediocre at best and at worst duplicative of those provided by other groups. For a philanthropic institution, a lack of clarity on giving strategy can often mean that the organization gives too many little grants or is only supporting a few organizations with personal ties to the institution's board of directors. It's therefore important to carefully review the mission statement and strategic plan of an organization, both of which should be prominent on the group's web site. You should be able to quickly discern what the core activity or activities that the group is engaged in (or for a foundation or other giving program, the kind of nonprofits to which it donates), who the primary audience is, its history and reason for existence and what it hopes to accomplish in the future.

Consultant and author Doug White offers the following observation and advice on mission statements and strategic plans: "Most charities want to save the world, and they say that in their mission statements." But that's not enough. According to White, the mission statement and strategic plan should answer one simple question clearly and specifically: "Who cares if your organization closes its doors tomorrow?"

You usually find the mission statement and strategic plan in the "About Us" section of the web site (beware if an organization's web site doesn't have such a section). Here's an example of a strong mission statement:

The Reading Connection is a 501(c)(3) organization dedicated to bringing books and a lifelong love of reading to children in housing crisis.

From this one sentence, it's clear what the organization advocates (literacy) and who it serves (homeless children). The Reading Connection's web site also provides a detailed history of the organization, as well as how and why it expanded its services over time.

Here is an example of a less effective mission statement:

The mission of Family Health International is to improve lives worldwide through research, education and services in family health.

From this statement, it's not clear what actual services this organization provides (for example, does the organization conduct clinical or policy research?), who the organization serves (do they provide information directly to families? to educators?), or how it makes a difference.

To be fair, many organizations may be stuck with a mission statement adopted 20 years ago, and staff will readily tell you that they despise it. That's why a strategic plan can be so important. The plan should complement and clarify the organization's mission statement, clearly articulating where the organization has come from, what challenges it has faced, what it will do in the future and why its services are unique. While neither the mission statement nor the strategic plan will tell you everything you need to know about the organization, they are good indicators of the savvy of the organization's leadership.

Effective leadership

There are two major leadership groups at any nonprofit organization or foundation: the board of directors (or for foundation, the board of trustees) and the operational managers (the executive director and vice presidents). It's important for you to find out how these two different groups work with each other to guide the organization. Again, you can't know everything about either the board or the executive director without working for them, but you can get some information from the organization's web site and from informational or job interviews.

The board's role is tricky—it should help the organization grow financially and programmatically, provide some oversight of the executive director but not micromanage day-to-day operations. In the case of foundations, the board of trustees also makes the final decisions on which organizations will receive grants. Many boards are too large or too small—either indicates that the board is unable to effectively oversee the organization. A board with 20 or more members is unwieldy and unlikely to easily come to decisions.

Visit Vault at **www.vault.com** for insider company profiles, expert advice, career message boards, expert resume reviews, the Vault Job Board and more.

V/\ULT CAREER LIBRARY   93

Moreover, many members on a large board are there in spirit only and do not providing any kind of real leadership or support beyond showing up for board meetings. A board of four or five people has too much on its plate and cannot effectively implement a plan they might devise. Moreover, one member of the board may dominate over the others. This is especially true at foundations, where one family member on the board is the decision-maker in all grant-making and may often be at odds with the executive director. There's no magic number for the number of board members, but there should be enough people to spread responsibilities around and to allow for a diversity of opinion. Moreover, board members should have many different backgrounds and expertise, from fundraising to policy to marketing to management. And board responsibilities should be clearly defined with by-laws and a committee structure. From the web site, you should be able to find out the number of board members and their backgrounds. The rest you may have to assess in your interviews with the organization's staff.

Like a for-profit business, the executive director or president's influence over an organization's culture, management style and stability cannot be underestimated. Any decision he or she makes (from dress code to budgeting) impacts every single employee. Ideally, the executive director is knowledgeable about the focal issue for the organization, but also is well versed in management. You want to work for someone who understands that the staff is the most important asset and who is not afraid of managing in crisis. Many nonprofit organizations are founded by charismatic and passionate individuals who have no head for business and no idea how to cultivate a professional and collegial work environment. Beware these leaders. Most organizations post a biography of the executive director on their web sites; review this carefully to find out how long he/she has been at the organization and where he/she comes from. If he/she founded the organization and have no previous management experience, chances are he/she is not the best manager. Some experienced fundraisers simply won't work for an organization where the founder is the executive director or president. You can find out more about the executive director in your interviews with staff. It's important to get an opinion on the executive director from more than one person at the organization.

Finally, you want to ask questions about the relationship between the board and the executive director. Expect that there will be some tension, as you would expect in any supervisor/employee relationship. However, there should be respect for the board's expertise, a sense that the board is aware of the organization's challenges and a generally collegial relationship between the executive director and individual board members. The relationship between staff and the board is particularly important at a foundation, where staff and the executive director spend a large portion of their time educating board members on the various nonprofit organizations that have applied for grants and working with board members to define the directions of grant-making.

Choosing the Right Work Environment

Like in any industry, you have to be picky about where you work. Different nonprofits and charities have different environments and not every one will be right for you. Below are some key qualities that will distinguish different organizations and help you find the perfect fit.

The importance of teamwork

As important as a strategic plan or a diverse board of directors may be, it is absolutely essential that you join an effective team of experienced fundraising or philanthropic giving professionals. These are the people who will teach you the ropes of fundraising, philanthropy and life at a nonprofit. Beyond collective experience in different aspects of the field, you want to find a team that is inherently collaborative, where information sharing is expected and welcomed. The grant writer should know when the next membership mailing is going into production, just as the program officer for the arts program at a foundation ought to know the grant cycle for the environmental program. Be wary of a nonprofit or giving institution that caters to a "star" fundraiser or one particular expert; you won't learn what you need to. Most development professionals believe collaboration is critical to effective fundraising. A wealthy individual may not just give a large donation each year; they may have contacts at large foundations, may be best friends with the CEO at a large corporation and may be revising their will. The fundraising team must work together to "not leave any money on the table," as stated by a planned giving specialist. Philanthropic giving professionals can't work in a vacuum either, especially given the complexity of the nonprofit community and the demands of donors. At Merrill Lynch, for example, a team of financial advisors assists wealthy clients in establishing family foundations and donor-advised funds to ensure that the assets are well managed, that the opinions of all family members are taken into account and to ensure that donations are distributed most effectively to charitable organizations. The ideal team in either fundraising or philanthropic giving will be open to teaching you all aspects of field and to sharing their victories and challenges. An effective and

Visit Vault at www.vault.com for insider company profiles, expert advice, career message boards, expert resume reviews, the Vault Job Board and more.

VAULT CAREER LIBRARY   95

collaborative team is also likely to keep things in perspective, foster a sense of humor and roll with the punches.

Mentoring

Just as everyone can name a teacher that influenced their lives, most fundraisers and philanthropic giving professionals can name one person that took the time to mentor them. Their mentor provided informal training, created new opportunities to build skills, helped to navigate the internal politics of an organization or was simply encouraging. Mentoring relationships are particularly important in the nonprofit world because many groups and giving institutions do not have the resources to provide formal training. On the corporate side, financial firms may have rigorous training programs for becoming a certified advisor in philanthropy, but there aren't structured ways to learn how to effectively collaborate with nonprofit organizations. Sometimes the most valuable teaching experiences in this field is by observation, like sitting in on a meeting with a major donor or listening in on a conference call where a foundation program officer helps facilitate a planning exercise with a grantee. Mentors are also critical networking resources, helping introduce you to others in the field or writing letters of recommendation to help you advance your career. One fundraiser advises, "For new people coming into the field, the No. 1 thing you must do is find a mentor, and don't let it be just anybody. It has to be someone who really knows the business."

While mentoring in a nonprofit setting has received more attention in the last few years, few organizations have formal programs where the human resources department matches employees with mentors. You should ask about mentoring opportunities in interviews and find out if your potential supervisor has given any thought to mentoring. Try to get as many specifics as possible; ask if you can establish a formal mentoring relationship with a written agreement of goals and objectives, if there are opportunities to observe your colleagues in action and if he or she is willing to introduce you to others in the field. In a corporate setting, ask if there are opportunities to mentor with someone involved in community relations or philanthropy for the company.

The size of an organization

Another question to ask yourself is what size organization you would like to work for. There are many more small, scrappy nonprofit groups than large, established organizations out there, just as there are more small businesses than large corporations. Working for a smaller organization has advantages. Because resources are tight and they employ fewer staff, you will have more of an opportunity to take on many different activities and may advance more quickly to a management position. You may also have more opportunity to be creative and work independently. On the other hand, the lack of resources usually translates to lower salaries, skimpy benefits and less infrastructure, like dedicated human resources professionals. Larger nonprofits and foundations generally offer the most competitive salaries and benefits, as well as training opportunities. On the down side, you are more likely to be pigeon-holed into one particular specialty in fundraising or philanthropic giving rather than learning about the field as whole.

It's important to keep in mind where this discussion started—each nonprofit organization is different, and there are few generalities that you can apply no matter what the size or the group. The one general principle you can rely upon is that dysfunction will happen, whether you work for a nonprofit with a $1 million budget or a $25 million budget. It's much more important to find an organization with the features described here than to make an arbitrary (and uninformed) decision about the level of effectiveness of the group and the quality of the fundraising or giving team based on size.

Transitioning Careers

Some of you reading this guide have considerable experience from years of working in the for-profit world. If you are looking to transition out of your current job and into fundraising or philanthropic giving, you don't have to start over. In fact, you can broaden your experience while staying employed where you are now.

Where you are coming from

Fundraising and philanthropic giving is often a second career (or as one fundraiser described it, a "last career"), and many who are successful in the field draw upon their experiences from a previous career life. Among the many professional fields that lend themselves to fundraising and philanthropy are the following:

- **Sales and customer service**—A major donor officer is really another kind of sales representative, identifying and cultivating relationships with potential customers who are interested in a product—in this case a cause

Visit Vault at **www.vault.com** for insider company profiles, expert advice, career message boards, expert resume reviews, the Vault Job Board and more.

VAULT CAREER LIBRARY   97

and an organization. A creative, compassionate, persistent, and savvy salesperson is a major asset to any nonprofit organization.

- **Financial management**—If you are one of those rare people who love both numbers and people, you will do well in fundraising, where an understanding of budget development, cash flow and revenue projection is critical to success and advancement in the field.

- **Banking and wealth management**—Many philanthropic giving professionals are stockbrokers and bankers who assist wealthy clients in establishing foundations or other financial instruments to give money back to the community. With a sophisticated understanding of how to grow assets combined with a familiarity with nonprofit organizations and the ways they tick, you can be a powerful asset to your financial firm or to a foundation.

- **Law**—Those with any kind of experience with the law can make great fundraisers, especially as planned giving officers, who often assist donors in writing up complex financial agreements with nonprofit organizations. Likewise, lawyers can advise wealthy clients on how to establish and run family foundations.

- **Food service and event planning**—Caterers, grocers and restaurant managers can apply their expertise to organize fundraisers for a nonprofit, especially if they know how to squeeze tight budgets to pull off sophisticated and well-managed events. Experience dealing with high-maintenance clients and difficult vendors is also a plus for nonprofit organizations that rely heavily on fundraisers largely run by volunteers and where many services are donated.

- **Direct response marketing**—The principles of direct mail, telemarketing and e-mail solicitation are the same, whether you are working for a major retailer or a nonprofit organization. Someone who has made a career in the for-profit world in direct response marketing can do very well in nonprofit world, from coordinating a program at a nonprofit, working at an agency that specializes in fundraising for nonprofits, or as an independent consultant.

- **Database design and management**—The donor relations database that stores wide-ranging information on past, current and prospect donors is one of the most important tools of a fundraising operation. Someone with experience in Access or Oracle can easily find a place at a nonprofit or as a consultant helping to customize databases to meet a nonprofit's particular needs.

- **Research and data analysis**—If you enjoy poring over annual reports, tax documents, newspaper clippings, stock performance charts to identify trends or if you thrill to calculating mean, mode and median in Excel, there's a position for you as a prospect researcher or direct response analyst at either a nonprofit or at a fundraising agency.

• **Technical writing**—A thorough and persuasive writer is a valuable commodity in the nonprofit world, where a well-written proposal can determine if an organization gets that major grant from a foundation or six-figure pledge from a longtime donor.

• **Public relations and communications**—While they may not have the same resources as a major corporation, nonprofit organizations understand the importance of media relations and brand positioning, especially in attracting foundations and major donors. A seasoned communications specialist can quickly make the transition to fundraising, especially in developing membership programs and in establishing partnerships with corporate donors.

Steps you can take

The next step is to get some experience working with nonprofit organizations. Here are few projects that you can probably take one while still at your place of business. In fact, many of these projects can yield important benefits for your company, including strengthening ties with local communities, boosting morale, generating positive media coverage and improving business practices.

• **Volunteer as a consultant**—You can work with an organization of your choice on a specific project that allows you to apply your expertise and learn the nuances of working for a nonprofit. For example, if you have expertise in direct response marketing, you can help a nonprofit group develop a membership acquisition campaign. Some progressive businesses may give you the time to take on such a project. Timberland and Wells Fargo Bank, for example, allow employees to take paid time from work to volunteer. And there are organizations, such as the Taproot Foundation, that pair volunteer consultants with nonprofits.

• **Create or run a company grants program**—Many businesses, both small and large, establish modest grant-giving programs, where a volunteer committee of employees manages a pool of funds derived from a small percentage of sales or profits. An example of such a program is the one at Smartwool, an outdoor retailer that sets asides money from its sales for two grant programs supporting breast cancer charities and environmental advocacy respectively. A committee of employees runs both programs, from designing the application process to making decisions about the organizations that receive grants. Getting involved in a company grant-giving effort, or helping start one, provides a great opportunity to make connections with local nonprofits, as well as learn the ropes of philanthropic giving. The marketing director at Smartwool—who led the creation of the company's grant program—argues that you can make a compelling case to upper management that a focused grant-giving effort can elevate a company's profile with the media and strengthen customer loyalty.

• **Organize a company-wide volunteering activity**—Many organizations like Habitat for Humanity, homeless shelters and youth programs welcome a chance to partner with a business that can provide a steady stream of volunteers, or secure a large number of volunteers for a single project, such as building a new home. You can organize a volunteer day, where your employer gives everyone the day off to work on a project. Or you can initiate a longer-term volunteer recruitment campaign. Either way, you are demonstrating leadership and commitment to your company and to the nonprofit community.

• **Convince your company to sponsor a nonprofit**—There are many ways that the business community can support nonprofits, from hosting fundraising events to providing in-kind services, such as communications support or financial advice. If there is one particular nonprofit organization that you think is a good match for your organization (for example, the organization caters to potential customers, or key community leaders are on the board), see if you can persuade your employer to develop a long-term relationship with the group. If you are successful, you have built experience in corporate relations that is extremely attractive to most nonprofits.

• **Involve your company in cause-related marketing**—For many businesses, social movements are important to the bottom line. For example, Luna Bar is deeply involved in breast cancer awareness because women in their 40s and 50s are the company's primary customers. So Luna Bar partners with various breast cancer groups to develop advertising campaigns and promotions around the issue. Such cause-related marketing projects can be time-consuming, but also provide a terrific creative challenge and leadership opportunity.

• **Fundraise for a nonprofit through a matching gift program**—Another way that companies encourage employees to give back to their communities is through a matching gift program, where contributions up to a set amount made by employees are matched by the company. You can initiate a matching gift drive for a nonprofit organization, encouraging employees to give small donations that the company matches. This is another activity that demonstrates leadership, as well as prowess in selling an organization and cause.

• **Educate your company about socially responsible business practices**— There is a rising tide of companies with business models that link profit-making demonstrates leadership, as well as prowess in selling an organization and cause.

- **Educate your company about socially responsible business practices**— There is a rising tide of companies with business models that link profit-making with social good—from equitable treatment of workers (such as Starbucks' commitment to providing all workers health insurance) to healthy living (such as Whole Foods promotion of organic products). Whether you work for a small business or a multinational corporation, there are opportunities for you to promote social responsibility in small and large ways. One small step is to recommend energy-saving policies for your office. Another is to suggest new partnerships. For example, you could recommend to your human resources department a staffing agency that trains and places welfare recipients or at-risk youth. These activities demonstrate to a potential nonprofit employer that you have commitment to social change, as well as an understanding of what motivates businesses to commit to social change. You can also show your ability to think creatively about partnerships between businesses and nonprofits.

Visit Vault at **www.vault.com** for insider company profiles, expert advice,
career message boards, expert resume reviews, the Vault Job Board and more.

VAULT CAREER LIBRARY   **101**

VAULT CAREER GUIDES
GET THE INSIDE SCOOP ON TOP JOBS

"Cliffs Notes for Careers"
– FORBES MAGAZINE

Vault guides and employer profiles have been published since 1997 and are the premier source of insider information on careers.

Each year, Vault surveys and interviews thousands of employees to give readers the inside scoop on industries and specific employers to help them get the jobs they want.

"To get the un-varnished scoop, check out Vault"
– SMARTMONEY MAGAZINE

VAULT

ON THE JOB

Chapter 8: Fundamentals of the Field

Chapter 9: Fundraising and Philanthropic Giving Career Tracks

Chapter 10: Fundraising Career Snapshots

Chapter 11: Philanthropic Giving Career Snapshots

Fundamentals of the Field

Like many other career fields, there are generalists in fundraising and philanthropic giving, and there are specialists with in-depth expertise and knowledge in a particular kind of fundraising or gift giving. The field continues to grow and diversify, so it is difficult to describe every sort of job that you may stumble upon in the classified ads. This guide touches upon many different career avenues, but provides more in-depth profiles of the most common career tracks and the most common kinds of consultants. But first, it's important to know a bit more about the fundamental strategies, responsibilities, and day-to-day activities undertaken by fundraisers and philanthropic giving professionals.

Begging for Money: The Fundamentals of the Job

It would seem that from either side of the fence—as the philanthropic giving professional looking out to the sea of nonprofits or as the fundraiser looking to land the big fish donor—the primary focus is money, either asking for it or distributing it. Well, let's throw that notion back out to sea, for most professionals in the business will quickly let you know that the focus of their work is fundamentally different.

Professional fundraising

People generally have one of two reactions to the whole notion of professional fundraising. It's either, "God, how awful to beg people for money all day," or "How hard can it be to ask people for money all day?"

Here's the most worst-kept secret among fundraisers: You actually spend very little time "begging" for money. In fact, if you are asking every person you meet to write a check (and you've seen those eager young folks on street corners with their clipboards), or running through a list of telephone numbers like a telemarketer, you are unlikely to have much success.

The motto of the professional fundraiser is very simple: people give to people. So in order to get someone to invest in your organization, you need to help that person get invested in you and that organization. And that's about establishing and strengthening a relationship with people who care about your cause. As one fundraising consultant puts it, "No matter if you're creating an individual donor campaign or writing a letter of inquiry to a foundation or meeting with a possible major donor to your organization, it's all about nurturing and building relationships for the long haul."

So asking for money from someone who deeply cares about your organization is the easiest thing in the world. The hard part is finding those people, establishing a rapport with them, and giving them the right information and arguments to convince them that their support of your organization over time will make a fundamental difference in the world. Therefore, a fundraiser's daily activities (no matter what his or her particular specialty) revolve around five basic strategies:

Identify the right people—If you surround yourself with wealthy people, this may seem obvious and easy. As one fundraiser for a national environmental group states, "If you happen to be best friends with Bill Gates, sure, chances are he'd support your cause." But if your best friend with a trust fund doesn't care about the issue that your organization addresses, then you actually don't know the right people. In fact, identifying potential donors, also known as "prospects," takes careful research. A successful fundraiser develops a list of potential donors who (1) have the ability to give, (2) the interest in your issue, and, (3) feel connected to your organization. Most large nonprofit organizations (those with budgets of $10 million or more) employ either a part-time or full-time prospect researcher solely responsible for identifying likely prospects and keeping fundraisers apprised of changes in people's finances and their giving habits. The more information you have, the more likely you are to get someone interested in your organization.

Establish a relationship—Fundraisers spend the vast majority of their time finding ways to get to know and engage potential and existing donors, whether they are program officers at a foundation or people writing up their wills. They meet with donors, invite them to events and informational presentations, alert them to important events, inform them of major victories and simply thank them for their support. Like any good friendship, a strong relationship with a donor is open, honest and warm. As described by a fundraiser:

"One of the best moments I've ever had in fundraising was when a major funder told me that she had worked with hundreds of nonprofits and had 'never seen it done better' than by us. Her accolade spelled out everything I work for: not only was she donating at a major level, but she completely believed in us and the organization, and in turn, we could be completely open with her, use her expertise and, of course, count on her for continued funding. She has even helped get us new funders."

This is the kind of relationship a fundraiser hopes to have with every donor.

Ask at the right time—Yes, there comes a time when you need to sit down with a donor and ask for that check, or in the case of a foundation, submit that proposal for support. But it's all in the timing. You may have the most enthusiastic donors in the world, but if they are in the midst of starting a new business, they may not have the money to spare. And if that foundation's assets have been hit by a bad break in the stock market, they may not be able to fund a six-figure grant request. You also need to know if these donors have already given or are about to give to another organization with a similar mission, and are therefore tapped out, or if a foundation board is about to undergo strategic planning and fundamentally changes the direction of their giving interests. Again, you need to *know* your donors to know when to ask for money.

Thank the donor—This may seem like another obvious step in fundraising, but the importance of a prompt and proper thank you for a gift cannot be overemphasized. Every donor—whether he or she has given $5 or $5 million—wants to know that his or her gift has made a difference, and that you as a fundraiser appreciate the person behind the gift. Indeed, that thank you alone can guarantee another gift in the future. Most fundraising operations have a rule of thanking major donors (including foundation officers and corporate community relations directors) within 48 hours of receiving a gift with a personalized thank-you letter from the executive director, often coming on the heels of a phone call from the development staff person. The process of thanking members for their donation is often more elaborate than the membership drive itself, for the staff must generate personalized thank-you letters for hundreds or thousands of donors and send out the membership gifts. The procedures for generating these thank-you letters is also known in the business as the "acknowledgement process" and is often supervised by the development assistant, with input from other development staff that have been involved in cultivating the relationship with the donor.

Strengthen the relationship—To paraphrase The Carpenters' classic ballad, you've only just begun when your donor writes that check or that grant comes in. Your donor needs just as much time and attention afterwards, especially if you think he or she is capable of giving more money in the future. A good fundraiser reports back regularly to donors, telling them how their money was spent, informing them of new activities or directions, and engaging them with others in the organization. A fundraiser is also likely to be the one to discuss problems and challenges with donors, which can be just as important as outlining the opportunities that an organization is pursuing. For example, many fundraisers need to explain how shrinking state and federal budgets impact the organization, both positively and negatively.

Professional philanthropic giving

The same basic framework for relationship building holds true for the philanthropic giving professional who gives money away, the only real difference being that you are looking to give (rather than ask) at the right time and to the right charitable cause. Whether you are advising someone with a charitable trust or supervising a grant-giving program at a foundation, you want the money to make the most impact as possible. Therefore you need to identify the organizations that fit the interests of the donor or the guidelines of the foundation and that you believe are effective in what they do. You also need to build a relationship with those groups, understand their unique role in the nonprofit community, their challenges and capacity needs, and their strategies for addressing an issue. And you need to track the progress of the groups to whom you donate, both to assess the effectiveness of your gift or grant and to better understand the challenges and opportunities that they face.

As was true 140 years ago when the first foundations invested in education for freed slaves, philanthropic giving professionals are *active* participants, and more than ever want to build long lasting partnerships with the nonprofit organizations that they care about. Moreover, donors at all levels look for creative ways to support communities, causes and organizations, and this means that partnerships take many different forms and include many different players. Giving institutions often establish and drive these partnership— community foundations in particular bring together wealthy individuals, community leaders, policy experts, mayors, county commissioners, Members of Congress, businesses, activists and nonprofit organizations to address the problems of a community, such as immigration, homelessness or health care coverage. But sophisticated donors, such as those who made it rich in the dot-com boom of the late 1990s, also deeply invest in organizations and issues to become important partners for social change.

So in truth, fundraising and philanthropic giving boils down to people and the relationships between donors, organizations and causes. Money is the means to an end and not to be forgotten. But most fundraisers and philanthropic giving professionals would describe themselves as more than money managers or salespeople. A good fundraiser may be able to work a cocktail party, chatting up the entrepreneur who just sold his company or the socialite with the big inheritance. And an effective philanthropic giving professional is keenly aware of his or her responsibility to make sound investment decisions to grow foundation endowments and donor-advised funds. He is also perfectly willing to use money as an incentive to ensure cooperation from nonprofit organizations. But the best in the field consider themselves advocates for a cause, a calling beyond schmoozing and sound investment portfolios. They are mediators and facilitators, building crucial relationships toward successful philanthropy in that larger sense of serving people, communities and causes.

Is this a higher calling? Many in the field will say yes. The director of development at a breast cancer awareness group describes the most successful fundraisers and giving professionals as possessing the same qualities of great social leaders and thinkers. They have Martin Luther King Jr.'s passion about a cause; President Clinton's charm and confidence to make a case for someone to donate; Stephen Hawking's deep knowledge about an organization, its programs, its fundraising practices, its financial health; Sigmund Freud's listening skills; and Lance Armstrong's resilience when the inevitable "no" comes your way.

Practical Skills

Of course, no one person has all of these qualities, and there's no requirement for saintliness in this field. But a successful fundraiser or philanthropic giving professional generally comes to work each day with passion, empathy and optimism. The best in the field are confident and thoughtful, carefully engaging with donors and grantees, gathering information and making timely decisions on when to ask for money, when to give money and when to pull back. They develop a confidence in their own analysis and in gut instincts to read people and situations. And that confidence comes in cultivating a range of practical skills, such as:

Active listening

Beyond engaging in small talk at a fundraising dinner, professionals in the field gather a great deal of information critical to strategy and decision-making through active listening and careful questioning. Both fundraisers and philanthropic giving professionals must understand the perspectives, interests, needs and trepidations of donors and grantees, expressed both in conversation and body language. For the major gifts officer, a hesitation in speech, an offhand remark or a hostile demeanor tells him/her that this is not the right time to ask for that big gift. For the foundation officer, the note of tension in an executive director's voice when talking about a partner organization can say a lot about how a collaborative campaign is working and whether it's time to delay a grant renewal. Like reporters, the best fundraisers and philanthropic giving professionals are able to adjust their listening and conversation style to the personalities of the people with whom they are engaging. They also know to ask the same question in a number of ways, for each time they will get a different answer and one more piece of important information.

Affinity for research

Philanthropic giving professionals and fundraisers also collect information through careful research. Fundraisers troll the Internet for press releases and newspaper articles, as well as review annual reports and tax forms, to identify prospective donors or just catch up on the giving activities of current donors. Grant writers compile all sorts of research to flesh out a grant proposal, including statistics that illustrate a problem (such as illiteracy rates or incidences of domestic violence) and position papers on complex policy issues. Philanthropic giving professionals, especially foundation staff, initiate all sorts of research, including commissioning white papers from academics on complex social issues, as well as conducting polls and focus groups.

Critical analysis

The next step beyond information gathering is analysis. A smart fundraiser or philanthropic giving professional not only understands and easily articulates the mission and activities of a nonprofit organization, but can also discern strengths and weaknesses in activities or campaigns, assess effective and dysfunctional partnerships, and identify where there are gaps in funding and/or capacity. With a bird's eye view of nonprofit organizations, fundraisers and philanthropic giving professionals may see what others in an organization cannot—that one program specialist is carrying all the weight for a complex campaign, that an executive director is not seeing how key strategies connect, or that several organizations are engaged in the same work in the same community. Unafraid to use money as a motivation, the fundraiser or philanthropic giving professional often pushes program and campaign specialists to thoroughly conceptualize and explain their work. For example, a grant writer during a planning session or a foundation officer at a site visit may make an executive director aware of key partners with whom she must work, that she needs to re-evaluate why a particular strategy or service is critical, and that she needs to more clearly identify how to measure the impact of her work.

Storytelling

Like the best communicators, a talented fundraiser can weave a clear and compelling story about the organization for which he works, about the need the organization fills and its unique approach to a social problem, and why it's so important to make a donation right now. Fundraisers actually need to spin this story in different ways depending on the interests of donors. It is rare that a grant writer can use one proposal over and over and over again with different foundations, for example. And a talented major gifts officer will adjust his pitch depending on what he hears from the donor during lunch. It takes creativity and a deep understanding of what the organization does to tell these stories, but it also takes judgment. There's a fine line between a dramatic tale of hope and triumph and a tall tale that stretches the truth about an organization's experience and success. The philanthropic giving professional can play a similar role as storyteller, especially as an advisor to donors. A foundation officer or donor advisor often serves as the advocate for potential and existing grantees, explaining to less informed trustees the often complex partnerships between nonprofit organizations working on the same issue and why one organization deserves continuing support because it plays a unique and vital role in a community or in addressing a thorny social issue.

Collaborative spirit

Fundraising and philanthropic giving are inherently collaborative activities. Fundraisers rely on each other, the executive director, the board of directors and program specialists to identify and cultivate donor relationships. Appeals and proposals to donors and foundations are group writing projects, with everyone from the executive director to the program specialist to the communications director reviewing and editing drafts. Likewise, foundation officers or donor advisors work closely with boards of trustees, their peers and a network of nonprofit organizations to make thoughtful decisions about how to grow investments to be used for philanthropic purposes and how to give that money away. If you don't play well with others, don't get into this field or into the world of nonprofits generally. As one financial advisor puts

Visit Vault at **www.vault.com** for insider company profiles, expert advice, career message boards, expert resume reviews, the Vault Job Board and more.

VAULT CAREER LIBRARY   111

it, "If someone at a nonprofit is not a good team player, chances are that he or she is not going to be in that job for very long."

Comfort with money and number crunching

For all of the lofty allusions to social change and saintliness, the fundraiser or philanthropic giving professional must be comfortable with cash and numbers. Beyond asking for that next donation with ease, a fundraiser must master basic financial management, including overseeing expense budgets for fundraising activities, calculating revenue projections and cash flow, and presenting detailed financial information to donors that request or require it. A healthy respect for and relationship with the financial staff at your nonprofit organization is essential. A familiarity with Excel and basic accounting vocabulary doesn't hurt either. For some philanthropic giving professionals—primarily donor advisors at investment management firms—review and analysis of financial information is a key aspect of their jobs. Most fundraisers and philanthropic giving professionals alike are quite comfortable reading annual reports, tax forms and stock performance charts.

Day-to-Day Activities of a Fundraiser

As described earlier, fundraisers or development professionals (no matter what their specialty may be) engage in a range of activities beyond needling a donor for money. These activities are as follows:

Analysis, planning and goal-setting

At least on a yearly basis, if not more frequently, fundraisers assess progress with donors, tally up the gifts that have come in so far, and recalibrate revenue projections. Such analysis—which includes systematically tracking interactions with donors, coming up with calculations for determining the likelihood of a gift coming in and when, and identifying new prospects and ways to engage them—is critical for setting fundraising goals and prioritizing activities throughout the year. For major gift officers and grant writers, the process may be informal, since no one can read the mind of a wealthy individual or a program officer. Such fundraising professionals may simply develop a calendar of activities for the next year, a rough estimate of revenue based on what came in the previous year, and an educated guess on what new money can be brought in. Major gift officers will also prioritize their donors, identifying those that deserve more special attention and more frequent visits.

The analysis is more rigorous for membership programs that secure donations by sending print or electronic appeals to several thousand donors at different times during the year. Each mailing or Internet appeal provides a range of quantifiable information about a large number of donors, including the percentage of people who respond to any given appeal, the average size of donation and where donors are located. By looking over the performance of past appeals, membership specialists can come up with formulas for determining the average gift size from members, the cost and revenue from renewing membership gifts and the cost and revenue generated from acquiring new members. Membership specialists will also spend a great deal of their time planning the production schedule for appeals, which may go out to thousands of donors at different times of the year. The bigger the organization, the larger a project this is, and the more outside help you need, including designers, printers and mailing specialists.

Information about past trends and future projections is critical to developing the organization's operating budget; after all, you generally don't want to spend more than you think you will accumulate in revenue. Most fundraising/development teams therefore develop a written annual fundraising plan with financial goals, which is then presented to and approved by the board of directors. Boards and executive directors may request more frequent analyses, perhaps on a bimonthly or quarterly basis, so they can keep track of contributions and revenue over the course of the year.

Research

Fundraisers devote some part of their time (although most admit not enough of it) to research on current donors and prospects, which may include scanning trade publications such as *The Chronicle of Philanthropy*, Google searches of individuals, review of 990 tax forms, and looking over past interactions documented in paper files or in a donor relations database (described in more detail below). Any little piece of information could be useful when meeting with a donor or deciding when to ask for a gift, including a marriage or divorce, a death in the family, a recent retirement, the graduation of a child from college, the most recent grants distributed by a family foundation, a stock split or a financial disaster. Most fundraising/development teams try to keep track of this kind of information on all of their major donors, board members and institutional donors (including board members and program officers of foundations, as well as upper management at corporations who support the organization). Grant writers will conduct more in-depth searches on foundations to keep track of upcoming deadlines, changes in giving priorities and submission processes, as well as changes in leadership. Foundation web sites are important sources of information, but there are also two major databases devoted to foundations—Foundationsearch (www.foundationsearch.com) and the Foundation Center's foundation directory.

Meeting with donors

For major gift officers and planned giving specialists, getting to know donors is the heart of the job. The Internet has certainly changed the way fundraisers interact with donors, but face-to-face meeting are the primary and preferred form of connection. So fundraisers are often out of the office at lunches and dinners, lectures and awards ceremonies; many also attend family events, including funerals and weddings, depending on the relationship with the donor. Fundraisers also spend a lot of time arranging meetings—tracking down donors to pin down a time and place, as well as setting up events where donors can get to know one another. In addition, fundraisers will set up meetings for donors to meet program specialists; in fact, many donors would rather talk to those on the front lines implementing the mission of the organization rather than the fundraisers. However, fundraisers try to participate in all meetings with donors, both to keep the meeting focused and to gather as much intelligence as possible on the interests and quirks of their donors. It's important to remember that the primary purpose of these meetings is to help the donor to connect with the nonprofit and its mission rather than ask for money. The time for the big ask will come some time in the year, but a fundraiser may visit with the donor two or three times before asking for a donation, depending on the size of the donor's wallet.

Depending on the size of the nonprofit and the scope of its work, fundraisers may be on the road to see donors a significant amount of time. And most fundraisers have a budget for fundraising visits, which others in the organization can look on with suspicion; it's sometimes hard to understand how a three-hour lunch is going to help the bottom line. Grant writers and membership coordinators will also have contact with their particular set of donors, but usually on a more limited scale, since proposals and appeals are the primary vehicle for communication.

Writing appeals and proposals

Most donors will not give without some kind of written request in hand. Foundations generally require the submission of a proposal describing the work that the requesting organization would like to have funded, and many major donors now ask for the same. As described above, membership programs are based on a series of appeals (both paper and electronic) sent to donors throughout the year requesting modest donations. So fundraisers, no matter what their specialty, spend a great deal of their time writing. A proposal can be anything from a two-page letter to a 25-page treatise. Appeal letters tend to be between two and four pages in length. There are formats, formulas and protocols for these materials, but there is also a great deal of personalization, depending on the interests of the donor in question. Grant writers in particular are glued to their computers, often working on several proposals in a given week.

Keeping up with program activities

Fundraisers can't do their job working in isolation from the rest of the organization; they need to be able to describe and write about ongoing activities, changes in direction or strategy, as well as successes. So fundraisers are often chasing down program specialists with questions about their work, sitting in on strategy meetings, as well as reading newly released reports (or at least the executive summary) and other information materials produced by the nonprofit for which they work. Fundraisers can also be important participants in program planning meetings, providing information on what they hear from donors about the organization's activities and what current and prospective donors (especially foundations) are funding. Since foundations require detailed descriptions of program activities and often ask some of the more difficult questions about the importance and impact of those activities, grant writers tend to spend more time and energy understanding program than other fundraisers. They can often be the most knowledgeable in the organization about program goals, activists, challenges and achievements, especially since most staff are focused on their small piece of the larger organizational pie.

Thanking donors

Personalized letters, calls and visits from the executive director, appreciation events, distribution of T-shirts and other gifts—all sorts of activity revolves around thanking donors for their gifts. As described above, thank-yous or acknowledgements are considered to be as important as the gift itself, and fundraisers are always trying to find ways to thank donors. Development associates and coordinators, the administrative staff for fundraising teams, are often charged with managing the thank-you process, including letters of acknowledgement to each and every donor. These letters are more than a

Visit Vault at **www.vault.com** for insider company profiles, expert advice, career message boards, expert resume reviews, the Vault Job Board and more.

VAULT CAREER LIBRARY   115

formality; they are a requirement by the Internal Revenue Service for donors that wish to deduct gifts from their taxes. Donors must prove that (1) they have given a gift before the end of the tax year, and (2) that they have not received any goods or services for that gift.

Managing systems and processes

Busy fundraising/development teams work with hundreds of major donors, dozens of foundations and thousands of members. They may be sending dozens of mailings and conducting scores of donor visits each year. So systems and processes must be put in place to ensure that proposal deadlines are met, that donors receive prompt replies to information requests, that appeals are sent to the correct addresses and that fundraisers have the information to frame conversation with donors. Most development offices struggle with maintaining some kind of information tracking system, the cornerstone of which is a donor relations database designed to store and analyze information about current donors and prospects. Several software companies have designed such databases, but most need to be customized, since every fundraising team functions a little bit differently. For example, most databases are not designed to help manage all of the cultivation steps involved in acquiring planned gifts, especially for a sophisticated team at a larger organization. Most offices maintain extensive paper file systems as well. Development associates and coordinators are the masters of the database and spend much of their day on data entry. Yet most fundraisers, no matter what their role, spend some time compiling information for the database or passing along information to those in charge of the database. Larger development offices will employ a database manager charged with ensuring quality control of data entry, training staff and pulling reports, profiles and mailings lists as needed. Team managers will spend significant amounts of time assessing systems and processes, including data entry, sending acknowledgements, maintaining deadline calendars and general quality control to ensure that donor names aren't misspelled and that proposals aren't riddled with typos.

Updating donors

Fundraisers also generate all sorts of reports, letters, newsletters and e-mails to keep donors abreast of the latest accomplishments and challenges of their organization. Many of these updates are at the demand of the donor; foundations require at least one written report over a 12-month period detailing how their grant funds were used and the impact of their support. So grant writers often lead the charge in crafting such reports on programs and activities that the whole fundraising team may send to donors. Fundraisers also keep track of the publications and other informational materials that the program staff may generate and send these along to donors. Answering requests for information is also an important activity, and most development teams take any phone call or e-mail from a donor seriously, no matter how silly or frivolous the question or request may be. Membership staff are often on the front line, the first responders to requests from a toll-free hotline or designated e-mail address. This often means that they are on the receiving end of a rant from someone who doesn't really understand what the organization does or the ramblings of a lonely widow in the middle of the country.

Success and Failure—Examples of Effective and Defective Fundraising

There is no one way to woo a donor, but there are some sure-fire ways to ensure that you never hear from one again. Here are two case studies of fictional organizations engaged in fundraising—one illustrating how effective fundraising can work (and all the effort it takes), and the second describing how a dysfunctional team can sabotage itself.

Success Story: Friends Services of Mississippi

The year 2005 marked a turning point in the fundraising efforts for Friends Services of Mississippi, a small, Quaker-based organization of 30 employees that finds temporary housing for displaced families. The organization was overwhelmed with requests after Hurricane Katrina left so many homeless and helpless. Luckily, a surge in donations in the aftermath of the storm allowed Friends Services to bring on temporary staff and new volunteers to place as many families as possible in hotels, empty apartments and with individuals giving up space in their homes. Friends Services also partnered with the Salvation Army, Red Cross and other Quaker groups across the

Visit Vault at **www.vault.com** for insider company profiles, expert advice, career message boards, expert resume reviews, the Vault Job Board and more.

V/\ULT CAREER LIBRARY   **117**

country to place families in temporary housing. The development team was careful to capture as much information as possible about all new donors, including home and e-mail addresses, religious affiliations, preferred methods of communication, and how donors had heard about the organization. This information was collected on the web site—which had been revamped a few months before the storm, largely to help collect online donations more efficiently and information about first-time donors—as well as through follow-up e-mails, phone calls (when the donor gave their phone number) and thank-you letters with a survey attached. The team also worked closely with volunteer coordinators to compile similar information about all new volunteers.

At the end of 2006, the development team came together for a retreat to determine the best way to keep this new pool of donors and volunteers engaged in the organization. In preparation for the meeting, the director of development worked with the membership coordinator to analyze the information they had compiled. A few patterns emerged. First, most of the new donors gave through the web site. Second, most had heard about the organization because of a story profiling organizations that were quick to provide assistance to hurricane victims that was published by Associated Press and run in local newspapers across the country. The vast majority of donations came from out of state and from individuals who had no religious affiliation. Most preferred to be contacted by e-mail. Volunteers, on the other hand, tended to come from neighboring states and had heard about the organization through their church. Only a handful of volunteers gave donations, but a few gave sizable ones of more than $500.

After a presentation of findings from the membership coordinator, the team engaged in a vigorous brainstorming session followed by a lengthy discussion of what activities were actually feasible given staff and resources (most of the staff had been forced to reprioritize their work in order to keep up with influx of donations and the follow-up information gathering, and many had routinely kept late hours). Eventually, the team outlined the following plan: the membership coordinator would develop a short electronic newsletter, which would profile hurricane survivors who had successfully settled. The newsletter would not include a definitive request for a donation, but would give the reader the option to donate by clicking on a link to the web site. The newsletter would be followed a month later with an electronic appeal asking donors to double their previous gift. Volunteers would be sent a personalized letter signed by the executive director and the director of development thanking them for their service. The letter would include a donation form and a return envelope, as well as a profile of a hurricane victim. The major gifts officer would personally follow up with those volunteers that gave $500 or more, meeting with each of them for lunch or dinner in the next few months to give them an update on the organization's activities. And at the end of the year, all volunteers and recurring donors who gave before the hurricane would receive an appeal letter with the profile of hurricane victims and the Associated Press article. In addition, the major gifts officer would send the article and a list of all the newspapers that carried it to existing major donors.

Over the next week, the director of development mapped out a time-line for these activities and scheduled a biweekly meeting with the team to discuss progress. While the electronic newsletter took longer to develop than originally anticipated, the plan proved extraordinarily successful. The major gifts officer was able to persuade one of the volunteers who also gave a donation, an entrepreneur with a successful pizza franchise, to initiate a matching gift challenge, where he would donate an additional $10,000 if other donors could match it. He also organized a giving campaign through his pizza chain, sending out coupons for a free pizza to everyone who donated $100 or more to Friends Services. The matching gift challenge was featured in the electronic appeal. Through the update and the electronic appeal, more than two-thirds of first-time donors gave another gift, many of whom gave twice as much. Through the visits with volunteers, the major gifts officer raised an additional $25,000 from volunteers on top of the challenge gift. And the annual appeal was the most successful ever, raising an additional $30,000 over past appeals. Donations from major donors also increased, with three new gifts of more than $25,000. In the end, the team exceeded its fundraising goal for the year by more than $300,000. As a reward, the director of development gave the team a four-day weekend and a floating holiday to make up for all the long hours they had put in to implement the plan.

Horror Story: Institute for Forward Thinking

The director of planned giving at the Institute for Forward Thinking—a think tank in Washington, D.C., focused on building bipartisan consensus around major policy issues—was about to tear her hair out. Six months ago, she had worked with her three-person team on a calendar of mailings to be sent to existing members encouraging them to join the Legacy Circle, a group of donors who have committed to incorporating a bequest to the Institute in their will. She discussed the

Visit Vault at **www.vault.com** for insider company profiles, expert advice, career message boards, expert resume reviews, the Vault Job Board and more.

VAULT CAREER LIBRARY   **119**

mailing schedule with the vice president of development, who was delighted that the director of planned giving was adding one extra mailing this year. It had been tough to find the money for the extra mailing, but the planned giving coordinator had negotiated a reduced price with the company that had been handling the printing and distribution of these mailings for years.

But unbeknownst to the director of planned giving, the director of membership had planned a renewal appeal to be mailed at exactly the same time, something that was never discussed at the weekly development meetings. The scheduling problem only came to light after the database manager realized that he was pulling nearly identical mailing lists for both directors. When confronted with the scheduling conflict, the director of membership wouldn't budge. The last membership mailing was nearly a month late because typos were found in the letter after it had gone to the printer, and a program specialist (who happened to see a copy of the discarded letter in the trash) had objected to language about health care policy. The initial meeting between directors had ended badly, and the director of planned giving was still steamed by the director of membership's comment that planned giving mailings are "second class." The vice president of development intervened and brokered a deal—the membership renewal mailing would go out as planned, and the Legacy Circle letter would follow six weeks later. It was a lot of mail for members to receive in a short period of time, but it was acceptable to all parties involved.

Yet things just got much worse. The database manager, overwhelmed with information and training requests, neglected to remove from the planned giving mailing list the addresses of donors who had already joined the Legacy Circle. The mailing had gone out three days ago, and the director of planned giving had already received three phone calls from angry donors asking why they had received a mailing to join a program that they were already a part of. In fact, she had spent an hour on the phone with one donor who threatened to rewrite his will, declaring that he "didn't want to give a dime to an organization that was so incompetent." Now she is working on an apology letter to be sent to all of the Legacy Circle donors, a letter that she doesn't know how she is going to pay for with her tight budget. She prayed that the vice president of development would let her go over budget so that she wouldn't have to abandon a mailing.

Day-to-Day Activities of a Philanthropic Giving Professional

The following overview describes the wide variety of activities that philanthropic giving professionals engage in on a day-to-day basis.

Analysis and planning

No philanthropic giving professional wants to throw good money after bad, so analysis and planning is a huge part of their day-to-day lives. Many philanthropic giving professionals, especially program officers at larger foundations, are experts in a particular field—from health care to child care to environmental policy to nonprofit management—and as such continue to research trends in their expertise, reviewing white papers, meeting with other experts and their peers at other foundations and commissioning studies. There's also a fair amount of self-analysis involved in philanthropic giving, with many foundations in perpetual strategic planning that foundation officers lead or facilitate. Some foundations have set up elaborate feedback mechanisms, hiring consultants to survey grantees about their perceptions of the grant-giving institution, which the foundation officers must absorb and respond to. Philanthropic giving professionals also take a close look at the programs they have funded, trying to determine if and how their grants make a difference. This means careful review of reports they receive from grantees and sometimes hiring yet another consultant to meet with nonprofit leaders, program specialists, policy makers and community leaders to study the effectiveness of a campaign or program.

Planning often goes far beyond the giving institutions; foundations in particular are often engaged in developing activities with the nonprofit organizations that they fund. To this end, foundation officers often lead program planning efforts with grantees. Going one step further, many larger foundations may develop their own campaigns and programs to address an issue (much to the annoyance of executive directors and program specialists at nonprofit organizations looking for funding), and bring their grantees on board. If they aren't directly engaged, many grantors offer tools for the program planning, including informational materials or planning grants. Many grant applications are geared toward forcing a program planning process, requiring answers to questions or articulation of goals that can only come from deep thinking on the part of the requesting organization.

Financial management

Many philanthropic giving professionals are primarily investment specialists with backgrounds in portfolio management, stock trading and general banking. Their primary responsibility is to make sure that client funds (whether for a foundation, wealthy individual or a nonprofit with an endowment) continue to grow. These financial managers, usually known as donor advisors, work at all sorts of institutions, including asset management firms, private foundations and community foundations. They are generally not investment analysts, but portfolio managers reviewing recommendations for investment and meeting with senior management and/or wealthy individuals to go over investment strategies. Daily activities will include meeting with investment analysts, reading through analysts' reports, reviewing and preparing performance reports for clients, answering inquiries from clients and preparing and delivering presentations on investment strategies to clients. For foundations, financial managers will spend a lot of time calming the fears of the board of trustees, who may be too involved in making investment decisions. If the financial advisor works for an investment firm rather than the foundation itself, it can be important customer services for the advisor to run interference between the board and the senior management at the foundation. For more information on the activities of portfolio managers, refer to the *Vault Career Guide to Investment Management.*

Meeting donors and grantees

Most philanthropic giving professional work hands on with their clients (if they are advisors) and with their grantees. They are therefore often out of the office with the people they advise and fund, learning about new programs from their grantees, discussing financial strategies with individuals and boards, and attending fundraising events that they have sponsored. Just attending scores of fundraising events will fill the schedule of any philanthropic giving professional, even if they wanted to stay holed up in their office. Fundraisers consider direct engagement an important part of the cultivation process and invite foundation officers, donor advisors and community development directors to lectures, planning sessions, board meetings, dinners, awards ceremonies, ground breakings and press events. Working into the evening is therefore routine for the philanthropic giving professional. Most believe the face-to-face engagement is critical to developing good relationships and truly understanding the needs of their clients and grantees. One director of a corporate foundation likes to deliver large checks to grantees in person to demonstrate his commitment to the organization and the community.

Bringing together stakeholders

In keeping with the role of facilitator and community leader, granting organizations often convene meetings and planning sessions, bringing together all the parties involved in a particular issue or social problem, including nonprofit groups, government officials and business leaders. Community foundations in particular are emerging as an important facilitating force over the range of issues that impact any given place—from health care to education to conservation strategies. These meetings usually require much more than sending invitations, especially when an issue is contentious, such as land protection or reproductive rights. Negotiating and wheedling with reluctant partners may take much more time than the meeting itself, although most grantors are not afraid to wield the power of the purse to motivate participants. Again, some nonprofit organizations seeking funding can see these meetings as a nuisance, especially when they involve a complex policy issue. It's not unheard of for foundation officers to interfere with high-level politicians on a policy issue without consulting their grantees.

Establishing and reviewing grant-making procedures

While not all philanthropic giving professionals are directly involved in giving grants, most provide some advice to clients and institutions on how to give grants—to meet legal and tax requirements, to ensure efficiency and to facilitate constructive discussions around giving priorities. Lawyers and financial advisors may specialize in assisting wealthy families in establishing foundations or other giving mechanisms, such as donor-advised funds that are investment accounts set up for the express purpose of charitable giving. Beyond an understanding of law and finance, these professionals must have an ability to navigate family dynamics. For a dysfunctional family, a foundation may not be the best mechanism for giving away assets, for it may only facilitate lengthy family squabbles. So financial advisors and lawyers spend considerable time assessing their clients needs through surveys and interviews to help them focus their giving priorities. They then use their expertise in law and/or finance to establish the giving mechanism. Setting up a foundation is like setting up a small business or nonprofit; the lawyer or financial advisor must choose the form of foundation (usually established as 501(c)(3) charitable corporation, like other nonprofits), craft by-laws and file for tax-exempt status. If someone decides to establish donor-advised funds, decisions must be made on where to establish the fund. Community foundations have long managed donor-advised funds and now many commercial banking institutions can do the same.

As part of their self-analysis, foundations are perpetually reviewing and refining their grant-making policies, especially when there is turnover on the board or with staff. This may mean refining their grant applications or changing the review process within the institution. Many foundations are taking advantage of the Internet, working with consultants to set up online applications and databases listing past grantees and the projects the foundation supported.

Reviewing proposals

When in the office, those involved in grant-making programs spend a good deal of their time looking over proposals describing the activities that a nonprofit group would like to see funded. Proposals may or may not carry much weight, depending on the grantor. If there is a longstanding relationship with a nonprofit organization, a proposal may only be a formality, used only to document that the organization is indeed spending a grant on charitable activities. For other grant-giving bodies, proposals are essential to evaluating the worthiness of an organization and a project. Some foundation officers will work with fundraising staff and program specialists through a series of draft proposals, ensuring that the potential grantee is thinking through all aspects of the project. It can be tedious and frustrating to review dozens of proposals, especially when your day is already crowded with meetings and site visits. Foundation officers routinely complain about the quality of writing, the inability to follow directions clearly stated on the web site, and the number of typos that they find.

Preparing for board meetings/review committees

Philanthropic giving professionals involved in grant-making have various levels of authority in awarding grants, depending on the structure and philosophy of the grant-giving institution. Some foundations and donor-advised funds leave it up to the foundation officers or donor advisors to make the grant-making decisions. Then approval by a board of trustees is largely a formality. In other cases, there are many steps to approving a grant, including review by the rest of the foundation staff, review by a grants committee at a corporation or review by the board of trustees. Philanthropic giving professionals may therefore spend a fair amount of time preparing for these review processes. Some are required to put together briefing books for their board members, which usually include a summary of the proposal and some analysis of the organization and the proposal. It's a common practice with corporate giving programs to have a committee of employees that meet regularly to review grants. The program officer at the corporate foundation or the community development officer usually facilitates these meetings, often taking the committee through a rigorous process of ranking proposals by various criteria.

Shuffling paperwork

All activities in philanthropic giving involve paperwork. There are the papers to file when establishing a foundation or donor-advised fund, and there are the investment reports sent out to donors about the growth of their investments. These describe corporate donations that go to upper management, there are tax forms to file detailing gift giving for any given year, the briefings and reports to boards of trustees so they can approve grants, and there are the proposals and reports that every potential and existing grantee provides to a grant-giving institution. It's an endless cycle of reviewing, submitting, and filing of paper, and there's no real escape from it, no matter what your expertise.

Philanthropy at Work—Examples of Effective and Ineffective Philanthropy

Effective philanthropy doesn't just happen with the appearance of a pot of money. Here are two fictional case studies of what can happen when everything goes right, and wrong, in the work of giving money away.

Successful Philanthropy: The Paul M. Verhoeven Family Foundation

You just couldn't wipe the smile off of his face, not after that phone call. A partner at a national law firm had just heard from *The Silo*, a relatively new online magazine focused on fostering in-depth reporting on environmental issues targeted toward the X and Y generations. *The Silo's* president had called to share some exciting news—she had hired an extremely well-known and respected reporter from the *Los Angeles*

Visit Vault at **www.vault.com** for insider company profiles, expert advice, career message boards, expert resume reviews, the Vault Job Board and more.

VAULT CAREER LIBRARY   **125**

Times, once a finalist for the Pulitzer Prize, to do a regular series on climate change. Because of the recently established endowment made possible by a $2 million gift from the Paul M. Verhoeven Family Foundation, *The Silo* could keep this reporter on indefinitely.

The lawyer had made the foundation and the gift happen. Ten years ago, a client of the firm, Paul Verhoeven, a siding manufacturer whose operation resided in Europe, had approached the lawyer about setting up a family foundation. The lawyer spent a lot of time with Paul and his family, meeting with them as a group and individually to explore their various giving philosophies. Paul's children (then in their 20s) were reluctant to take part in the foundation's operations, expressing concern that it would take too much of their time to run, especially once their father passed away, and that they may be forced to spend a significant amount of time in the United States in order to continue its operation. Paul expressed frustration at his children's lack of interest in philanthropy. But after facilitating a series of planning sessions with the family, the lawyer proposed a plan that made everyone happy, sparking a new sense of purpose and enthusiasm among the kids. The lawyer proposed the establishment of a family foundation with a primary focus on the environment and public education. The entire family would serve on the board of trustees, with Paul as board chair for five years. The foundation would be aggressive in its grant giving with the intention of fully spending down the endowment Paul had set aside for the foundation in a 30-year period. Under this plan, Paul would work closely with the lawyer on setting up grant-giving procedures, which the children expressed little interest in. The limited time frame also ensured that the children would not be saddled with the day-to-day management of the foundation for the rest of their lives, allowing them to stay in Europe and only travel for periodic board meetings. The children were also excited about the primary direction of the foundation, which married their interest in civic participation and the environment. The lawyer had also connected Paul with a highly competent donor advisor at one of the prominent New York financial firms to manage the foundation's assets.

Over the years, the lawyer remained actively engaged with the foundation, keeping track of environmental groups, both in the United States and abroad, with activities and philosophies that matched the intentions of the family. Three years ago, he'd come across an article about an interesting startup nonprofit, *The Silo*. He forwarded the article to the family, suggesting that they may want to invest. The family was hesitant to fund a fledgling group and ultimately declined the first grant proposal. But the lawyer continued to follow the *The*

Silo's progress and growth, sending along to family member articles that the 'zine published.

Six months ago, *The Silo's* president called the lawyer and asked for a face-to-face meeting to discuss growth plans for the magazine. The lawyer arranged a meeting for when Paul would be in town on business. It couldn't have been more successful. Paul was thoroughly impressed with *The Silo's* president, a savvy young woman with an MBA from Stanford. She presented a five-year plan to double the organization's staff and revenue from contributions, advertising and partnerships, with socially responsibly businesses. Luckily, the manufacturer's eldest daughter (who had been the most vocal in her concerns about funding the magazine) was also in town and attended the meeting. At the next board meeting, the foundation approved a $2 million grant for *The Silo's* endowment, the largest grant that the foundation had given thus far. *The Silo's* president had sent a heartfelt thank-you letter to every board member and the lawyer, thanking them, "for facilitating a new kind of journalism that activates and engages a whole generation in environmental advocacy." And now it really looked like *The Silo* was going to make that dream happen.

Dysfunctional Philanthropy: The Boots Unlimited Community Development Fund

The community development director at Boots Unlimited, a shoe and retail manufacturer centered in Denver, Colorado, was about ready to resign. She just couldn't get a commitment from the leadership at the company for the three-year-old grants program, the Boots Unlimited Community Development Fund. Trying to expand the company's profile in the Denver area beyond sponsoring tables at fundraisers, the community development director had spent two years trying to establish the program, pulling together a volunteer review committee made up of employees from across the company. She convened the group in the evenings after work to come up with grant-giving guidelines and a grant selection process that wouldn't take up too much time and energy. After several presentations at staff meetings and numerous offline conversations with the CEO, the management team had reluctantly given the green light, committing to matching employee donations to the fund. And the CEO donated $15,000 of his bonus to the fund.

But with the CEO's departure (he had been forced out as the company prepared to go public), the grant program languished. Employee donations to the fund were down, and the review committee was completely overwhelmed with grant requests from local nonprofit organizations. Team managers were starting to complain that

Visit Vault at **www.vault.com** for insider company profiles, expert advice, career message boards, expert resume reviews, the Vault Job Board and more.

V**A**ULT CAREER LIBRARY   **127**

members of the review committee were spending too much time on the fund and not enough time on their actual jobs.

Yet the community development director did not want to see the program die. So she spent several weekends with the review committee (which had dwindled from 20 employees to a committed group of five) developing a new plan for saving the program. They decided to ask for a dedicated staff person to process grant applications and make preliminary funding recommendations. And they wanted the company to direct 5 percent of online sales profits to the fund. The community development director put together a comprehensive proposal (once again on her own time), including a cost-benefit analysis highlighting results from a recent survey sponsored by the Outdoor Industry Association in which the majority of consumers cited community involvement as an important factor in their purchasing decisions.

Unfortunately, it was now clear that the new CEO has no interest in the program. At the meeting with the community development director (which took nearly eight weeks to schedule), he took several calls and finally cut the presentation short. He was happy to continue the existing program, he said, but only in its current form and only if employees could continue to keep up with their workload. He was, however, willing to send out an e-mail encouraging employees to donate any proceeds from stock options that they cashed in once the company went public. The community development director dreaded the upcoming review committee meeting; she was sure that at least two more members would quit when they heard the news.

Fundraising and Philanthropic Giving Career Tracks

Your career path as a fundraiser or a philanthropic giving professional is not necessarily straightforward. It depends one your chosen specialty and the kind of institution you want to work for. Moreover, many professionals in the field move back and forth between fundraising and philanthropic giving positions. The following chapter maps out some of the most common career tracks.

Career Track for Fundraisers

The career path for most fundraisers has many twists and turns. With strong demand for fundraisers (even with just a few years of experience) and the pressure that comes with the job, fundraising professionals tend to be transient beings, often staying no longer than two years at any one organization. They move on because of organizational dysfunction, stress, boredom, or often because they are offered a salary or promotion at another organization that they can't refuse. So fundraisers frequently make lateral moves or even what appears to be demotions if moving from a smaller to a larger nonprofit. A director of development at a small organization, for example, may take a manager position as a much larger, national group. Or he or she may jump in an out of the consulting pool, spending a couple of years working independently for a variety of organizations until he or she is wooed by a nice salary, benefits and an interesting organizational mission.

So it's difficult to map a typical career path. But there is a progression of junior to senior positions, as described below. Please note that these position titles are not uniformly applied across the nonprofit sector. The director of development at one organization is equivalent to the vice president of development at another, or vice versa. Likewise, a grant writer at one organization is equivalent to an institutional relations officer or a foundation relations director at another. In reviewing job descriptions, the best indication of the level of position usually is in the number of years of experience required to take on the job.

Visit Vault at **www.vault.com** for insider company profiles, expert advice, career message boards, expert resume reviews, the Vault Job Board and more.

V∧ULT CAREER LIBRARY   129

Associate

Your first position in the fundraising field (especially if you have just graduated college) will likely be that of an associate or assistant, an administrative position where you will keep track of donor files, enter information into the donor relations database, schedule meetings and manage correspondence. Your direct supervisor is usually the director of development or the vice president of development, depending on the size of the organization. The associate position is viewed as a learning one, and most supervisors will give you a range of special projects to help you become familiar with all aspects of fundraising, from researching donors to working with vendors for a special event to assisting in analyzing the results of a membership appeal. Salaries are low—you are unlikely to make more than $35,000 to $40,000 even at the largest organizations.

Coordinator

The next step up the ladder is the development coordinator, who usually has somewhere between two and five years experience in a particular aspect of fundraising. The coordinator is a specialized administrative position at a larger nonprofit with a development department made up of several teams, each focused on a different kind of fundraising (institutional, major gifts, membership and planned giving). Each team will have a coordinator that handles filing, database entry, scheduling and usually plays a lead role in processing gifts—meaning that he/she ensures that information about a gift is entered into the donor relations database, that the finance department understands the nature of the gift and how it is to be spent, and that an acknowledgement is sent out in a timely manner. Coordinators also manage the calendar of deadlines, help research donors and prospects and may be the primary contact for vendors that assist with mailings, publications and special events. The coordinator position can be a stepping off point leading to a manager/officer position, and to that end, a coordinator usually takes on special projects that provide hands-on training in a specialty. For example, an institutional relations coordinator may draft smaller proposals and reports to foundations and corporations in order to gain enough experience to become a full-fledged grant writer/institutional relations manager. Most development coordinators who are successful are promoted to a manager/officer position in two years. Coordinators can make as much as $60,000 a year, depending on their level of experience.

Manager or officer

Front line fundraisers usually have a title of manager or officer and have at least two years experience in the field. It's at this point in their career that most fundraisers develop a specialty, focusing on grant writing, membership, major gifts or planned giving. Managers/officers usually have a portfolio of donors that they are charged with raising money from and fundraising goals that they develop with the director that supervises them. There is second subset of managers that specialize in systems related to fundraising; these include prospect researchers and database specialists. Managers/officers generally do not have supervisory duties.

There are varied paths to the manager/officer position, especially if you have previous job experience. Many people with backgrounds in for-profit industries can transition into these positions. Those with significant experience in sales and/or direct marketing are attractive candidates for manager/officers with a membership or major gifts team. Likewise, those with specialties in other nonprofit activities can move laterally to become a manager/officer. This is especially true for grant writers, who often have an extensive background in technical writing and/or other program-related work.

The pay scale for these positions is largely tied to experience; pay can be as low as $40,000 and as high as $150,000. Experienced major gift and planned giving officers (with at least eight years of experience) who are not interested in moving into a director position are at the high end of the pay scale.

Director

The director title means different things depending on the size of the organization. At small to midsized nonprofits, the director of development may be the most senior development person, in charge of the entire fundraising operation and reporting to the executive director. A director of development will oversee planning and goal-setting, manage a small fundraising team usually comprised of three or four managers and an associate, and will work closely with the executive director on engaging the board of directors in fundraising activities. In theory, a director of development is a generalist with knowledge and/or experience in most forms of fundraising. In reality, the level and quality of experience can widely vary; many have experience in one particular kind of fundraising, usually major gifts. Most have at least five years experience in the field; at midsize organizations, the director of development will have 10 years or more.

At a larger organization, the development department will have a number of directors, each managing a team of fundraising specialists. The director of planned giving will manage a team of a couple of officers and a coordinator, the director of institutional relations will manage a team of grant writers and a coordinator, and so on. These directors have deep knowledge of their particular area of fundraising, usually at least eight to 10 years. They develop strategies and set fundraising goals, troubleshoot problems and inefficiencies in process, manage and train team members, and are the primary liaison to the most important donors. They also manage expenses for their team; this is an especially important task for the director of membership, who may oversee a multimillion dollar direct mail budget.

Salaries for directors depend on the size of the organization, but these experienced fundraisers are in high demand. At midsized and large organizations, they can pull in between $80,000 and $200,000 a year. Some directors of development are paid more than the executive director. However, these are also high-pressure positions, responsible for meeting fundraising goals and ensuring that operations run smoothly. Many work long hours and are always in need of more resources. There's a reason why there is high turnover and many at this level make the decision to become consultants.

Vice president

Mostly found at large nonprofit organizations—including national advocacy groups, hospitals and universities—vice presidents are fundraisers with at least 10 or more years experience in fundraising and at least five years experience managing a fundraising team. (However, some smaller and newer nonprofit groups are adopting the title of vice president of development for the equivalent of a director of development position.) A vice president of development runs a sophisticated fundraising operation of at least 20 people working in teams. There's generally a desire for vice presidents to have advanced degrees, especially a master's in public administration, master's in nonprofit management or a master's in business administration. Most vice presidents have also spent a significant portion of their careers working at large, national organizations and possess a depth of knowledge about a particular subsector of the nonprofit world. For example, a vice president of development at a university (often known as the vice president of institutional advancement) will have significant experience and knowledge in university fundraising. The largest nonprofits often recruit vice presidents from the corporate world who may not have specific fundraising experience but are talented managers and strategists.

Beyond strong management abilities, vice presidents are political creatures navigating the various interpersonal conflicts between directors, different departments and the board. The pay can be substantial; a 2006 salary survey by the *Chronicle of Philanthropy* revealed that a vice president of development make more than $300,000 at the largest nonprofits with budgets of $50 million or more. The pressure and time commitment can be equally hefty.

Executive director/president

Highly experienced and talented fundraisers are often attractive candidates for the top management positions at nonprofit organizations. Most executive directors spend at least 50 percent of their time fundraising, and it never hurts to have extensive contacts with foundations, major donors, and corporations, as many fundraisers do. So don't be afraid to aim high.

Career Track for a Philanthropic Giving Professional

The path of advancement for a philanthropic giving professional is equally hard to follow, since there are a variety of institutions involved, from law firms to investment banks to foundations. In general, you cannot enter the field without significant education, training and experience. So usually you are already working your way up the ranks in your profession as a lawyer or investment advisor or as a program specialist at a nonprofit organization. Your career path, therefore, depends upon your specialty and the kind of institution you are working for or that you aspire to work for. The following is a brief description of career paths through various kinds of institutions:

Foundation

According to the Foundation Center, the nonprofit organization that tracks trends in foundation giving, more than 70,000 foundations operate in the United States today. There are three major categories of foundation—private, corporate and community. The vast majority are private ones set up as nonprofit organizations and run by a board of trustees. However, a very small number of foundations maintain professional staff. The Foundation Center's 2006 survey of more than 20,000 foundations with assets of more than a $1 million revealed that only 3,500 employed any staff at all, and most employed one person to manage day-to-day operations.

Positions at foundations are therefore highly coveted and difficult to get. Most who run them are highly experienced financial advisors and nonprofit administers with a host of advanced degrees. At the largest foundations, there are entry-level positions, either program or grant assistants, that take care of administrative tasks, such as answering the telephone, filing and organizing proposal submissions. The next level up is a foundation officer who manages relationships with grantees and usually has some level of authority in awarding grants. Most foundation officers have advanced degrees in either nonprofit management or in a particular policy or social issue. There's no guarantee that a grants administrator will be promoted to program officer; in fact, you won't be unless you have the proper education and experience for the job. Only the largest foundations have another layer of leadership, foundation directors, that manage a team of foundation officers focused on a particular focal issue, such as the environment or health care. Foundation directors are usually leaders in their field. They will have served as executive directors at recognized nonprofit organizations or conducted significant research in the field at a university. The highest level of advancement is the president or executive director. At a small foundation, the executive director may be the only employee.

Large community foundations (such as the California Community Foundation serving the larger Los Angeles area or the New York Community Trust serving New York City and beyond) will have a slightly different make-up of staff, largely because they are managing a significant pool of funds from individuals. These foundations are actively soliciting donations from individuals, so they may employ dedicated fundraising staff, primarily major gift officers. Community foundations may also employ in-house investment advisors, who are there to assist individuals grow their philanthropic funds.

Salary at foundations is influenced by size—the largest foundations offer the most generous compensation. According to the Council of Foundations 2006 salary survey, the median salary for a program officer is around $70,000; the median salary for an executive director is around $115,000. This means that more than half of foundations offer less or more in compensation. The turnover rate at foundations is very low; a major factor in employee loyalty is the small number of these jobs that are available.

Law firm

Lawyers can build an expertise in philanthropic giving in a variety of ways— navigating the process for establishing nonprofit organizations, helping nonprofit clients refine their operational policies, serving on boards and assisting wealthy clients with their estate planning, including starting up foundations. There are law firms with a wealth planning and/or philanthropy practice, and it's worth researching these firms if you are fresh out of law school and have an interest. The path of advancement is the same as any other lawyer. You will start as an associate lawyer with the hopes of one day making partner.

Salary will depend on the size of the law firm. According to the Association of Legal Career Professionals, the median salary for an associate at a large law firm (more than 500 lawyers) is $125,000; the median salary at a law firm of two to 25 lawyers is $67,000. There are also jobs for lawyers experienced in philanthropy at the various other giving institutions, including foundations, investment banks and social venture operations.

Investment firm

If you are involved in managing philanthropic funds for the wealthy, also known as high-net-worth individuals, you are likely to work for the private client services division of an investment institution—either an investment consultant operation, an asset management firm, an investment bank or a large global firm that combines the three functions. These investment managers are specialists with many years of experience in asset management under their belt, many with advanced degrees, and all are Certified Advisors in Philanthropy (CAP). Some have extensive experience managing endowment funds for foundations and other nonprofit organizations, and therefore their clientele is the nonprofit organizations themselves. To become a CAP specialist, you will need to work your way up the ranks as a broker and/or portfolio manager and complete many hours of continuing education. For more information on investment management as a career, refer to the *Vault Career Guide to Investment Management.*

Because these professionals are highly experienced and educated, salaries and bonuses are equivalent to senior financial advisors.

Corporation

There are two avenues through which corporations give money away—they can set up a separate, nonprofit foundation built off of a percentage of company profits (usually around 5 percent), or they establish a team focused on philanthropic giving, known by several names. A corporate foundation usually functions like any other described above. The size and shape of a corporate community development, community relations or corporate

Visit Vault at **www.vault.com** for insider company profiles, expert advice, career message boards, expert resume reviews, the Vault Job Board and more.

VAULT CAREER LIBRARY   **135**

citizenship department can vary widely, depending on the size of the company and its commitment to philanthropic activities. Corporate citizenship is now seen as a core business principle, and so philanthropic activities of all sorts are often woven into day-to-day business operations. Banks, for example, will operate grant-giving programs, as well as micro-lending and other social venture initiatives.

A community development team is usually comprised of some combination of coordinators, specialists or managers supervised by a director or vice president. A coordinator-level position is the most junior and manages the administrative aspects of the corporate involvement program, such as processing grant applications and managing other team members' schedules to ensure that there are corporate representatives at key fundraisers and other community events. Within smaller corporate involvement teams, coordinators may manage some giving efforts, such as an employee giving program, including United Way donations and matching gift applications. These are generally not entry-level positions; it's expected you will have at least some experience in public relations, communications or philanthropic giving. A specialist or manager is usually the primary public face for community relations, working closely with local nonprofit partners to develop relationships. They are also the ones to attend fundraisers or other public events hosted by the charities that they sponsor. In a corporation with offices around the country or around the world, community relations specialists or managers may be in charge of a particular region, creating and managing philanthropy initiatives and developing relationships with nonprofit organizations in that region. Specialists/managers are usually seasoned public relations specialists (with at least four years of experience) who work with senior management in various parts of the company to incorporate philanthropic activities into an overall communications strategy for the company. Higher up the chain is a director or vice president of community relations overseeing all philanthropic activities and working with senior management to set priorities in philanthropy. You will most likely need an advanced degree for a director position (usually an MBA) and at least seven years experience in corporate philanthropy.

According to the Boston College Center for Corporate Citizenship, median salaries range between $50,000 for coordinators and $140,000 for vice presidents. The breakdown is as follows: coordinators are likely to make between $50,000 and $60,000, managers make between $80,000 and $90,000, directors make between $110,000 and $120,000, and vice presidents make between $130,000 and $140,000.

Federated charity

Organizations like the United Way and Jewish Charities that collect and distribute money to other charitable organizations are a kind of hybrid nonprofit operation, functioning like any other nonprofit but also like a foundation. The two major activities of federated charities are managing the collections of donations from partner organizations, usually corporations, and operating a grant-giving program. Federated charities establish chapter organizations across the country that operate autonomously from one another. Like foundations, there are very few of these chapters that employ large staff, usually those found in major metropolitan areas. At smaller United Way chapters, a tight-knit group of employees many handle many different activities, from collecting donations to reviewing grant applications. Larger United Way chapters will hire specialists in donation collection or grant giving respectively. Positions related to collecting donations are much like those for a fundraising team. There are assistants focused on administrative tasks, officers/managers charged with building relationships with potential donors (primarily local businesses and corporations) and directors charged with managing teams. The grant-giving positions are similar to those at foundations; most officers and directors have extensive experience in a particular social issue and are often recruited from local nonprofit groups. Because of the strong connection to the business community, there is a fair amount of cross pollination for leadership positions, with corporate executive transitioning to vice president and executive director positions at local United Ways. As you would expect, executives at larger corporations are usually courted by United Way chapters in metropolitan areas that can offer more generous salaries.

The salary ranges at federated charities are equivalent to those of other nonprofit organizations in their region. As you would expect, rural chapters pay employees far less than those in urban areas. In urban areas, salaries are likely to be comparable to the larger nonprofit organizations and foundations.

Social venture operation

It's nearly impossible to describe the typical social venture operation, since there are many different kinds of social ventures out there. Banks may manage a micro-lending program or low-interest loans to foster community development. A nonprofit organization may run some for-profit business operation that funds charitable activities. A relatively new invention is the social venture fund, a favorite vehicle of the retiring dot-com and technology tycoons. Social venture funds are something between a foundation and a

Visit Vault at **www.vault.com** for insider company profiles, expert advice, career message boards, expert resume reviews, the Vault Job Board and more.

VAULT CAREER LIBRARY **137**

venture capital effort, and therefore employee a combination of experts in a particular social issue (not unlike a foundation officer) and seasoned investment professionals. This is a small but growing subsector of philanthropic giving, but the number of positions within these institutions is limited. You may be able to work your way up through a social venture group as an administrative assistant, but generally you will need some combination of experience in nonprofit management, philanthropy, banking and/or investment management to advance upward. A master's in business administration is likely to be a prerequisite for advancement, especially one from a university with a course curriculum focused on socially responsible business and/or social venture activities. Salary information is tough to come by, given how new and diverse this group of philanthropic giving professionals is. For more information, check out the Social Venture Network (www.svn.org); the web site provides profiles of different kinds of organizations, from retail businesses to venture capital funds to nonprofit organizations.

The Consulting Path

With experience, independent consulting is another viable, and often lucrative, career path for both fundraisers and philanthropic giving professionals.

Uppers and downers of consulting

The wear and tear of everyday life at a nonprofit or foundation and the lure of a fat consultant fee, have led many fundraising and philanthropic giving professionals to go out on their own. The perks are like those of any independent consultant—among them the freedom to set your own hours and the chance to work on a variety of projects with a range of clients. Consultants are often glad to disentangle themselves from what they view as oppressive office environments; as one fundraising consultant states: "I like challenge—I don't like politics." Some consultants feel they have more power to make change in dysfunctional nonprofit operations. "It seems as a consultant that your word is worth more," say the same consultant. And you can make some serious cash; one planned giving advisor confided that he made twice as much on his own than he did as a full-time employee.

There are a multitude of different kinds of consultants in the fundraising world—from those that provide general advice and support to those that assist with membership and planned giving to those that simply assist with hiring the right fundraiser. Likewise, all sorts of consultants assist with philanthropic giving; there are many independent financials advisors and lawyers that specialize in helping individuals set up charitable-giving vehicles with no affiliation to a large investment institution or law firm. Foundations hire consultants for all sorts of projects—for position papers on hot-button issues, systems to evaluate grant-making practices and strategic planning for themselves and their grantees, to name a few.

While the money may be better (especially for fundraisers), there are plenty of demands, not the least of which is the anxious executive director who wants results quickly (especially since he is paying you so well), or wary staff who may not exactly understand what benefit you bring to the organization. This is a complaint heard often among consultants specializing in planned giving, a part of the fundraising field that isn't very well understood by most people, even other fundraisers. For the grant-writing consultant, you will not escape deadlines of grant makers or those inconvenient periods in the summer and winter when foundations often expect proposals. Both fundraising and philanthropic giving consultants must contend with difficult clients who assume you are available at any time; one grant-writing consultant complained of regularly receiving phone calls from a particularly stressed-out staff person after 9 p.m. As a fundraising consultant, you are likely to work with smaller nonprofits with fledgling fundraising departments—or no fundraising staff at all. There is some risk that some of these organizations are financially unstable. It is, therefore, important to negotiate contracts where you get some money up front.

How to break into the consulting world

As is true for any consultant, contacts and networking are critical to establishing a steady base of clients. For the fundraiser, you will need to demonstrate an ability to bring in the money, and potential clients will most likely ask how much you have raised for other organizations. Potential clients may be looking for someone with experience fundraising for similar kinds of organizations. A hospitals or university, for example, will want consultants that have raised money for other hospitals and universities. However, the demand is high for fundraisers of any kind and with any experience, especially if you want to devote yourself to a particular sector of nonprofits and if you have previous experience as a program specialist. One freelancer with a little more than a year of grant-writing experience (but several years working as an environmental advocate) lined up a full plate of clients within three months. In fact, grant writers and planned giving specialists will frequently start receiving requests for assistance if they are

Visit Vault at **www.vault.com** for insider company profiles, expert advice, career message boards, expert resume reviews, the Vault Job Board and more.

V/\ULT CAREER LIBRARY **139**

perceived to have any expertise at all, whether or not they are interested in freelancing.

If consulting on your own feels a little daunting, there are many firms that specialize in different aspects of fundraising and philanthropic giving (as a lawyer or financial advisor at a firm, you are already a consultant of sorts). Like most consultants, you will work for a number of clients at any given time. You will learn a lot from those around you, especially if you are relatively new to the field. However, the pace can be grueling, since the firm rises and falls with the number of billable hours and the number of clients served. Agencies that specialize in growing membership-based fundraising programs are known for their particularly brutal work environments, especially if they are involved in fundraising for fast-paced, high-pressure political campaigns, in addition to fundraising efforts for nonprofit organizations. Yet these agencies will hire someone with little or no experience in fundraising, so they can be a good place to cut your teeth. Pace and pressure may not be a concern for the lawyer or investment advisor, since it's expected that you would give up most of your time to a respected firm— and be handsomely compensated for it.

Keep in mind that certain practices are considered unethical among fundraising consultants, especially charging clients based on a percentage of donations that come in. All of the various associations for fundraising professionals expressly condemn this practice. Some fundraising consultants set rates based on the size of a nonprofit's budget, discounting fees for smaller organizations. There are other important rules, such as a fundraising consultant should never be paid with grant funds, unless the nonprofit has explicit approval from the grant maker or the grant is for general capacity building. Otherwise, this is also an unethical practice and can cause a foundation to revoke a grant.

Requirements for philanthropic consulting

On the philanthropic giving side, it can be difficult for a lay person to discern any real difference in experience or expertise between someone calling themselves a financial advisor, a money manager or a registered financial advisor. There are a lot of frauds out there with minimal experience in financial management who simply acquire the necessary registration from the state and/or federal government. Education and certifications distinguish a true expert. An experienced philanthropic advisor should have at least a four-year degree in finance, if not a masters in finance, a masters in business, and/or a law degree. They should also have at least two different certifications as a certified financial planner (CFP) and/or a chartered financial analyst (CFA), as well as a certified advisor in philanthropy (CAP). Accountants involved in financial management should have a CPA, as well as a certification in financial planning. The certifications signify that the individual is not only educated but experienced in the field of financial management; a CFA will have at least three years experience in the field. While the title of personal financial advisor can mean many things, if they are dealing in securities they fall under the regulation of Securities and Exchange Commission and must follow strict rules and regulations. In addition, ethical financial advisors will work on a fee-only basis, not on commission, thereby protecting the client from many conflict of interest issues in recommending investments. Ethical financial advisors, according to the National Association of Personal Financial Advisors, will be familiar with all current rules and regulations (which change quickly in the financial world), will continue in their education as advisors, keep clients' financial information private and will inform clients in writing of any conflict of interest that arises.

Visit Vault at **www.vault.com** for insider company profiles, expert advice, career message boards, expert resume reviews, the Vault Job Board and more.

VAULT CAREER LIBRARY   141

Fundraising Career Snapshots

The following profiles cover some of the most recognized fundraising specialties: grant writers, planned giving officers, major gift officers, membership specialists and special event coordinators.

Institutional Giving/Grant Writer

The grant writer—also known as a proposal writer, foundation relations manager or institutional giving officer—occupies a special, superhero-sized place in the fundraising world. True-life, fairy-tale stories about lifesaving (or organization-saving) grants abound. Richard Linklater received a $2,300 grant from a Texas-based nonprofit, supporting independent film, to complete *Slackers*, the movie that established his career. On the other end of the scale, Conservation International—one of the largest environmental organizations in the world—received a $261 million grant from the Betty and Gordon Moore Foundation for a range of special projects to protect biological diversity worldwide. Such stories perpetuate a myth that the grant writer is the one person who can keep a nonprofit organization afloat, or at least allow staff to embark on that next exciting project. However far from the truth this may be—and in fact it is, as you've read in this guide—the myth persists each time a sizable grant is awarded to an organization.

What does a grant writer do?

A grant writer crafts funding proposals to convince grant-making institutions—foundations, corporations and government agencies, primarily—to give money. In the simplest terms, a grant proposal describes a grant seeker's mission, programs, activities, and how much money the grant seeker needs to undertake its work. The proposal may describe the grant-seeking nonprofit generally or a specific project. A successful grant proposal also outlines all the compelling reasons why a grant-seeking nonprofit, and the work described in the proposal, makes a difference in the world. (A more in-depth description of the components of a standard proposal is provided in the shaded box on page 148.)

Obviously, almost every aspect of the job requires that the grant writer write clear and concise prose, and more importantly, be able to produce clear and concise prose at a regular clip. Assuming that a nonprofit is successful at institutional fundraising, the grant writer will have many deadlines and cannot afford to procrastinate. Generally, proposals are between five and 10 pages long and can be the most in-depth discussions of program activities that an organization has on paper. In fact, the grant writer is often the first person to document all aspects of a program or project and therefore plays an important role in helping flesh out that program. It is often the grant writer that asks the most difficult questions about activities, knowing that the grant maker will ask the same tough questions. The grant writer is therefore a crucial player in program planning for the organization and can often lead this process.

Unlike other fundraisers (particularly major gift and planned giving officers), grant writers are less likely to work directly with funders, although there are opportunities to interact with staff at foundations, government agencies and corporations with grant-making programs. Most of the time, grant writers collaborate closely with a nonprofit's leadership—primarily the executive director, but also with other managers—and with program specialists on building relationships with grant makers. Most foundation officers, community relations officers and government administrators want to hear the inside scoop on any issue from program specialists, or they want the executive director to show up for a meeting to demonstrate how important the grant-maker is to the grant-seeking organization.

A grant writer is also a financial manager of sorts, working closely with a nonprofit's accountant or director of administration to develop budgets for projects and programs, and also with program staff on how they spend grants. At larger nonprofits, a finance department may produce financial documents for grant makers and employ a grants manager to oversee expenditures to grants; but more often than not, the grants writer is as knowledgeable as the organization's leadership and financial officers about program expenses and how a particular grant ought to be spent.

Uppers and downers

• Writing grant proposals can be a creatively rewarding exercise. Ultimately, proposals tell a story about a nonprofit organization doing good work, and it can be a fun challenge to shape the story for grant makers of widely varying interests. Most grant writers also enjoy and appreciate the collaborations with program staff, and grant writers generally develop closer relationships with them than other fundraisers.

- There is great fulfillment in helping strengthen a nonprofit's work by asking the questions that push program staff, and even the nonprofit's leadership, to think ahead. Ultimately, the grant writer can be a driving force in planning a nonprofit's next steps. Busy program staff will take the time to look far into the future when a large grant is at stake.

- If you don't enjoy writing and if you aren't a little bit pushy, then this is not the job for you. You will be overwhelmed by the number of deadlines, by the recalcitrant program staff person who doesn't return your phone calls and by the demands of an executive director who is going to pay attention to big-dollar grants. As rewarding as the experience of working with your program staff can be, there are downsides to collaborative writing. It can be irritating to get five different sets of comments on a draft, to have a program person give negative, unhelpful feedback or for someone to simply not respond until after the proposal is submitted.

- Grant writing is also one of the more intense fundraising jobs. After all, there is pressure associated with always having strict deadlines. And it takes a great deal of time and energy to write proposals day after day after day, especially if program activities are not fully developed or if program staff have trouble articulating what they are trying to accomplish. As a result, grant writers tend to work longer hours than most in the nonprofit world, especially when that six- or seven-figure proposal is due. Many submission deadlines fall at inopportune times, such as the first of the year or in the middle of summer, so you are a little crazed while the rest of the staff is planning vacations.

- Some grant writers may not have an inner accountant waiting to emerge and will find the preparation of financial documents (project budgets, revenue projections and expenditure reports) tedious. Filling out the forms that often accompany grant proposals (this is especially true for government grants) is not a lot of fun, nor is the process of compiling auxiliary materials, such as press clipping and publications, partnership agreements and letters of support. At larger nonprofits, you may have assistance from a development coordinator for these more administrative aspects of institutional fundraising; however, you are most likely on your own at a small nonprofit.

Visit Vault at **www.vault.com** for insider company profiles, expert advice, career message boards, expert resume reviews, the Vault Job Board and more.

VAULT CAREER LIBRARY   **145**

So what, exactly, are a grant proposal's moving parts?

If you have spent some time in the corporate consulting world, you will quickly recognize the similarities between a grant proposal and a pitch letter to a potential client. In essence, you are trying to explain through a grant proposal that the work you want potential funders to support is (1) essential for solving the problem or issue to which the grant-seeking organization is dedicated; and, (2) that you are the only organization that can successfully undertake this work. Proposals vary in length; the general rule of thumb is five to 10 pages. However, a grant writer will most likely write a significantly longer proposal for large, multiyear grants; it is not unusual to submit 25 pages for a grant of $1 million or more.

Grant makers will have different requirements for the format of proposals; some will simply accept any kind of narrative and some require written answers to specific questions. Generally, a grant proposal is made up of the following narrative sections:

Introduction/Executive Summary: Usually written last, this summary or introduction captures the highlights of the proposal, including the basic need/problem that the grant-seeking organization is trying to address, the overarching goal of the project and the major strategies and activities that the organization will undertake. The introduction will also include the formal request for funding, generally a sentence, such as: "The Hightown Community Orchestra respectfully requests a $10,000 grant to support its highly successful music appreciation program." *(No longer than one page.)*

Problem/Needs Statement: What follows is a discussion of the issue that the grant-seeking organization is attempting to address and why the project described in the proposal is so urgently needed. Most needs statements are peppered with statistics demonstrating the scope of a problem and also describe major challenges and significant opportunities that make it possible to solve the problem. For example, the proposal for the Hightown Community Orchestra might describe how little funding the local school system currently provides for music programs and also cite recent studies revealing a correlation between music appreciation initiatives and higher literacy rates. A common mistake of beginning grant writers is in spending too much time on the needs statement and not enough understanding and describing the activities associated with the project that the grant will be funding. Program staff can be part of the problem; they may provide a wealth of information about the issue and very little about the work to address it, often because staff haven't thought through the full breadth of work they need to undertake. *(One-two pages.)*

Goals and Objectives: Before diving into the specific activities of the proposed project, grant-makers uniformly require that you provide a list of goals and objectives for the project. The distinction between goals and objectives is a bit tricky; both state a specific change or vision that you hope to achieve. In the grant-giving world, a goal describes the overarching, ambitious change you are striving for, such as ensuring that students throughout Hightown are exposed to and develop an appreciation for classical music. Objectives are smaller, measurable goals that indicate you are progressing toward your larger vision. For example, an objective toward the goal of music appreciation might be to develop a curriculum where at least 50 high school students gain a rudimentary knowledge of great composers of the 18th Century. *(Half a page.)*

Description of Strategies and Activities: This section should be the longest of the proposal and should not only outline specific activities ("The Hightown Community Orchestra will hold host three workshops over the next year for high school students focused on major composers of the 18th century"), but also why these activities are the most strategic ("We believe these workshops complement the current curriculum for student orchestra players, since none of the local high schools offer a class in music history"). A strong proposal answers the basic who, what, where, when and why for each of the major lines of work that the grant-seeking organization will undertake. This is usually the most difficult, and tedious, section to write. *(Four or five pages.)*

Evaluation Measures/Indicators of Success: As discussed in more depth in the chapter on trends, grant makers, especially foundations, over the past decade have paid increasingly more attention to measuring the impact of their grant giving. They are therefore requiring groups applying for grants to describe how they will quantitatively and qualitatively measure progress toward larger goals. If there are specific tools that an organization can use (surveys, for example), they would be described in this section, as well as a list of outcomes that indicate success. For example, the Hightown Community Orchestra might measure success based on a quiz students take at the end of each workshop with the hope that 60 percent will score well. The orchestra may then follow up with a survey of those students, measuring how they are incorporating classical music appreciation into their education and/or daily lives. Ideally, all nonprofits would spend the time and money to develop and use rigorous self-evaluation tools, including surveys and case study analyses, or at least adopt a list of indicators for determining the effectiveness of any given project. However, it is far more likely that the grant writer will need to force program staff to think through how they evaluate progress for a project only because of a grant requirement. *(One page.)*

Overview of the Organization's History and Qualifications: Most nonprofits have developed boiler-plate language for this section to describe the founding of the organization, its mission, and a brief history of major accomplishments. The grant writer may need to tailor information based on the primary interests of the grant-makers. For instance, the Hightown Community Orchestra may want to describe in more detail the success it has had in educating students on music history to a foundation that cares about expanding after-school programs. *(Two or three paragraphs.)*

Project Budget Narrative: This is a short summary of the project budget (a separate document accompanying the proposal) that outlines the major expenses and the major sources of revenue for the project. A grant seeker may also indicate in this section how it will specifically use the grantor's funds; for example, the Hightown Community Orchestra might state that it will use a $10,000 grant to support the advertising and outreach for bringing students to the music history workshops.

Conclusion: As a grand finale, proposals usually includes a paragraph or two that once again summarizes the need for a grant and that thanks the potential grantor for all it has done to support the organization. The concluding paragraph also restates the specific request for funding. The conclusion of the Hightown Orchestra proposal might end with: "The board of the Hightown Community Orchestra deeply appreciates the commitment that the foundation has made to the educational needs of Hightown's children and its continuing investment in arts and music programs."

There are two other pieces that you will almost always include with the proposal: a cover letter and a budget. The cover letter can be an important communication to the potential funder; it's an opportunity to point out anything unusual in the grant proposal or highlight a particular accomplishment. The budget is equally important. In fact, many grant-making boards and foundation officers review the budget first to really understand what the foundation or corporation would be funding.

For those embarking on a fundraising career right out of college or graduate school, a grant proposal has many similarities to a standard term paper. You are trying to convince the reader of a general thesis (i.e., if you fund this work, then the world will be better) and then support it with facts and additional arguments. You are also trying to anticipate questions the reader might have about your thesis. If you're struggling to organize information for a proposal, think of it as an essay, and arrange information supporting the strongest argument first.

A Day in the Life of a Grant Writer

This is the day in the life of a fictional grant writer who works for a $5 million regional nonprofit organization with a mission to expand respite care services for families with mentally ill children.

9:00 a.m.: Come into the office, turn on the computer in your cubicle and scan your e-mail. The executive director has sent a message asking for the latest stock report for a well-known retail company. He is meeting tomorrow with the company's owner, who has an autistic child and recently established a small family foundation with a focus on improving services for the mentally ill.

9:15 a.m.: Search the MSN Money web site for the monthly closing prices of the retail company's stock. You print a chart of stock prices, an article announcing a recent stock split and the foundation's proposal submission guidelines posted on the foundation's web site. You consult with your boss, the director of development, on what additional information to provide. She suggests that you remind the executive director that he was going to speak with the company's owner not only about a personal gift but also about approaching the foundation to fund a new project, a web site for families needing respite care for mentally ill children. You dash off a quick note to the executive director to accompany the packet you have pulled together.

10:15 a.m.: Start on your main project for the day—a draft proposal to a large foundation describing your organization's biggest, most

Visit Vault at **www.vault.com** for insider company profiles, expert advice, career message boards, expert resume reviews, the Vault Job Board and more.

VAULT CAREER LIBRARY   **149**

complex program, which is a statewide outreach and education initiative for low-income families with mentally ill children. You have a lot of questions about how a new lecture series at local community centers will build upon a number of outreach events the organization sponsored last year, including a poorly attended lecture series at local libraries. You review your notes from a recent meeting with program staff, and call the director of community outreach to discuss how these new lectures will be different from the previous ones and how she hopes to encourage greater attendance.

12:30 p.m.: Run out and grab some lunch from the deli across the street. You bring it back to your desk so that you can continue to work through the proposal draft.

1:30 p.m.: Look up at the clock and see that you have a half-hour to finish preparing for the monthly meeting of the public policy team. You finalize a short presentation on the status of existing foundation funding for a campaign to lobby the state legislature for greater health care coverage for respite care. You add a summary of the history, interests and submission deadlines for three foundations you and the director of development have identified from prospect research. You stick your head into your boss' office to see if she will be joining the meeting. She is on the phone with the chair of the board discussing the elements of the next fundraising report and presentation to for the next board meeting. You quickly make a note to yourself to provide her with a quick summary of grants that have come in this month.

2:00 p.m.: Join the policy meeting. The director of public policy starts a discussion about whether to partner with a regional mental health center with strong connections to state officials. You remind the team that one of the foundations you have identified as a prospect is also funding the center. You also ask a number of questions about this partnership and how the two organizations would work together to engage officials at the state's department of mental health.

3:15 p.m.: Return to your desk and resume drafting the proposal. You complete the section on the lecture series and turn your attention to creating the budget. You recall a conversation in the hallway with the director of administration, who mentioned that rent would be going up next year. You call the director to figure out if you should adjust the percentage added to the program expenses for overhead.

4:30 p.m.: Finish a draft of the budget and e-mail it to the program director and the director of administration for review. The executive director calls to thank you for the stock information and to ask what he should highlight about the new project in his meeting tomorrow. You go over with him the overall structure of the web site and remind him that there will be a chat room devoted to parents with autistic children.

5:15 p.m.: Turn your attention back to the draft proposal. People are starting to leave the office, so it's quieting down. You figure if you can plow through another 45 minutes, you can complete the draft.

6:05 p.m.: Look up from a completed draft and see that it is time to go. You quickly look over the draft and see that there are a lot of questions highlighted in yellow. You decide to review it one more time tomorrow before sending it out to program staff and for comment. Your boss is still around and you ask if she wants to see the draft before or after program staff have reviewed it. She opts for after the program staff review and asks that you flag for her any remaining program questions that remain unanswered. You turn off the computer.

6:15 p.m.: Just as you are about to head out the door, the executive director calls again. The program officer at another large foundation contacted him. She said that she reviewed a proposal describing the health care coverage campaign and is recommending to the foundation's board an increase in funding by $50,000. The executive director compliments you on your work on the proposal, adding that he can now hire a new outreach person to enlist psychiatrists and pediatricians in the campaign. You make a note to write a thank you to the foundation officer tomorrow. As you close the door, you think about asking your boss to hire a freelance grant writer to help with three proposals due next month.

Visit Vault at **www.vault.com** for insider company profiles, expert advice, career message boards, expert resume reviews, the Vault Job Board and more.

V∧ULT CAREER LIBRARY   **151**

Planned Giving Officer/Specialist

Every fundraiser acquires some kind of specialized expertise, whether it is designing the perfect membership appeal or mastering the art of writing the compelling grant proposal. But the expertise of the planned giving officer is perhaps the most technical, the most obscure, and the most mysterious in the fundraising world.

A grant from a foundation or a donation in response to an appeal is generally a straightforward transaction; the donor or foundation sends a check to the nonprofit organization, which is then deposited into the nonprofit's bank account. A planned gift is not nearly so simple, although just as lucrative for the nonprofit organization. Most people are familiar with the bequest, where someone includes a clause in their will donating assets to a nonprofit organization. But as described earlier, this is only one kind of planned giving vehicle. There are a variety of complicated financial arrangements between donors and nonprofit organizations that involve all sorts of assets, from land to art to jewelry to mutual funds to life insurance policies. Many planned giving vehicles provide a donor with significant tax breaks — for example, retirees over the age of 70 and a half can donate up to $100,000 from their IRA accounts to charitable organizations and not count the withdrawal as income on their taxes. Or a planned giving arrangement can provide a yearly income to a donor; such is true for charitable gift annuities and charitable remainder trusts.

A planned giving officer is therefore charged with educating potential donors about the different kinds of planned giving vehicles available and their benefits. They then work with a donor's financial and legal advisors to design planned giving agreements that best fit the donor's long-term financial and philanthropic goals. Once an agreement is in place, the planned giving specialist ensures that donors receive benefits promised to them, such as monthly income checks from charitable gift annuities and remainder trusts. They also assist lawyers and financial managers to ensure that agreements (especially bequests) are executed as the donor intended. In this role, planned giving specialists may oversee anything from interpreting a clause in a will to the appraisal and sale of assets. Thus planned giving specialists acquire a unique range of knowledge around tax law, estate planning, and investment management.

To identify potential candidates for planned gifts, the planned giving specialist works closely with others on a fundraising team — especially the membership director and major gift officers — to cull through the list of existing donors. Strong candidates for planned gifts are those who have consistently donated to a nonprofit organization for at least five years, no matter what size the gifts may be. Once prospects are identified, the planned giving officer designs focused marketing initiatives, which usually include tailored appeals and newsletters that highlight the benefits of planned gifts. And like any other fundraiser, planned giving officers meet one-on-one with donors to update them on major activities that a nonprofit organization is engaged in, to better understand the donor's financial and philanthropic goals, to go over a planned giving agreement, and to field questions about planned giving. While the demographics of planned giving donors is changing, the vast majority are older, usually well into retirement. A planned giving officer must therefore be attuned to the needs of the elderly and be willing to engage in conversations about death and loss. They must also be prepared to deal with older individuals with serious physical and mental disabilities.

A planned giving agreement is a legal and binding one that requires great care and knowledge to create. While standard agreements exist, and there are software packages that help to customize them, every agreement must be tailored to correctly express the donor's intent, to conform to changing tax regulations, and to meet the needs of the nonprofit organization. It's then no surprise that many planned giving officers are also lawyers with backgrounds in tax law and estate planning.

Once overlooked by many nonprofit organizations and fundraising professionals, planned giving is now considered an essential part of any successful and diversified fundraising operation. The retirement of the baby boomer generation is a major factor; this wealthy segment of the population will be leaving behind trillions of dollars in assets. What's more, they are now at a stage of life when they are thinking about the mark they will leave on the world once they die.

Uppers and downers

- Given the newfound appreciation for planned giving, and because of the technical knowledge is takes to secure such gifts, planned giving officers are some of the highest paid fundraisers. Training and experience is critical, but there are numerous courses offered by the Association of Fundraising Professionals and the National Committee on Planned Giving. Another avenue for training is with one of the many specialized businesses that support planned giving operations, including marketing firms and software vendors. With training and a few years under the tutelage of an experienced planned giving officer, you can easily command a salary of

Visit Vault at **www.vault.com** for insider company profiles, expert advice, career message boards, expert resume reviews, the Vault Job Board and more.

VAULT CAREER LIBRARY   **153**

$100,000 or more in a large city or at a university. With a few more years' experience under your belt, you can go out on your own as a planned giving consultant. Such consultants are particularly well paid and rarely lack for clients.

• Planned giving officers spend time with donors from all walks of life who are usually among the most dedicated to the organization. These are people who may have donated to an organization for decades and are delighted to make significant contributions that they otherwise didn't think they could. It's hard not to be inspired by these donors.

• As stated above, most planned giving donors are elderly, preparing for their eventual death or grieving the loss of a loved one. Many are grappling with long-term illness, including senility. It can be an illuminating, inspiring, or depressing experience to talk with someone at this stage of life. You may be spending a great deal of time on the phone with someone who is very lonely. What's more, each planned gift that comes in feels like a mixed blessing. The gift can be a sizable donation of millions of dollars. Yet it means that a cherished donor, or even a friend if you have been working with them for a long time, has died. If you are not comfortable facing mortality, this is not the right specialty for you.

• Because the gifts are so complex and take years — or even decades — to come to fruition, planned giving officers are often underappreciated by organizational leadership and their own fundraising colleagues. There's no predictability to a bequest, so when it comes in, few realize how many years of cultivation a planned giving officer invested to make that gift happen. And few at nonprofit organizations really understand how charitable remainder trusts and charitable gift annuities work, or how much money they can bring in.

• Moreover, many executive directors and financial departments don't understand the infrastructure needed to build a successful planned giving program. They don't understand why planned giving officers are paid so much more than other fundraisers and may be reluctant to expand staff because of the expense. Leadership may also object to investing in the many different consultants needed, including knowledgeable and ethical lawyers and tax specialists. Finally, financial staff may not fully understand the accounting practices for recording and managing these complicated gifts. The planned giving officer is often put in the frustrating position of continually educating executive directors, controllers, and accountants on the finer points of planned giving. Even worse, they may spend a great deal of time correcting for past mistakes that could lead to costly litigation.

Princeton University, for example, is in the midst of a major lawsuit with the heirs of an alumnus whose donations grew over time to more than $100 million. If the heirs convince the court that Princeton violated the terms of the giving arrangement, they will take back every dime.

Key associations, websites, and resources

National Committee on Planned Giving (www.ncpg.org): national association for fundraisers involved in planned giving that provides educational workshops and DVDs, hosts a national conference, and manages a network of local councils for planned giving professionals. The committee also establishes and educates members on ethical practices in planned giving, and serves as the primary liaison to Congress on policies and incentives to encourage and facilitate planned giving. The website offers online tutorials on planned giving and houses an electronic library for members.

American Council for Gift Annuities (ACGA) (www.acga-web.org): nonprofit organization that educates donors, fundraisers, and other nonprofit staff about charitable gift annuities. One of the primary services ACGA provides is a table of suggested charitable annuity rates that most nonprofit organizations with charitable gift annuity programs use. The ACGA website offers a basic primer on charitable gift annuities designed for donors, but it is useful to anyone wanting to learn more about this particular kind of planned gift.

Leave a Legacy (www.leavealegacy.org): public education campaign sponsored by the National Committee on Planned Giving aimed at providing more information to donors on planned giving options, primarily on how to establish bequests. The website provides boilerplate language for bequests, as well as stories of donors.

Examples of planned giving arrangements

Bequest: A donor includes a provision in their will directing that assets be donated to a nonprofit organization. There are a number of different kinds of bequest provisions. The donor could list specific assets to be donated to the organization, or direct that a certain percentage of the entire estate be donated, or require that assets be donated if other beneficiaries die. This is the most common and most popular form of planned gift.

Charitable Gift Annuity: An arrangement where a nonprofit organization takes ownership of a donor's assets and in return provides the donor with a

Visit Vault at **www.vault.com** for insider company profiles, expert advice, career message boards, expert resume reviews, the Vault Job Board and more.

VAULT CAREER LIBRARY   **155**

yearly income based on a fixed percentage of the value of those assets. The percentage rate is based on the donor's age, so the older the donor is, the higher the rate will be. The American Council for Gift Annuities publishes the rates that most charities use. Here's an example of a charitable gift annuity: an individual might donate $100,000 in stock to an organization when they are 65, and the organization provides a payment of $6,000 a year (the six percent rate determined by the person's age) until the donor's death. If the individual gave the $100,000 gift of stock at age 70, they might receive $7,000 a year; the percentage rate is higher because the donor is older. The charitable organization works with a bank or investment management firm to manage the assets in keeping with state regulations and to distribute yearly payments.

Charitable Remainder Trust: An arrangement where a donor places assets into a trust, and upon the death of the donor, the assets go to a designated charity or charities. However, during the donor's lifetime, he/she receives income from the trust based on a percentage of the value of the assets (usually between 5 and 10 percent). This kind of planned gift is somewhat rare and is usually appropriate for assets valued at $250,000 or more.

Charitable Lead Trust: An arrangement where a donor places assets in a trust, and each year a nonprofit organization (or number of organizations) receives a donation based on a percentage of the value of assets in the trust. Upon the death of the donor, the assets return to the donor's heirs, who do not have to pay any estate taxes on those assets. These planned giving arrangements are extremely rare, largely because the benefits to the charity and the donor are tangible only if the donated assets are worth one million dollars or more. According to one planned giving specialist, you may come across one such gift during your entire career.

A Day in the Life of a Planned Giving Director

This is the day in the life of a fictional planned giving director at a $20 million nonprofit organization focused on changing environmental policies. She supervises two employees — a planned giving officer and a planned giving coordinator.

9:15 a.m.: After chatting with the receptionist, drop your coat on your office chair and listen to voice mails while turning on your computer. The most important one is a frantic message from an elderly gentleman in Colorado who has not yet received his charitable gift annuity check, which was supposed to arrive two weeks ago. He receives around $10,000 a year through the annuity arrangement, an important supplement to his income now that he is no longer working. You quickly get on the phone with your customer service representative at the bank that manages the assets and payments for your organization's charitable gift annuity program. He promises to sort out the problem. Twenty minutes later, just as you finish sorting through your emails, your customer service representative calls back. He explains that the bank recently converted to a new software system for generating checks and some checks were not printed and sent on time. You get a commitment from him to print the check today and send it out overnight. You call the gentlemen in Colorado and explain the situation. He's hard of hearing and you have to repeat yourself several times, but he's also quite funny and thanks you profusely for looking into the problem. You put a note in your Outlook calendar to call the bank tomorrow to make sure the check went out, and to call the donor to make sure he received the check.

10:30 a.m.: Review a draft bequest agreement that you received yesterday afternoon from a donor who has consistently given $15,000 annually for the past six years. You met with the donor six months ago, a 63-year-old widow with an impressive stock portfolio and a handsome home in Sun Valley, Idaho. She and her husband used to go fly-fishing in Glacier National Park, and she was delighted to hear about your organization's efforts to fight a flawed pollution policy now moving through Congress, a policy that would reverse a tough standard for capping air pollution levels in and around national parks. She made it clear that she wants to make a sizeable bequest to the organization, and you offered to provide her with some boilerplate language for her will. But she insisted that her lawyer, a personal friend of her late husband, draft the agreement. You had suspected it back then, but now you are sure the lawyer has never handled a

Visit Vault at **www.vault.com** for insider company profiles, expert advice, career message boards, expert resume reviews, the Vault Job Board and more.

V/\ULT CAREER LIBRARY   **157**

charitable bequest before. First off, he misspelled the organization's name and did not made it clear which assets would be donated. In addition, the bequest would go toward the clean air initiative that should end in the next two years. The woman is pretty healthy, so you expect that your organization will be stuck with a bequest that it can't use. You leave a message for the woman's lawyer briefly explaining the problem and ask that he call you back.

11:30 a.m.: Grab your coat and head out the door for a brown bag lunch at the local Planned Giving Council. You make an effort to attend these workshops sponsored by the chapter group of the National Committee on Planned Giving, and you're particularly interested in this one because a friend of yours, a planned giving consultant, will give a presentation on how to educate board members about the complexities of planned giving. You are having such a hard time convincing the board to change some long-standing policies around the planned giving program; maybe your friend can offer some insights.

1:35 p.m.: Return from the lunch and see that there is a message from the estate planning attorney that you keep on retainer. He asks that you send over for his review another problematic bequest agreement that you two had discussed yesterday. You shoot an email to the Planned Giving Coordinator and ask her to email the agreement over to the attorney. You also send an email to your friend, the planned giving consultant, praising him for his talk and asking when he might be available to discuss the possibility of giving a presentation to your board.

1:55 p.m.: Look over your weekly list of phone calls to donors that you keep in Outlook. You have 12 calls to make, regular check-ins with committed donors with whom you have already finalized planned giving agreements or who have indicated that they have arranged for a bequest. You scan the list and see that it's time to catch up with one of your liveliest donors, a 61-year-old woman living in Santa Fe who recently retired after selling her highly successful retail clothing business. She and husband travel extensively, vowing to visit every national park and national monument in the world. Last year, you helped her establish a charitable remainder trust, as well as a bequest agreement designating at least $1 million in stock and other assets to your organization.

The donor picks up the phone and greets you warmly. She's home from a recent white water rafting trip down the Green River in Utah.

She regales you with a hilarious story about how she and her husband attempted to sneak a pint of scotch in a thermos along on the trip, only to lose the thermos when capsizing in the first rapid they encountered. You ask if she's had a chance to read the latest newsletter that your organization publishes. There's an article about the pros and cons of carbon offset programs. You know she'll be interested because she and her husband are considering some investments in technologies aimed at reducing carbon emissions. She hasn't gone through all of her mail yet, but is glad to know about the article. Before getting off the phone, she once again asks you to come for lunch when you are next in Santa Fe. She also offers to get you tickets to the Santa Fe Opera.

2:45 p.m.: After leaving messages for a couple of other donors on your list, finish preparing for a meeting with the membership and online communications teams to develop a mini-campaign focused on educating 30-something members about the organization's planned giving program. You are excited about this effort, which will largely focus on a series of electronic appeals directing these members to a special web page with information and hints on how they can set up simple bequest trusts.

3:05 p.m.: Walk down to the main conference room for the meeting. You are a little disappointed that the Director of Online Communications has not spent any time thinking about the web page. There's a lively discussion on how to encourage donors to use My Space and Facebook pages to share information with their friends about planned gifts. You all agree to research the idea further and see what success other nonprofits have had with this approach. The Director of Membership offers some great suggestions for images to use on the website and in the electronic appeals. Everyone leaves with assignments, including you. You need to draft a short appeal for the Director of Membership and the Vice President of Development to review in two weeks.

4:30 p.m.: Return to your desk to find on your chair a pile of acknowledgements. These are customized thank-you notes to donors and their attorneys who recently signed off on planned giving agreements. The Planned Giving Coordinator whom you supervise finally caught up on these letters after a week-long vacation. You also see that your Planned Giving Officer has left for your review a proposal for a planned giving arrangement. You're pleased that she has convinced this donor, a somewhat grumpy 57-year-old man who owns a small boat-building and outfitting business in Maine, to consider a

Visit Vault at **www.vault.com** for insider company profiles, expert advice, career message boards, expert resume reviews, the Vault Job Board and more.

VAULT CAREER LIBRARY   159

significant planned gift. You decide to leave the proposal for later and begin to review the acknowledgements. In scanning the thank-you letters, you quickly become annoyed that the coordinator misspelled the name of one of the donors. But as you continue your review you also see that she took to heart some suggestions you gave on personalizing these letters. You decide not to upbraid her for the typo and instead make a mental note to send an email praising her for these acknowledgements.

5:15 p.m.: Finish reviewing the acknowledgements and begin to think about leaving for the day. The phone rings and it's the attorney for the widow in Sun Valley. You explain in more detail how the clean air initiative that the widow wishes to leave assets to is a short-term campaign designed to end with the next Congressional elections. You also explain that with so many lawsuits brought against nonprofit organizations for failing to fulfill a donor's intent after they die, your organization needs to be extra careful in crafting bequest agreements. He seems to understand the problem, so you suggest sending to him the boilerplate bequest agreement that you had wanted him to review in the first place, which gives your organization much more flexibility in using the widow's assets. He agrees.

6:20 p.m.: Hang up the phone with the attorney. You consider making a few more phone calls, or starting to review the draft proposal given to you earlier, but decide it all can wait until tomorrow. Before leaving you take a quick minute to look at your calendar for the next few months, wondering if you can fit in a trip to visit donors in the Southwest, including the woman in Santa Fe. You decide to set up a short meeting with your Planned Giving Officer to coordinate travel plans for donor visits through the end of the year.

Major Gifts Officer

The job of the major gifts officer may be the most straightforward in the fundraising business. You are tasked with building relationships with wealthy people and asking them for money. It seems simple—perhaps even glamorous.

Simple? Keep in mind that as a major gifts officer at a large, national nonprofit organization, you will be charged with bringing in millions of dollars each year. To reach your fundraising goals, you will need to build a rapport with perhaps 100 donors or more scattered across the country, all with different quirks and concerns. And it's not necessarily easier to raise a few hundred thousand dollars at a smaller, local organization. Unless you join a nonprofit organization with loads of contacts with the wealthiest people in your area, it's going to take a lot of time, energy, planning and cajoling to convince donors barraged with fundraising requests that your organization is the most worthy among dozens that serve the community.

So it takes more than optimism, a love of good food and a fondness for schmoozing to become an effective major gifts officer. While major gifts officers are often gregarious and serve an important role as the face of the organization for donors, they engage in careful research, coordination and prioritization to keep those donors happy and ensure that the gifts keep coming.

What does a major gifts officer do?

The most fundamental activity of a major gifts officer is building a network of contacts, both with wealthy individuals and people who know the wealthy. At a larger, more established organization, you will start with an extensive network from which to build on; at a smaller organization, you may be starting with only a handful of existing donors. Either way, the methods for expanding the web of contacts are the same—you scheme with those closest to the organization to make new contacts. You work with your board of directors to reach out to those they know in the community, encourage your existing donors to introduce you to their friends and business associates and collaborate with your fellow fundraisers to identify individuals who give small amounts now but have the ability to give much more in the future.

Then you try to make a connection with existing and potential donors in pretty much any way you can think of, without annoying them. Most major gift officers try to either meet face-to-face or get on the phone with each of

Visit Vault at **www.vault.com** for insider company profiles, expert advice,
career message boards, expert resume reviews, the Vault Job Board and more.

VAULT CAREER LIBRARY   **161**

their donors once a year. They also may host gatherings of donors to thank them for their support or to provide them with information about an organization's activities. And they send letters and e-mail updates tailored to pique the interest of individual donors. The personal touch is essential, as is understanding the particular, and often peculiar, needs of your donors. Some will only give in response to a letter, will never attend informational lectures or events or eagerly look forward to the yearly luncheon at their favorite restaurant. Planning and coordination are key activities; it's hard to overestimate the time it takes to schedule a year's worth of personal visits, events and phone calls.

Not every major donor gets the same level of time and attention; it's nearly impossible to do, and it's not necessarily a good use of the major gift officer's time. Thus, major gifts officers spend time prioritizing their donors, looking over research they have compiled and making some judgment calls on when a donor is ready to give and how much. Major gift officers keep detailed records of their interactions with donors, usually housed in a donor relations database. A review of all interactions with a donor can be an important part of the prioritization process; if the donor has given the same amount for a few years and revealed in last year's meeting that they would be coming into an inheritance, that's a donor worth spending some time to cultivate.

Many major gifts can be secured with a lunch and a handshake, but it's more and more common that wealthy donors want detailed written proposals describing how their money will be used. Major gift officers are therefore spending more time than ever before at the computer writing these proposals or working closely with grant writers to tailor existing proposals going out to foundations. And lunches to get to know the donor are rarely just that; more so than in previous times donors want to understand how their gift will make a difference to an organization and to the community at large. So major gifts officers must have a firm grasp on an organization's approach and activities and be quick on their feet to answer difficult questions.

Uppers and downers

• Work with major donors can be glamorous. You may have the opportunity to dine at fancy restaurants, attend elaborate parties and rub elbows with the rich, powerful, and famous. A seasoned major gifts fundraiser can build an impressive rolodex with the addresses and phone numbers of the elite in their community and beyond. But it's important to note that lunching and partying is only one aspect of the job.

- There's a scarcity of experienced and successful major gift fundraisers, and nonprofit organizations are willing to pay top dollar to recruit them. According to the *Chronicle of Philanthropy*, someone with as little as five years experience and a demonstrated track record of landing large gifts can have their choice of jobs. And they may get frequent calls from recruiters even if they've only been at a new job for a few months.

- More than any other fundraiser, major gift officers must love spending time with all sorts of people. If you are easily bored or intimidated at large, public events or if you are easily annoyed by the idiosyncrasies of human beings, this is not the right job for you. You will meet with smart, articulate, talented people who will inspire you. You will also meet with spoiled, unhappy, and self-centered people who will waste your time. And you will need to accommodate them all. Some people thrive on the challenge. Some people cringe at the thought of it.

- Depending on the size and scope of the nonprofit organization, you may spend a great deal of time traveling. For some, that's a major benefit of the job. For those with families, it can be a major stressor. Either way, travel wears you out over time. Many major gift officers who have been in the field for a while will negotiate limited travel schedules.

- The vast majority of major donors are older, often retired with many years of professional experience. They may or may not appreciate a fresh, young major gifts officer knocking on their door. Many major gifts officers in their 20s report that they have trouble building a rapport with these older donors, especially if the donor has been giving for a long, long time. Some leave the profession before their careers take off, feeling frustrated, disrespected and ignored.

Visit Vault at **www.vault.com** for insider company profiles, expert advice, career message boards, expert resume reviews, the Vault Job Board and more.

VAULT CAREER LIBRARY   163

A Day in the Life of a Major Gifts Officer

This is the day in the life of a fictional major gifts officer at an independent school for girls. The school's annual budget is $6 million.

10:15 a.m.: Arrive at work a little late today. You were out until midnight the night before with a donor, a recently divorced alumnus of the school with a thriving management consultant practice. While you had only arranged to have dinner with her to talk about her annual gift, she's rediscovering the singles scene, and she convinced you to join her for a drink at a new martini bar. You kept yourself to a glass of wine and also secured a $15,000 gift, $5,000 more than the donor gave last year. You shoot the donor an e-mail thanking her for the fun time and her generous gift. Then you document last night's meeting in the donor database, making a note that the donor did well in the divorce settlement. You also put a reminder in your Outlook calendar to call her in a month to remind her to send the check, if it hasn't already come.

11:05 a.m.: Review your to-do list for the week to see what you can accomplish before 3:30 p.m., when you need to leave the office to catch the 4 p.m. train into the city. You and the school's president are meeting one of the school's most important donors for dinner. She's an alumnus who is now a successful illustrator and author of children's books. Her most recent book was a finalist for the Caldecott Award, and sales have been very good. The donor recently left the board of directors for the school to focus on her writing career but remains active in fundraising. For years, the school's president has casually discussed with the donor the idea of dedicating one of her books to the school, as well as a portion of the profits. Now that the donor is on the verge of celebrity status, the president feels like it's the right time to make a formal pitch to her. You're a touch skeptical; the donor is extremely enthusiastic about the school, but you're just not sure she's quite ready to take this next step.

You decide you don't really have the energy to make a bunch of phone calls to donors, but figure your time would be better spent pulling together a request letter for a donor who gives $25,000 annually. He doesn't like chatting on the phone at all—you found that out the hard way when you first started the job and he abruptly hung up on you— but instead prefers to receive a letter updating him on the school's activities. You run down to the grant writer's cubicle and ask for any recent reports to foundations, especially any that focus on the school's performing arts activities. The donor's daughter is an alumnus who is now a struggling actor in New York. The grant writer agrees to e-mail you a couple of reports sent to foundations in the past few months. The grant writer teases you about the dark circles under your eyes, asking how many martinis you put away last night. You smile and say the usual—five or six.

12:15 p.m.: Head to the lunchroom (which is really a closet fitted with a counter, a refrigerator, a coffee maker and a microwave) to heat up your leftovers from last night. You head to your desk and eat your pasta while reviewing e-mails. You see the grant writer has sent you three reports. You open the first attachment and scan it. There's a lot of good information. As you finish up your lunch, you begin to cut and paste paragraphs into a blank document.

2:35 p.m.: Finish a rough draft of the letter and decide you need a cup of coffee—the red wine last night did not help your sleep and you are dragging a bit. You meet your boss at the coffee maker. You two chat about the dinner this evening. She had hoped to join you for the dinner, but she needs to prepare for the upcoming board meeting, which is at the end of the week. You two briefly review the elements of the pitch, and she reminds you to go over with the president the letter you and the director of development wrote last week outlining the request. She wishes you good luck and heads back to her office.

2:55 p.m.: Return to your desk and finish pulling together two briefing packets on the donor you will visit this evening (the request letter will have to wait until tomorrow). Yesterday you printed a profile from the donor database that includes all interactions that you, the director of development and the president have had with the donor over the past two years. You also copied several news articles about the donor and the reviews of her book. Now you print two copies of the proposal letter and head down to the president's office to go over all the materials. He's on the phone with the board chair when you get to his office and you stand outside waiting for him to finish. You only get 10 minutes with the president, so you quickly review the proposal letter with him. He then suggests that you grab your coat and overnight bag; you two can take a cab together to the train station.

4:00 p.m.: Sit down next to the president and settle in for the two-hour train ride into the city. Now you have the chance to discuss the briefing packet and the dinner this evening. He rereads the proposal letter. He compliments you on it, particularly the paragraph referencing the donor's own experience as a scholarship student. He then looks over the donor profile and asks for more detail about your meeting with the donor from three months ago; he's confused about a note referencing the donor's concern about the quality of the current writing curriculum. You clarify the note—she was not concerned per

Visit Vault at **www.vault.com** for insider company profiles, expert advice, career message boards, expert resume reviews, the Vault Job Board and more.

V/\ULT CAREER LIBRARY   **165**

se but wanted more information on how the school planned to integrate creative writing into the overall curriculum. You also tell the president that you sent a follow-up letter after the meeting describing to the donor some of the exercises that various teachers assigned to students with a focus on writing, including a research paper students wrote in their advanced algebra class. The president scribbles some notes on the proposal letter about the school's approach to writing and a fledgling effort to offer a science writing unit for juniors. You make a mental note to yourself to be more careful about how you describe donor conversations in the database.

6:25 p.m.: Arrive in the city and grab a taxi to the hotel where you will be staying overnight. The president heads off in a different cab; he's staying with a friend. You decide to take a quick nap before dinner. Unfortunately, it's hard to sleep because your room faces a busy street. You think about changing rooms, but decide against it. You can sleep on the train tomorrow.

7:30 p.m.: Meet the donor and the school's president at the restaurant, a fancy Asian fusion place. You are afraid it's going to be too noisy to talk, but the donor thought ahead and reserved a table in the corner. The food is delicious and the conversation goes well. The donor is definitely interested in the idea of dedicating a book to the school and would like to donate a higher percentage of proceeds than you expected. But she would rather have the donation go toward expanding the school's writing curriculum. The three of you discuss various ways that could happen, including using proceeds to support an endowed position for a creative writing teacher. She seems to like that idea very much. She asks that you revise the proposal letter to reflect this tentative agreement. The conversation then turns to more personal matters. She discusses the excitement and boredom of book tours. She's about to head off for three weeks to give readings at 30 different bookstores around the country.

9:45 p.m.: Head back to the hotel after leaving the donor and the president at the restaurant. They've decided to get a drink at the bar next door, but you beg off. You've got to get some sleep. Besides, you need to be up by 6:30 a.m. to catch 8 a.m. train back home. Thankfully, it's quiet out on the street. Before drifting off, you remind yourself that the donor's birthday is next week and that you need to go out and get her a card.

Membership/Direct Marketing Specialist

For those of you that like math and analysis, you might want to consider a career as a membership or direct marketing specialist.

We've all received those letters in the mail—from Easter Seals, Habitat for Humanity or a local group—asking you for $15, $20 or even $50. You probably throw most away and wonder, "Why do these charities spend time and money on these appeals and how on earth do these charities survive on such small donations?" The truth is that these small donations, even when a very small percentage of people respond, are often the bread and butter upon which an organization thrives.

Let's do the math: If you mail an appeal to 50,000 people who you know have some sort of interest in your cause and only 2 percent of those that receive the mailing give an average of $20, you will have acquired 1,000 new members and raised somewhere around $20,000. Now some portion of those donations pays for mailing costs. But next year, you send another appeal, which generally costs far less than the first appeal. It's likely that two-thirds of these members will give again, and probably give more, let's say an average of $50. You will then have raised at least $33,000 from that same group of people. And let's say you send more than one appeal to them a year, and they give more than once in a year. So if you keep expanding your pool of new members and retaining a good portion of the ones you already have, you quickly raise significant amounts of money for your organization.

So $20 donations from thousands and thousands of people do add up; look at recent efforts by MoveOn.org and the presidential candidates, who are more and more relying on small donations from hundreds of thousands of people. At a national organization with half a million members, you are likely to raise at least half if not more of a multimillion-dollar budget. Furthermore, membership donations can go toward core operations and infrastructure, activities of an organization that other funders are not eager to support.

What does a membership/direct marketing specialist do?

Like any other fundraiser, a successful direct marketing/membership specialist knows how to identify the right people to solicit and determine the most effective way to ask for a donation. With thousands of people giving the same way each year, perfecting an approach becomes less of an art and more of a science. The first and most important step is to build a list of potential and existing members. Luckily, there are many millions of donors out there that already give to other organizations. Does that mean that they are committed to one and only one organization? Usually not—most are giving small gifts to a number of organizations. So direct marketing specialists borrow, rent or exchange lists of potential donors. Most nonprofit organizations with a sophisticated direct marketing/membership program hire a list broker, who can arrange for the organization to rent a wide range of lists—lists of donors from similar organizations, magazine subscribers who might have an interest in a particular cause or consumers who purchase certain kinds of products indicating their interest in a particular issue. For example, someone who subscribes to *Mother Jones* magazine might be interested in a progressive cause, such as health care reform. Or a woman purchasing organic baby products could be interested in an organization that promotes organic farming. As you can probably guess, list brokers also keep detailed demographic information to offer profiles of potential donors.

The direct marketing specialist then develops an appeal package—usually including a letter asking for a donation, a return envelope and a pledge form—that's sent out to potential or existing members. And as part of an overall mailing plan, the specialist will design a series of experiments or tests to find the best lists and create the most effective appeal packages. Direct marketing testing is like any other scientific experiment. You have a control group and a test group. If you are testing to see if a new list you recently rented is effective, you send your appeal to lists that you already know brings in donors, along with a subset of a new list. Then you compare results. If you are testing elements of an appeal package, you send a control group a package you know attracts donors and then send a test group a package with one element that has changed—the design of the pledge form, the content of the letter or sometimes simply the kind of envelope you use. Then you compare results of the two packages. Like any other scientific experiment, you only want to change one variable at a time; otherwise you don't really know what worked and what didn't.

Mail is only one way to attract members, especially since e-mail is such a pervasive form of communication. So direct mail specialists apply the same principles of identifying lists and designing appeals for electronic donors. And as despised as it is, soliciting gifts via the phone is very effective, especially if a written appeal follows. Membership specialists also conceive of and design activities and strategies to retain members and deepen their relationship with an organization. To this end, membership fundraisers send out periodic newsletters to members (both print and electronic), thank-you gifts and invitations to special events.

Naturally, planning and analysis are fundamental activities for the direct marketing specialist. Marketing and mailing plans are developed well ahead of time, and specialists follow a strict calendar of deadlines. Direct marketing programs have many moving parts, from the acquisition and maintenance of lists to the development of appeal packages to the simple process of mailing the appeals to the right people to cashing thousands of checks and sending thank-you notes. There are many different outside vendors involved—banks that handle the check deposits, direct mail writers that craft appeals, graphic designers to lay out copy and pledge forms, mailing houses that personalize and mail the letters. Direct marketing specialists therefore spend a great deal of time working with and pushing vendors to make sure that appeals go out on time.

Where do membership/direct marketing specialists work?

There are two setting in which direct marketing specialists work—they are either employees of nonprofit organizations running direct marketing/membership programs, or they work for an agency that manages direct marketing efforts for many different organizations. The atmosphere at a direct marketing agency is intense; you're expected to work quickly and for long hours on numerous accounts. Running a direct marketing program at a nonprofit organization may be slightly less demanding, depending upon the size of the program. But some find it frustrating working within an organization where everyone feels like they have a say in how the membership program works. Those who have worked at an agency and move to a nonprofit organization can find the pace maddeningly slow.

Uppers and downers

• While analysis is critical to the job, there is a lot of room for creativity in direct marketing fundraising, especially as new technologies emerge. Our ever-increasing reliance on e-mail, as well as the explosive popularity of YouTube, MySpace and Facebook are providing exciting new opportunities to try different approaches to build membership programs.

• It's one of the few jobs where you can quickly rise in the ranks with very little training or experience. Direct marketing agencies often hire young people straight out of college, and they are quickly thrown into the game.

Visit Vault at **www.vault.com** for insider company profiles, expert advice, career message boards, expert resume reviews, the Vault Job Board and more.

VAULT CAREER LIBRARY   **169**

The pace and demand is draining, but you learn the tricks of the trade very quickly. You can quickly rise within the agency or move on to a membership coordinator position at a nonprofit organization.

- Since direct marketing is an essential tool for many for-profit industries, there's an opportunity for anyone with experience in this kind of marketing to transition over to a nonprofit organization without starting their careers over. That said, for the most part, nonprofit groups do not have the same resources for direct marketing activities as big businesses. That can be viewed as either a fun challenge or a big frustration.

- Like the grant writer, the direct marketing/membership specialist is driven by never-ending deadlines, and the pace and pressure can be fierce. The end of the calendar year is one of the busiest times for the membership specialist since many people are inclined to give right before the holidays— either out of the giving spirit or to make sure they can take a deduction on their tax return. The frenzy around sending appeals and processing checks can put a serious dent in holiday merry-making.

- Some of your nonprofit colleagues simply don't believe that direct marketing is a science, and they will want to push on to you their gut feelings about an appeal. This can be frustrating, especially since testing often demonstrates that gut instincts are simply wrong. For example, most think that a donor is unlikely to give another gift if they've just received an appeal. In truth, testing shows that people are more likely to give another gift if they receive a second appeal shortly after the first.

A Day in the Life of a Deputy Director of Membership

This is the day in the life of a fictional deputy director of membership at a Friends of the Zoo nonprofit organization that raises $7 million annually for a major urban zoo. The deputy director of membership is charged with managing communications with and fundraising from 25,000 members. He manages a membership assistant.

9:35 a.m.: Hang up your coat on the back of your office door and turn on the computer. After briefly perusing your e-mail, you log into the membership bank account to review yesterday's check deposits. Everything seems to be in order; yesterday's deposit was around $10,000. You expect that it will drop off a bit by the end of the month when the most recent renewal appeal will have been in members' hands for about six weeks. Now you begin to go through your e-mail. There are two important ones from your membership assistant. The first is about the BRE (business reply envelope) account—the account with the post office that pays for the postage on the return envelopes from members. The account is low on funds. You call the bank and authorize a transfer of a $2,500 into the account. The other message from your assistant is about the next appeal to lapsed donors. The vendor printing the letters and preparing the envelopes for the mailing called to say that they can't open the data file with the lapsed member addresses. You sigh. This is not the first time this has happened. You call your technical support representative at Raiser's Edge, the software company that created and helps you maintain the donor relations database that stores all the membership information. She's a nice woman but is relatively new at the company; you're beginning to feel like you and your assistant know more about Raiser's Edge than she does. You leave a voicemail message for the woman, asking that she call back immediately to resolve the problem with the data file. You finish reviewing your e-mail; the last one is a message from the contract copywriter you recently found and hired. She's sent the rough draft of the next appeal letter to members who give more than once a year.

10:10 a.m.: Begin your review of the appeal letter. You're very disappointed. You gave the writer very specific instructions on what to cover in the letter and the kind of language to use. You are particularly annoyed to see that she hasn't mentioned the birth of the new panda in the first page of the letter. It looks like you're going to have to rewrite it. You look at your schedule for the rest of the week; you can stay home the day after tomorrow to focus on the letter. If you finish by the beginning of next week, you can probably stay on schedule with the mailing.

You add an item on your to-do list: call your friend who is the membership director at a human rights watch organization and ask for recommendations for copywriters.

11:50 a.m.: Finish your first thorough review of the letter and look up at your e-mail. You see that you've received the latest layout of the electronic newsletter for members. The designer (someone you've worked with for years) has done a fabulous job, as usual. She's done a beautiful layout of photographs of all the baby animals that were born in the last six months. You think about pushing on to review the newsletter more closely, but your stomach is growling. You consider eating your lunch in the office, but you are really ticked off about the

Visit Vault at **www.vault.com** for insider company profiles, expert advice, career message boards, expert resume reviews, the Vault Job Board and more.

VAULT CAREER LIBRARY   **171**

disastrous renewal letter. So you decide to take the lunch you brought and eat it outside in the courtyard. You can see the children's tours come by as you eat, and that always cheers you up.

12:35 p.m.: Return from lunch and settle in to review the newsletter. You catch a few typos here and there, but otherwise everything looks good. You then click on the link to the web cam in the monkey habitat. You're able to get to the web cam but all you see is a dark screen. The web cam is such a great feature and you don't want members to be disappointed. So you call the IT guy and ask if there's a problem with the web cam. He doesn't know of any, but says he'll check it out. You also ask for him to come and check your computer to see if there's a problem with it. You send the newsletter on to your assistant to have her check all the links to make sure they are working and going to right pages on the zoo's web site.

You send a quick e-mail to the designer thanking her for all her hard work. You also ask when you two can sit down and start talking about images for the appeal and holiday cards that go out to all members at the end of November.

2:35 p.m.: Pull together materials for your meeting with your boss, the director of development, on the next "Adopt an Animal" acquisition campaign. You pull a performance report from the database detailing the returns from last year's campaign, which brought in 1,000 new members at the $50 level. In reviewing the report, you are reminded that one list of potential members did particularly well; it's the list of members of a national land protection group. You'll definitely rent that list again. You're talking with your list broker tomorrow, and you make a note to discuss if there are other national nonprofit groups that attract members with similar demographics. You also review your ideas for a test package for the acquisition campaign. You and your boss decided last year to test a new appeal letter, and you're getting together with him shortly to discuss the focus of that letter. While you've come up with a number of concepts, you really want to test a letter describing the zoo's burgeoning conservation programs. This letter may be a particularly good fit for the list from the national land protection group.

3:00 p.m.: Grab your assistant and head down to the director of development's office for the meeting. You see on his desk the samples of acquisition packages that you gave him last week. You all sit down for a little chitchat. Your assistant tells a funny story about one of the current "Adopt an Animal" members. Your assistant called the woman to get new credit card information for her annual gift; the woman name had come up on a list from the bank of credit card donors whose cards had expired. The woman was delighted to talk with your assistant, going on and on about the baby panda. The woman confided that she is pregnant with her first child and plans to name it after the panda, boy or girl.

You start talking about the next acquisition mailing. You present all of your ideas for the new appeal letter but stress your preference for one on conservation programs. Your boss is supportive, but he also wants to explore using some different images in the test package. He's really impressed with the montage of photographs that the San Diego Zoo used in their acquisition appeal. You remind him that it doesn't make sense to test more than one feature of the package, otherwise you won't know what really attracted new members. But you suggest trying a similar montage with the end-of-year appeal to existing members. Your boss likes that idea.

4:10 p.m.: Return to your office and the phone rings. It's the volunteer coordinator, who wants to talk about the lapsed member phone-a-thon that's coming up this weekend. You two worked together to create this initiative last year using volunteers to call members who have not given in the last 18 months and ask them to join up again. It was quite successful and significantly boosted the performance of the lapsed member appeal letter that landed in mailboxes a week after phone calls were made. You tell her to come on by. She's in your office 10 minutes later. She's excited because she's lined up 10 more volunteers than last year and she's gotten Whole Foods to cater a lunch for the volunteers on both days. You two go over the training agenda one more time and fine-tune the script that the volunteers will be using.

5:40 p.m.: Think about leaving for the day when the phone rings. It's the technical representative from Raiser's Edge. She apologizes for calling so late in the day, but she was talking with some of her colleagues about the problem. She begins to describe a different process for pulling the list out of the database. You ask if she could write up some instructions and send them to both you and your assistant, and you ask to have those instructions first thing in the morning so as not to delay the mailing any longer. She agrees and apologizes again.

6:05 p.m.: Shake off your worry about the data file and the delay in the mailing, grab your coat and head out for the day. You hear one of

Visit Vault at **www.vault.com** for insider company profiles, expert advice, career message boards, expert resume reviews, the Vault Job Board and more.

VAULT CAREER LIBRARY   **173**

the lions roar as you head toward your car. That gives you some ideas on how to start the acquisition letter: "What would it be like to never hear a lion roar again?" You're inspired to jot down a few phrases for the acquisition letter when you get home.

Special Events Coordinator

There are a wide variety of special events that nonprofit organizations host—marathons and bike rides, hikes and walks, white-water rafting trips, cocktail parties, awards luncheons, conferences, intimate dinners with board members and their friends, gala parties, auctions, benefit performances. The one thing that all of these events have in common is a person behind the scenes making sure that everything runs smoothly—that everyone has a drink in hand and the food is tasty, the keynote speaker is on time, there are enough chairs, all the trash is picked up, and the bills for catering and rental space are paid on time. That person is the special events coordinator.

It's not a job for everyone who dreams of becoming a party planner, because a special event for a nonprofit organization is more than just a party. Events are important vehicles for raising money, deepening connections with donors and the community at large and generating awareness about and enthusiasm for a cause. While keeping an eye on every detail of an event, the special events coordinator is also another important ambassador for a nonprofit organization.

What does a special events coordinator do?

Like any other fundraiser, the special events coordinator works to cultivate relationships with donors, using the special event as the invitation to give. To this end, a key activity for the special events coordinator is identifying the right donors to invite to an event. And that depends on the event itself and its purpose. For a bike ride, hike or walk, the primary aim may be to secure modest donations from a large number of people, not unlike a membership drive. The strategies and activities are therefore similar to those employed by a direct marketing fundraiser; the events coordinator may rent lists of potential donors and develop an invitation/appeal for those donors. If the goal is to engage a select group of major donors, then the approach will be similar to that of any other major gifts officer—a more personal invitation to donors tailored to individual needs and personalities.

A major fundraising component associated with most special events is obtaining sponsorships, usually from corporations and local businesses. A sponsorship is another word for donation, the only difference being that the business earns the right to publicly claim that it is a major sponsor of an event and the nonprofit organization hosting the event. These fundraising relationships are attractive to corporations because of the visibility; most businesses want to position themselves as contributors and partners to local charities and to the community. So the special events coordinator works closely with major donors and the fundraising team to gain access to executives and corporate giving officers and make the pitch for sponsorship. The relationship with a local business is likely to be more informal, and the special events coordinator may treat them like they would a major donor. Corporations are bombarded with requests for sponsorship and usually have a more formal decision-making process. Corporate giving officers usually handle these requests and may establish a process akin to that of a grant maker.

The great challenge of special events coordinators is how to make the most out of very little; most nonprofit organizations do not have the resources of corporations for hosting lavish events. Thus most special events coordinators rely heavily on volunteers and in-kind donations to pull a successful event together. So special events coordinators spend a great deal of time recruiting and training a pool of volunteers to work on special events and asking for free services and products, such as catering; design, production and mailing of invitations; rental spaces; and free publicity. Needless to say, close oversight over a limited budget is also an important responsibility.

Like any project manager, special events coordinators are only as good as their planning skills and attention to detail. Special event coordinators must also be able to work collaboratively with many different people, from volunteers to vendors to board members to the executive director. Since special events can serve many purposes, the coordinator must also build consensus and clarity on the overall purpose of the event; otherwise, the nonprofit organization may try to do too much with too little, with no success.

Visit Vault at **www.vault.com** for insider company profiles, expert advice, career message boards, expert resume reviews, the Vault Job Board and more.

V**A**ULT CAREER LIBRARY   **175**

Uppers and downers

• Events can be glamorous, especially at a larger organization. As a special events coordinator, you will get the chance to meet the elite in your community, even celebrities. But it's always important to remember why you are there—to make sure the event runs smoothly, and that means you will always be involved on some level with less glamorous jobs. As one special events director puts it, "If the trashcans are all full, and there's nobody else around, you are going to take out the trash."

• Special events can generate great enthusiasm for a nonprofit organization and a cause. It's inspiring to see hundreds or thousands of people train for a marathon or a bike ride in the name of social change. No less inspiring is the collaboration with dedicated volunteers who take time out of their lives to make an event a success.

• If you have experience in event planning for businesses, associations or corporations, you can easily move into a special events coordinator position at a nonprofit organization. That said, the lack of resources is a shock for many who make the shift to a nonprofit.

• Special event coordinators are among the lowest paid of fundraisers, perhaps because there are many who want to be involved in some form and the high cost of special events. Starting salaries are around $30,000, and you are unlikely to make much more than $75,000 annually.

• Most nonprofit organizations don't schedule events during workday hours, so you will be working weekends and evenings as a special events coordinator. Furthermore, the weeks leading up to an event can be brutal, for that's when things are likely to go wrong and you are the one who needs to fix them.

Corporate Giving Officer

The 21st century corporation places great emphasis on social responsibility, citizenship and community involvement. What this really means for business practices and day-to-day operations is not always clear, but for every corporation, philanthropic giving is an essential piece of their commitment to community and social policy. And behind the buzzwords are corporate giving officers who shape and manage the logistics of corporate philanthropy programs.

No one corporate giving program looks quite like another, but most have three common components—a grant-making process, an employee volunteering initiative and an employee matching gift mechanism. Corporate giving officers are charged with making sure that these different but complementary activities are streamlined and effective and with raising awareness about them both among employees and the general public. The corporate giving officer is therefore part foundation officer, part public relations specialist, part advisor and part administrator.

What do corporate giving officers do?

A corporate grant-making program is usually not much different from that of a foundation; in fact, many corporations establish independent foundations to distribute a small percentage of profits as grants to the nonprofit community. A corporate giving officer therefore engages in the same activities as a foundation officer. They help grant-seeking nonprofit organizations navigate the grant-making process, they conduct site visits to meet with grantors, and they evaluate grant applications. One big difference for many corporate grant-making programs is that there is an emphasis on sponsoring special events—gala dinners, conferences, benefit performances, among others. Special events can generate significant positive publicity for corporations.

Corporate volunteerism has taken on a new dimension and urgency; a robust program that encourages employees to volunteer at local nonprofits is seen by most executives as an important tool for boosting morale and a way of deepening connections into local communities. Coordinating a comprehensive program can be a massive undertaking, especially if the corporation has offices across the world. To provide employees with a range of opportunities, corporate giving officers will design volunteering events with local nonprofits, such as a day of building homes with Habitat for Humanity. They also establish mechanisms (such as an internal web site) for linking individual employees to nonprofit organizations. Another important role that the corporate giving officer plays is in assisting senior executives to serve on nonprofit boards of directors. Officers also set up and manage systems for tracking employee time devoted to volunteer activities, which are reported to the board of directors and publicized as part of public relations efforts.

The primary mechanism of giving for many corporations is the employee matching gift program—through which employees make a contribution to a charity that is matched by the corporation. As the administrator of these programs, the corporate giving officer is often fine-tuning automated systems

Visit Vault at **www.vault.com** for insider company profiles, expert advice,
career message boards, expert resume reviews, the Vault Job Board and more.

VAULT CAREER LIBRARY   177

that verify the legitimacy of nonprofit organizations, track amounts given to any particular charity and document giving patterns of employees. Corporate giving officers also work with senior management to establish matching gift criteria. For example, many corporations are currently grappling with policies around churches and faith-based charities, trying to find a balance between giving employees freedom of choice while managing conflict that can arise when a corporation supports a wide variety of charities with different belief systems.

Corporative giving officers also supervise internal and external communications related to corporate philanthropy programs. Working with senior management and communications specialists within the company, giving officers develop public relations campaigns to secure positive media attention for the company. They also supervise the development of various informational materials, which usually include an annual report focused exclusively on the corporation's community involvement. Internally, corporate giving officers make sure that senior executives across the company are apprised of philanthropic activities and create ways for employees to engage, usually through the company's intranet.

As you would expect, the larger the company, the more sophisticated and diverse the philanthropy program. In cases where a company has established many branch offices, such as banks, there may be local centers of philanthropy headed by one person that manages all grant-giving, employee volunteerism and communications for that community. But there's usually a central committee or department that oversees philanthropy across the country. IBM, for example, created a corporate citizenship council headed by the vice president of corporate community relations and includes division heads of many different departments, including environmental affairs and product safety, human resources, investor relations and supply chain management.

Uppers and downers

• In many ways, corporate giving officers take advantage of the best of two worlds—they work in a corporate environment with corporate salaries and resources, but engage with the nonprofit community in a deep and meaningful way. For someone who is tired of focusing on the bottom line but can't afford the pay cut that comes with jumping to the nonprofit sector, a corporate giving position can rekindle interest and enthusiasm in a company's mission and activities.

- Corporate giving officers work closely with senior management, giving them significant visibility within a company and access to top executives. Collaboration with the best and brightest in the corporate world can be an inspiration in of itself, as well as an important career booster. On the downside, engagement with the senior staff means you are at their whim and whimsy. At any given time, you might have too little or too much attention paid to you. It can be hard to get on the calendar of a busy executive; at the same time, when you have their attention, it can be hard to keep them from breathing down your neck.

- When faced with financial pressures, the corporate philanthropy budget is the first to be cut. After all, philanthropy may be important and a core business practice, but it doesn't make money, at least not directly. While your job may not be in jeopardy, it's certainly frustrating to make do with less.

- Generally, changes with the business impact giving strategy and structure, for better or for worse. Of large corporations recently surveyed by the Committee Encouraging Corporate Philanthropy, one-third have gone through a merger or acquisition in the last few years and as a result significantly revised their giving practices. Just like other business units, the corporate giving department can feel the stress and strain of merging corporate cultures.

Visit Vault at **www.vault.com** for insider company profiles, expert advice, career message boards, expert resume reviews, the Vault Job Board and more.

VAULT CAREER LIBRARY   179

Philanthropic Giving Career Snapshots

The following profiles cover some of the most recognized philanthropic giving specialties: foundation officers, corporate giving officers, donor advisors and social entrepreneurs, also known as venture philanthropists

Foundation/Program Officer

Perhaps the most prestigious job in the philanthropic giving world is that of a foundation officer, also known as a program officer. At the largest foundations, program officers are the elite, intellectual powerhouses behind philanthropy in America and the world. They are admired, courted and feared by fundraisers and nonprofit executive directors alike.

In the simplest terms, a foundation officer is the gatekeeper at a foundation, determining how to distribute a pool of grant funds each year to worthy nonprofit organizations. Foundations are themselves nonprofit organizations but with the single purpose of supporting other nonprofits through grant-making programs. A foundation is built from a pool of assets carefully invested over time. Those assets can come from a variety of places—from the pocket of a wealthy individual (in the case of a family foundation), a percentage of corporate profits (in the case of a corporate foundation) or from a group of different funds of varying size (as is true for the community foundation). Foundations with a single source of assets are referred to as private foundations; those with multiple sources are known as public foundations. By law, foundations are required to distribute 5 percent of their assets in any given year, and most give away about that much. However, some foundations are set up to dissolve at a point in the future and therefore program officers are tasked with spending down assets in a more aggressive manner. Like all other nonprofit organizations, foundations must establish a board of trustees to oversee operations. A foundation's board of trustees is ultimately responsible for the financial health of the foundation and the effective distribution of grant funds.

What does the foundation officer do?

As a gatekeeper, the foundation officer is the primary contact to nonprofit organizations seeking grants and the key coordinator of the foundation's grant-making process. Every foundation has a different way of doing business. Foundations that employ program officers—and this is a very small percentage of foundations, since the vast majority of foundations are run by volunteer boards of trustees—usually establish a formal and rigorous process for reviewing grant applications.

Most foundations today will not accept unsolicited grant proposals; there are simply too many groups seeking grant funding for program officers to keep up with requests. So the grant-making process usually begins as a series of conversations between foundation officers and the staff of grant-seeking organizations. Most of the time, initial contact is made by the grant seeker. An executive director meets a program officer at a meeting, a board member at a grant-seeking nonprofit has a business or personal relationship with a board member at a foundation or a fundraiser writes a compelling introduction letter to a program officer.

A foundation officer then must evaluate potential grantees, determining if they are a good fit for the foundation. The evaluation process usually involves interviewing staff at a grant-seeking organization, visiting the organization's facilities and/or the communities that the grant seeker serves, as well as meeting with leaders at other nonprofit organizations providing similar or complementary services. Program officers are also guided by the foundation's giving priorities, usually established by the person or corporation that established the foundation, and by strategic planning initiated by the board of trustees. It's not uncommon for a foundation to change its mission and giving priorities over time, especially if founding members pass on. For example, a wealthy entrepreneur may establish a foundation to fund nonprofit organizations in a particular community, such as his/her hometown, but not provide any other guidance on what kind of nonprofit organizations to support. But as that foundation matures, the board of trustees may survey the community and further refine the foundation's mission to meet particular challenges and needs.

If a foundation officer believes that a nonprofit organization is a strong candidate for funding, he/she will ask for some kind of proposal that makes the case for support. The proposal review process at each foundation is different; in some cases, foundation officers have the authority to approve or reject grant proposals with minimal interference from the board of trustees. At other foundations, there are lengthy and complicated review procedures, where the foundation officer serves as the advocate for the grant-seeking nonprofit organization at a series of meetings and presentations with foundation staff and the board. If approved, the foundation officer is then charged with monitoring the progress of the grantee; that may merely mean that they require the foundation to send along periodic progress reports. It can also mean more direct involvement; the foundation officer may want to help the organization further shape program activities and campaigns.

To be in a position to evaluate the potential of nonprofit organizations, you need expertise and experience. Foundation officers are therefore highly educated with a background in a particular issue, such as urban planning, reproductive rights policy or performing arts. They have also spent time working at nonprofit organizations in some capacity. It's important to note that the largest foundations are now looking to the corporate world for leadership, as evidenced by the recent change in guard at the Ford Foundation, the second largest foundation in the country (the largest is the Bill & Melinda Gates Foundation). The foundation recently hired a management consultant from McKinsey to take over as president.

Uppers and downers

- As a foundation officer, you are placed in an environment where you are encouraged to learn, like you would at a university, but with real world application. A key part of that learning process is meeting smart people at nonprofit organizations with deep commitments to making the world a better place. It's hard to overestimate how intellectually stimulating and deeply rewarding these interactions can be.

- As a person on the philanthropic giving side, a foundation officer doesn't feel the constant pressure of fundraising. The money is there, and sometimes there is a lot of it, depending on the size of the foundation. At large foundations, the office buildings can be well appointed, well located and quite modern. The William and Flora Hewlett Foundation, for example, built one of the most environmentally-friendly buildings in the country. But keep in mind that most foundations are on some level cost conscious, so resources aren't unlimited. A few scandals around compensation and overhead costs have caught the notice of Members of Congress, who have vowed to force foundations to spend more of their assets on grant-giving activities rather than salaries and office space.

- A larger foundation will feel more formal and corporate than your average nonprofit organization. That may mean more restrictive dress codes and generally a less relaxed working environment.

- If you move from a grant-seeking organization to a foundation, you're relationship with your former colleagues will change and change quickly, especially if you obtain a position at a foundation that funds similar work.

Visit Vault at **www.vault.com** for insider company profiles, expert advice,
career message boards, expert resume reviews, the Vault Job Board and more.

VAULT CAREER LIBRARY   **183**

You have to put some distance in the relationship and that can feel isolating. As one program officer states, "You learn pretty quickly when you are giving money away, that you can give signals inadvertently to people ... you want to be friendly because you want to be friendly, but that can be interpreted as a desire to fund them."

A Day in the Life of a Foundation Officer

This is the day in the life of a fictional foundation officer at one of the top-100 largest foundations in the country, with a mission to serve nonprofit organizations in an urban region crossing three states along the East Coast. In total, the foundation gives away $50 million a year. The foundation officer is part of a three-person team charged with giving $11 million in grants annually to arts and culture organizations in the region.

8:15 a.m.: Arrive at the office a bit early so that you can answer e-mails before the phone starts ringing. You've been tied up in so many meetings this week that you have a mountain of messages you haven't even opened yet. About a dozen are from grantees that have sent interim reports due at the six-month point of their grant terms. You shoot them all quick e-mails thanking them for the report and telling them you will get back to them with any questions. You scan through another six or seven e-mails with news clippings on various topics—reviews of local theater productions, a profile of the new executive director of the city's chamber orchestra and a feature article in the *Enquirer* (the primary newspaper for the region) on the status of performing arts in the region. You take a minute to read this article in full. It's centered on a report that the foundation funded and that you helped develop, a survey of performing arts organizations with commentary from several economists on the many ways in which arts and culture activities bolster local economies. You're glad to see that one of the economists that you brought on board to the project, a professor from New York University, is quoted in the article.

You respond to an e-mail from your boss, the director of the arts and culture program, confirming that you are available for lunch. There's also an e-mail from him asking for a list of the letters of inquiry to be considered at the next review meeting to occur at the end of the month. You quickly tick off the 13 organizations that have sent you letters, a three-page request summary that serves as the first step in the proposal submission process for the foundation. You also let your boss know that you have invited two other organizations to submit letters, and you expect to receive them by next week.

9:20 a.m.: Start returning phone messages; you had five from yesterday from various grantees. You call the grant writer at the natural history museum, who had a question about how to update outcome measures in the letter of intent that the museum is about to submit to you. You tell her it's not necessary to update them at all, that the ones submitted last year provided a lot of information to the foundation's board on how the museum was evaluating the impact of new programs on audience attendance. You leave a message for the director of development for a dance company giving her three days next month when you would be available for a site visit. You also ask that she send you a copy of the company's latest marketing plan to review before the visit; the grant the foundation gave last year was to help the company hire a new marketing director and a contract publicist. You're curious to see how the new hires are working out. Then you speak with the executive director of a small puppet theater, assuring him that it's perfectly fine to submit a letter of intent sometime next week. He is extraordinarily apologetic that the letter will come several days later than anticipated, explaining that the director of development and her assistant are both out with the flu.

10:15 a.m.: Join the monthly conference call for the Cultural Alliance, a consortium of arts organizations across the region focused on audience development. Your foundation is one of three funders that have invested in an online ticketing and audience management system to be managed by the Cultural Alliance that will allow a broad range of nonprofit arts organizations to manage tickets sales and demographic information. The software developer has set up these monthly calls to discuss progress on the system. Today, the developer is taking the group through an online presentation to introduce the web site and interface for the system. It's impressive and seems easy to use. The developer declares he is confident that the system will be up and running in time for three performing arts groups to use it for ticket sales next season.

11:35 a.m.: Step out the door with your boss for a meal at the Chinese restaurant down the block. This is a periodic lunch he schedules so that the two of you can catch up on things outside of weekly staff meetings. You spend most of the lunch describing the presentation by the software developer. Your boss asks if you could arrange a one-on-one meeting with him and the developer so that he can see the system for himself.

You two also discuss the upcoming planning retreat with the board of trustees. The foundation is entering the third year of its five-year

Visit Vault at **www.vault.com** for insider company profiles, expert advice, career message boards, expert resume reviews, the Vault Job Board and more.

V\ULT CAREER LIBRARY   **185**

strategic plan and the board has asked each of the four program teams to schedule a daylong retreat to discuss progress toward goals and lessons learned. Your boss wants you to give a presentation focused on various projects you are managing, including the performing arts report and various efforts to assist groups with audience development and marketing.

1:15 p.m.: Get back to your office to make a few more phone calls. You catch up with the development directors for two different organizations—a youth orchestra and an art gallery focused on displaying work by at-risk children—and schedule site visits. You also get in touch with the professor from New York University, who is about to catch the train down for a town hall meeting you have helped organize. The meeting is an outgrowth of the report project and is meant to bring urban planning experts and economists, city officials and leaders from the arts community together to discuss the impact of urban revitalization efforts on arts and culture institutions in the city. You assure the professor that he does not need to prepare extensive opening remarks but rather should be prepared to answer questions from the audience. He asks if you can join him for dinner beforehand, but you decline. You just don't think you have time today, especially since you need to try and review a couple of letters of inquiry today and tomorrow.

You notice that while you have been on the phone, you've received three voicemail messages. You don't have time to review them now, since you're a little late for a meeting.

2:05 p.m.: Run down the stairs for a meeting in the conference room on the regional arts and culture information project. A group of five funders, including your foundation, have joined officials at local art councils and state cultural agencies to create a new mechanism for capturing demographic information about audiences that attend art events, as well as financial data from arts organization to gauge their health and growth. Unfortunately, the project is going slowly. The group has spent many weeks deliberating on what kind of data to compile, a conversation that you think should happen later once you have hired a contractor to design the system. And now the group is struggling to put together a request for proposals in order to hire the contractor. Once again, the team reviews the draft request, which has gone through at least 10 iterations. It looks like everyone is finally ready to sign off on it, and you now hope the project can now move along at a faster pace.

3:45 p.m.: Return to your office and review your voicemail messages. None of them are urgent, so you decide to focus on the draft letter of intent you received yesterday. It's from a fledgling performing arts groups focused on incubating new theater and dance pieces. Six months ago, you read a glowing review in the local paper of one of their workshop productions and attended. You were impressed with the quality of the work and the sophistication of the production. You spoke to the artistic director after the performance and again, you were impressed by her level of sophistication, especially since you guessed she wasn't yet 30. After inviting her to your office for a longer conversation about the direction she wants to take the organization, you asked her to submit a letter of intent.

The basic concept described in the letter is exciting; the organization wants to link up with the local theater fringe festival to showcase new work and then promote those productions that are successful at the festival to other local theater and dance companies. Unfortunately, the letter is poorly written and riddled with typos. And the artistic director doesn't seem to quite understand what an outcome measure is. You just don't think the letter will make it through the first step of the review process. You decide to give the artistic director a call to talk about the possibility of a small planning grant for the organization; perhaps you can help them hire some contractors to help with fundraising efforts. You also make a note to talk with your colleague at another foundation with a technical assistance fund for small arts organizations.

4:35 p.m.: Leave the office in order to grab the train to the city. You should be able to get to the central library, where the town meeting is to be held, with just enough time to grab a sandwich beforehand.

5:30 p.m.: Arrive at the library full from a triple-decker sandwich from a nearby deli. The meeting starts in a half-hour, and you see that the panelists and a number of your colleagues from other foundations have arrived. You chitchat outside the meeting hall for a bit with your professor friend from New York University and a colleague from a community foundation. The primary host of the meeting, the president of the Cultural Alliance, takes the professor away to get fitted for a microphone. You and your friend from the community foundation complain a bit about the meeting earlier this afternoon. She is part of the team leading the regional arts and cultural information project and is just as frustrated as you that it's taking so long just to hire a contractor. As more people arrive, you two separate to shake hands with various participants, most of whom are grantees. But you're

Visit Vault at **www.vault.com** for insider company profiles, expert advice, career message boards, expert resume reviews, the Vault Job Board and more.

VAULT CAREER LIBRARY   **187**

pleased to see that members of the local actor's union have come, as well as some local store owners and one of the big real estate developers in the area.

6:15 p.m. Sit down as the town meeting gets underway. It's starting a bit late, but that's largely to accommodate a large crowd that came in at the last minute. The large meeting hall is three-quarters full. The discussion is lively and there's some strong statements made against real estate developers. You're glad that the facilitator, the director of the arts administration program at the University of Pittsburgh, is strong and unflappable. There's a rich conversation about the importance of festivals in creating a sense of unity in neighborhoods. The theater fringe festival and the Get on Your Feet Dance Jamboree are mentioned repeatedly—two festivals that your foundation has funded since their start.

7:50 p.m.: Grab a bottle of sparkling water at the drinks table and join the reception. You catch your boss' eye, and he wanders over. He joined the meeting about a half-hour late. He's very excited about the discussion of the theater fringe festival; it's one of his pet projects. You talk to him about the letter of intent you read this afternoon from the small theater group focused on new work. You all discuss ways that the foundation might find some mentoring opportunities for the artistic director around fundraising.

As your boss heads out the door, you catch up with the professor and congratulate him. You two talk a bit about how to build better relations between arts groups and real estate developers. He mentions an initiative in Chicago where the city arts commission worked with local foundations and bankers to convince a real estate developer to set aside a few units of artist housing in a new apartment complex on the south side of the city. The professor wonders out loud if it would be possible to replicate that model elsewhere. You make a mental note to continue this conversation with your boss; perhaps the foundation can find a little money for a study to determine the viability of such a project in this region.

9:15 p.m.: Arrive home after the reception. You're quite full (the hors d'oeuvres were tasty and you had one too many bruschetta) and quite tired. You send a quick e-mail to your boss to remind him that you will be working from home in the morning. You want a little quiet time to review letters of intent without interruption.

Donor Advisor

Supporting a charity can be as simple as writing a check once a year, or attending a volunteer event. But even individuals of modest means accumulate assets over time—life insurance policies, retirement accounts and property—some or all of which they may wish to devote to philanthropic giving. If philanthropy is important to you as part of your long-term planning—and it is to most Americans, no matter what their income—you will need the help of an advisor with expertise in setting up financial instruments and processes that provide you with flexibility in your charitable giving and the maximum tax benefits. That expert is known as a donor advisor.

Donor advisors come from varied backgrounds and work at many different institutions. Some are lawyers with expertise in estate planning; others are financial managers at investment firms; still others work at specialized consultancies focused exclusively on assisting individuals with their philanthropic giving. In all cases, donor advisors are knowledgeable in the wide variety of ways in which individuals can give to nonprofit organizations, have a basic understanding of tax law as it relates to charitable giving, can manage your assets or connect you with a reputable investment manager, and have the ability to guide you through a planning process to understand your needs and goals in philanthropic giving.

What do donor advisors do?

Planning is perhaps the most important service that a donor advisor provides. There are many questions that come up in thinking through a philanthropic giving strategy. Are there certain charities that you want to support over the long term? Do you need to supplement your income while supporting charities? Do you want to involve your family in the decision-making process? How do you want your assets to be distributed to charities once you have died? More questions emerge if you are a wealthy individual with diverse assets, such as stock options or shares in a family-owned business. An effective donor advisor will take some time to get to know you far beyond how much you earn. They will quiz you on your interests, passions and personal philosophies to help you formulate a giving strategy. It's not unlike forming a business; your advisor will help you articulate a mission and vision for your philanthropic giving.

With a mission for giving and personal financial goals in mind, a donor advisor will then identify the instruments and mechanisms that best meet your

Visit Vault at **www.vault.com** for insider company profiles, expert advice, career message boards, expert resume reviews, the Vault Job Board and more.

VAULT CAREER LIBRARY   **189**

needs. The most basic charitable giving tools are bequests inserted into wills leaving assets to specific nonprofit organizations and donor-advised funds, which are donations to public charities (primarily community foundations) that distribute these donations as grants to other charities. There are a number of more complicated giving tools, including charitable remainder trusts, charitable gift annuities and private foundations. Your advisor will then help you set up these mechanisms, which may mean writing the provision for your will, negotiating a charitable remainder trust with a nonprofit organization, or drafting and filing the paperwork for a private foundation.

In addition, your donor advisor usually handles the financial transactions associated with your charitable giving; this is especially true if you are working with an investment manager. Such transactions could include choosing the right investments to build your asset base over time or transferring assets to a giving instrument or charity (such as selling off property or stock options to establish an endowment for a private foundation). All financial dealings are closely monitored by state and federal regulatory agencies, but there is another level of scrutiny on those transactions linked

with charitable giving, since authorities are concerned that wealthy individuals are simply looking for ways to cheat the tax collector. Donor-advised funds in particular have come under fire recently; the Internal Revenue Service is currently reviewing regulations to ensure that such funds are actually used for charitable purposes. Donor advisors with a financial background usually have extensive experience in investment management and undergo specialized training focused on the rules and regulations that define legitimate philanthropic giving practices.

Finally, donor advisors will often help their clients set up processes for identifying charities to support. For wealthy individuals who establish private foundations, a donor advisor will assist in establishing a grant-making process and may serve as the foundation's primary administrator. Donor advisors may also screen nonprofit organizations for their clients to ensure that they are legitimate and effective. In addition, they may supervise the mechanics of gift giving, including writing checks and collecting acknowledgements from the nonprofit organizations that their clients support. In this role, donor advisors are not unlike foundation officers and if a private foundation grows, they are often brought as the first executive director.

Uppers and downers

- There are many different avenues to becoming a donor advisor, and it is often a path that a burned-out lawyer or investment manager finds appealing. As is the case for many jobs in philanthropic giving, you have the opportunity to build upon your existing training and apply it to good causes. And you can keep the paycheck that comes with being a successful lawyer or financial advisor.

- Developing an expertise in assisting wealthy individuals with their philanthropic giving can make you attractive to foundations (perhaps the most exalted institutions in philanthropy), especially if you are a talented investment manager. Positions at foundations are high-status, and therefore hard to come by, so any edge is advantageous. You may be a particularly strong candidate for a community foundation, which often manages a pool of donor-advised funds. Community foundations have emerged as a powerful force in philanthropy, often adopting some of the most sophisticated and innovative giving strategies. As a donor advisor at a large community foundation, you may have the opportunity to lead at the cutting edge of the field.

- Working with wealthy individuals is both an upper and a downer. For the most part, those who are intensely interested in philanthropic giving are smart, dedicated people with a sincere interest in making a contribution to society. In a few cases, however, a donor advisor may be managing for the capricious nature of a selfish and self-absorbed individual who happens to have a lot of money. Unfortunately, such a person expects a lot of attention, and as a donor advisor you may not have the authority to ignore unreasonable requests. You may also be dealing with dysfunctional family dynamics, especially if you are assisting a client in establishing a family foundation.

- Don't expect a major change of pace if you are already a practicing lawyer or financial advisor at a large firm. Expectations for commissions and billable hours will not lessen. However, new opportunities may open up to you, such as finding a position at a foundation or setting up your own practice. At that point, you may be able to slow down and work more regular hours.

Visit Vault at **www.vault.com** for insider company profiles, expert advice, career message boards, expert resume reviews, the Vault Job Board and more.

VAULT CAREER LIBRARY   191

Social Entrepreneurs and Venture Philanthropists

Over the past two decades, a diverse and growing category of philanthropic giving professionals has employed a variety of new strategies that harness money and an entrepreneurial spirit to address social issues. These professionals are known as social entrepreneurs or venture philanthropists.

The basic premise behind social entrepreneurship and venture philanthropy is that traditional mechanisms of philanthropic giving (particularly foundations and corporate giving programs) are important, but do not provide nonprofit organizations with critical, long-term support for infrastructure and stable growth. First conceptualized in the 1980s but more widely endorsed by the dot-com entrepreneurs of the late 1990s, venture philanthropy applies a variety of business practices used in the for-profit world to enhance nonprofit operations—including rigorous business planning to generate earned income and the creation of new capital markets. There are many, many iterations of the social entrepreneurship or social venture model, but we'll describe a few that dominate and the activities of those who oversee them.

Types of social entrepreneurship and venture philanthropy

The oldest and most commonly understood model is a hybrid of a nonprofit and a for-profit organization that provides services to the community like any other nonprofit organization but also sells services or products from which it can generate revenue. This model is often used by arts organizations, human services groups and nonprofits involved in community development. For example, many job training centers offer staffing services to local businesses for a fee. Nonprofit organizations may also purchase a franchise that generates funds to support core services. Ben and Jerry's, for example, will franchise its scoop shops to charities focused on job and skills training for disadvantaged youth. To run these revenue-generating projects, nonprofit organizations hire professionals with some combination of experience in business planning, operations and financial modeling, as well as nonprofit management. Since most of these social purpose businesses focus on assisting low-income and disadvantaged populations, individuals with experience in community organizing and social work are desirable. As a manager of these earned revenue operations, you will design and implement a business plan, market services, build strategic partnerships with vendors and potential consumers, educate and train staff in the nuances of for-profit activities, as well as ensure that nonprofit clients receive the training and experience they need to improve their life circumstances.

Another iteration of the model is a straightforward entrepreneurial enterprise, a small business that delivers a service or product that addresses a social need but also aims to make a profit. Examples of such businesses include software developers that create tools to encourage grassroots advocacy (GetActive Software), retail businesses that market items produced by impoverished or disenfranchised communities (Indigenous Designs), manufacturers creating building materials out of recycled products and developing replacements for toxic building compounds (IceStone), or contractors that design and manage construction projects for underserved populations (KaBoom!). In this guide, we make a distinction between these entrepreneurial pursuits that expressly focus on social change and those businesses that create a myriad of products and services but also adopt environmentally and socially responsible business practices, such as Starbucks and Google. The social entrepreneur described here is everything a successful entrepreneur ought to be—creative with business savvy, versed in finance and marketing, hardworking and ambitious, and someone who is likely to wear many hats as they build a business. They are also people who are invested in a particular cause and may have experience in nonprofit management and fundraising.

Yet another kind of social venture model is the consulting firm that provides technical support and advice to nonprofit organizations to build activities that earn income or to enhance a nonprofit's overall business planning. Some of these firms are nonprofit organizations themselves or are arms of foundations. This is an enticing career opportunity for would-be management consultants straight out of business school, or seasoned consultants tired of working with corporations. The work usually includes training and coaching staff in strategic planning, evaluating and improving accounting procedures, conducting cost-benefit analyses of fledgling for-profit ventures, developing business and marketing plans, and designing creative financing strategies.

Foundations, banks, and investment firms are engaged in another aspect of venture philanthropy: social financing. To give nonprofit organizations and social entrepreneurs greater access to capital, these institutions create all sorts of financing mechanisms, including low interest loans and lines of credit, diversified loan funds where individuals and businesses pool resources and spread loans out among many different social ventures to accommodate risk, and partnerships where nonprofit organizations invest in each other's activities. The Bill & Melinda Gates Foundation employs a particularly creative funding mechanism as part of its initiative to facilitate the development of vaccines. The foundation's advance market commitment

Visit Vault at **www.vault.com** for insider company profiles, expert advice, career message boards, expert resume reviews, the Vault Job Board and more.

V**A**ULT CAREER LIBRARY   **193**

guarantees a subsidy for the purchase of vaccines as they come on the market. Those involved in social financing engage in activities akin to a loan officer; they assess financial risk, provide advice and assistance in financial planning, and monitor loan payments. The level of engagement is usually deeper than that between a traditional loan officer and a small business. In most cases, loans and investment arrangements are made with people and organizations with little business background and almost no collateral, so social financing experts will get into the trenches to facilitate strategic planning, set up infrastructure and identify other sources of revenue.

Finally, a handful of private and community foundations, as well as a new generation of grant-making organizations referred to as social venture funds, undertake a modified version of grant-making commonly known as high engagement philanthropy. These entities function as both grantors and management consultants, distributing large, multiyear grants to a small number of nonprofit organizations but also providing intensive support in business planning, marketing and building infrastructure. Individuals involved in high engagement philanthropy generally come from the for-profit world with extensive experience in business planning and management; however, they work closely with experienced foundation officers to better understand the unique characteristics of nonprofit organizations and how to serve them.

Uppers and downers

- If you want to bring your training and experience in business planning and management to a cutting-edge and creative operation, look into social entrepreneurship. At this early stage of development, job opportunities are somewhat limited, but they are flexible and challenging. Moreover, there are numerous opportunities to create your own job, especially in starting a socially conscious business. Once you've landed a job, you will be encouraged to innovate, forge your own path and take risks, an exciting prospect for many.

- This particular brand of philanthropic giving is not for the risk averse. It's new, largely untested and the ultimate impact and success for social entrepreneurs is unclear. Many social purpose businesses and social venture funds will fail, leaving their founders and employees looking for new jobs. Moreover, there's no guarantee that foundations, nonprofit organizations, and banks will make a long-term commitment to social venture operations. To date, many nonprofit organizations have abandoned earned income projects before they got off the ground. Likewise, foundations have a tendency to jump on the latest trend and then quickly realize it ultimately doesn't mesh with their longstanding giving practices. For the moment, job security is certainly an issue.

Final Analysis

How selfish soever man may be supposed, there are evidently some principles in his nature, which interest him in the fortune of others, and render their happiness necessary to him, though he derives nothing from it, except the pleasure of seeing it.

Adam Smith, *The Theory of Moral Sentiments*

There are many prisms through which to view American society. While celebrating the wealth and influence that comes with being an American, most of us acknowledge that a complex web of interrelated social problems—poverty, sickness, environmental degradation, disintegration of family and moral values—threaten the very American notions of prosperity and freedom. We debate endlessly on what the solution may be to these very thorny issues. Yet no matter what perspective, no matter what side of the political, social or religious fence you make stake your claim, Americans show a deep commitment to social reform. We may not all agree on how to get there, or even what the ultimate outcome should be, but we agree to commit to change.

That commitment is reflected in the immense and powerful machine of philanthropy (in that larger sense of the word) fueled by the donation of time and money from nearly every American. Despite seemingly insurmountable challenges, the United States has built the most powerful network of charitable organizations in the world, and created an entire sector of the economy exclusively focused on social change.

This leaves you, the job seeker, with tremendous opportunity in the wide field of careers in fundraising and philanthropic giving. Whether as a development director at a small nonprofit organization or a program officer at the largest foundation, you have the opportunity to hone a diverse range of skills—persuasive writing, financial analysis, direct marketing, public relations and strategic investment, among others. And you have the chance to work at a variety of institutions and in a variety of settings—hospitals, universities, performing arts centers, zoos, investment and law firms, foundations, large and small consulting firms, corporations and on your own. What's more, you can make some money along the way, both for yourself and for a higher purpose.

The demand for your time, energy, and talents is high as the nonprofit sector continues to grow and mature. So join us in feeding the engine of change. You are needed.

Visit Vault at **www.vault.com** for insider company profiles, expert advice, career message boards, expert resume reviews, the Vault Job Board and more.

VAULT CAREER LIBRARY   195

APPENDIX

Glossary of Terms

501(c)(3) organization: referring to section 501(c)(3) of the Internal Revenue Code, a charitable organization registered with the federal government as a tax-exempt entity and defined as "a public charity or private foundation, which is established for purposes that are religious, educational, charitable, scientific, literary, testing for public safety, fostering of national or international amateur sports, or prevention of cruelty to animals and children;" donations to 501(c)(3) organizations are tax deductible.

501(c)(4) organization: referring to section 501(c)(4) of the Internal Revenue Code, a charitable organization registered with the federal government to receive tax-exempt status that is either devoted to social welfare causes or is an association of affiliated members; such organizations usually focus on lobbying efforts; donations to 501(c)(4) organizations are not tax deductible.

Acknowledgement: a formal letter from a nonprofit organization thanking a donor for a gift; such letters are not only important in maintaining relationships with donors but are also necessary proof for a donor to receive a tax deduction for a gift.

Annual report: a report produced by nonprofit organizations for the general public that describes activities and achievements of the past year, and summarizes financial information, including yearly revenue and expenses, as well as accumulated assets.

Appeal: a written request for a donation.

Appeal package: the range of materials sent to existing and/or potential donors as part of an appeal, including an appeal letter, a pledge form, and a reply envelope; appeal packages can be much more elaborate to include personalized stickers, testimonials, brochures and gift offers.

Acquisition appeal: a written request for a donation sent to individuals who have not yet given to a nonprofit organization but have the potential to do so.

Bequest: a planned gift where a donor includes a provision in their will directing that assets be donated to a nonprofit organization upon his/her death.

Board of directors/trustees: the governing entity of a nonprofit organization or a foundation; the primary responsibilities of a board is to supervise the executive director, provide guidance on the overall direction of the organization's work, and to ensure that the organization is financially stable; a board of trustees for a private foundation also approves all grant-making activities.

Visit Vault at **www.vault.com** for insider company profiles, expert advice, career message boards, expert resume reviews, the Vault Job Board and more.

VAULT CAREER LIBRARY **199**

Branding: a marketing strategy used by corporations and nonprofit organizations alike to define for consumers and donors the character and emotional appeal of products and services; through branding, nonprofit organizations try to distinguish themselves from other groups by building a recognizable look and feel that conveys the organization's unique values and mission.

Capital or major gifts campaign: an intensive, public fundraising initiative over a specific time line focused on securing new and significant funds for a nonprofit organization far beyond what they now receive from annual fundraising efforts, either to significantly expand operations, or to build, purchase or renovate a building.

Charitable gift annuity: a planned giving arrangement where a nonprofit organization takes ownership of a donor's assets and in return provides the donor with a fixed yearly income based on a fixed percentage of the value of those assets.

Charitable lead trust: a planned giving arrangement where a donor places assets in a trust, and each year a nonprofit organization (or number of nonprofits) receives a donation based on a percentage of the value of assets in the trust; upon the death of the donor, the assets return to the donor's heirs, who do not have to pay any estate taxes on those assets.

Charitable remainder trust: a planned giving arrangement where a donor places assets in a trust, and upon the death of the donor, the assets go to a designated charity; during the donor's lifetime, he/she receives income from the trust based on a percentage of the value of assets.

Combined Federal Campaign: a workplace giving program run by the U.S. Office of Personnel Management that allows federal employees across the country to donate a portion of their salary to designated nonprofit organizations.

Community foundation: a foundation that distributes grants from a pool of donations made by many individuals with a mission to improve the quality of life for a particular place or community; community foundations usually assist individuals with modest assets to establish and manage donor-advised funds and may provide guidance on which organizations to support with those funds.

Contributed revenue: income that a nonprofit organization derives from donations.

Corporate foundation: a foundation established with a percentage of profits from a corporation; not all, but many corporations establish foundations to carry out grant-making activities.

Corporate giving officer: a manager at a corporation charged with overseeing its philanthropic giving activities, which usually include grant-making, volunteer initiatives, and an employee matching gift program.

Development: another term for fundraising, referring to donor or resource development.

Development associate: an entry-level position at a nonprofit organization involved with administrative aspects of fundraising, including filing, scheduling, and database management.

Development coordinator: an administrative position at a larger nonprofit organization charged with overseeing systems and processes for a team within a development department focused on a specific kind of fundraising (direct marketing, planned giving, institutional donor relations); duties usually include processing gifts, maintaining files, writing acknowledgements and prospect research.

Director of development: at a smaller organization, the person in charge of all fundraising activities who usually supervising a small team of fundraisers.

Direct marketing: targeted communications promoting a product, service, or cause designed for specific consumers; the most common form of direct marketing is direct mail; in fundraising, direct marketing is a technique used to convince a large number of potential donors to make modest gifts to a nonprofit organization.

Direct marketing specialist: a fundraising professional charged with designing and implementing direct marketing initiatives to raise money for a nonprofit organization; a direct marketing specialist may be an employee of a nonprofit organization or may work for a direct marketing agency serving many different nonprofits.

Direct marketing agency: a consulting firm that specializes in designing and implementing direct marketing campaigns.

Donor: a person, business, or organization that financially supports a nonprofit organization; there are different categories of donors, including institutional donors, major donors and corporate donors.

Donor advisor: a financial or legal specialist who assists individuals in setting up financial instruments and processes for philanthropic giving.

Donor-advised fund: a donation to a public charity (usually a community foundation) that then disperses grants to other charitable organizations; donor-advised funds are a way for a donor to establish a grant-giving program without going through the complex process of establishing a foundation; the public charity receiving the donation usually invests it so it grows over time and consults with the original donor on grant-giving activities.

Visit Vault at **www.vault.com** for insider company profiles, expert advice, career message boards, expert resume reviews, the Vault Job Board and more.

VAULT CAREER LIBRARY   201

Earned revenue: income that a nonprofit organization derives from selling services or products.

Employee matching gift: donations that individuals make on their own that are matched by their place of business.

Endowment: an investment fund that nonprofit organizations establish to provide a steady source of income for a range of expenses, both general operating and for special projects and programs.

Event sponsorship: a particular type of donation where an individual, foundation, small business, or corporation provides funding for a special event and is publicly acknowledged as a sponsor of the event and the nonprofit organization.

Executive director: the job title often given to the head of a nonprofit organization.

Federated charities: a network of loosely affiliated chapter groups under the leadership of an umbrella organization that collect donations and distribute them to other charitable organizations; the most well-known example is the United Way charity network.

Form 990: the tax form that the Internal Revenue Service requires all nonprofit organizations registered as tax-exempt entities to file in order to make public their financial status; nonprofit organizations must provide information on annual assets, expenses and grants awarded (if the organization is a foundation).

Foundation: a nonprofit organization with the primary purpose of distributing funds to other nonprofit organizations through a grant-making process; foundations usually derive their funding from the investment of substantial assets provided by individuals or from a small percentage of corporate profits.

Foundation officer: a philanthropic giving professional who designs and manages the grant-giving processes at a foundation.

Funder: a person or institution that financially supports a nonprofit organization; the term usually refers to institutions that give money, including foundations, corporations, government agencies and social venture funds.

Funder network: a collaboration between grant-making organizations to develop giving strategies for addressing a particular issue or population; foundations usually pool funds to create a new grant-making initiative targeted toward the issue or population.

Giving circle: a tool for giving where a group of like-minded individuals pool donations and create a process for distributing small grants; most giving circles focus on a specific cause (such as helping children or the homeless) or are built on an affiliation (many African-Americans, Latinos and Asian Americans form such groups).

The Gospel of Wealth: an essay written at the turn of the 20th century by steel baron Andrew Carnegie, in which he declared that the accumulation of wealth served society as a whole and that the wealthy must make a commitment to curing society's problems; the essay documented a philosophy of philanthropy adopted by several titans of industry who then established some of the oldest professional foundations in the country, including the Carnegie Corporation and the Rockefeller Foundation.

Grant: a donation to a nonprofit organization usually to be spent over a specific period of time for a specific project or program; nonprofit organizations usually receive a grant through a formal process where the organization submits a grant proposal which is then reviewed and evaluated.

Grantee: a nonprofit organization that receives a grant.

Grantor: a grant-giving organization that provides a grant.

Grant proposal: a document (usually between five and ten pages) that a nonprofit organization seeking a grant submits to a grant maker describing activities to be funded with a grant; the proposal is meant to convince the grant maker that the organization seeking the grant is providing unique and important services that will have a significant impact on people or a cause.

Grant writer: a fundraising professional charged with crafting grant proposals to obtain funding from grant-making organizations.

High engagement philanthropy: a relatively new way in which philanthropic giving professionals engage in grant-making, usually through a social venture fund; instead of simply distributing grants to nonprofit organizations each year, philanthropic giving professionals make a long-term investment in a handful of nonprofit organizations and provide intensive support to improve and strengthen these organizations/operations.

Independent sector: a term used to describe the vast network of nonprofit organizations across the United States that work to improve the quality of life for Americans and people across the world; first coined in the 1970s by the Commission on Philanthropy and Public Needs (a research body created by the House Ways and Means Committee), the term is meant to recognize the separate and independent nature of nonprofit organizations in relation to government institutions and for-profit businesses.

In-kind gift/donation: a contribution to an organization other than money, including expertise, volunteer time, office space or equipment.

Institutional donor: an entity, rather than an individual, that gives money away; foundations, corporations, government agencies and social venture funds are all considered to be institutional donors.

Visit Vault at **www.vault.com** for insider company profiles, expert advice, career message boards, expert resume reviews, the Vault Job Board and more.

VAULT CAREER LIBRARY **203**

Institutional relations manager: a fundraising professional charged with developing relationships with institutional donors, such as foundations, corporations, social venture funds and governmental agencies; the term grant writer and institutional relations manager are often interchangeable.

IRA rollover: a planned giving arrangement where a donor designates a nonprofit organization as the primary or secondary beneficiary of an IRA investment account.

Lapsed member: a member donor of a nonprofit organization who has stopped making donations.

Letter of intent or inquiry: a letter (usually no more than three pages) that serves as a summary description of a project in need of funding that helps grant makers decide if they want to review a full proposal; because of the large number of nonprofit organizations seeking funding, many foundations require the submission of a letter of intent/inquiry as a first step in a grant-making process to narrow down the number of grant proposals staff review each year.

List broker: a consultant who makes arrangements to rent mailing lists for direct marketing campaigns; a list broker will help clients identify lists of consumers or potential donors most likely to be influenced by a direct marketing campaign, as well as work with the owner of the list to set a rental price.

Member: in the fundraising world, a donor who annually gives a modest amount to a nonprofit organization, usually between $5 and $999; a member donor may receive benefits for their donation, including newsletter subscriptions, discounts on events or products, or gifts such as T-shirts or mugs.

Membership coordinator: a fundraising professional charged with designing and implementing initiatives to attract and retain member donors, including direct marketing campaigns and member appreciation events.

Membership program: an ongoing fundraising initiative to attract and retain a large number of donors that annually give modest amounts (usually between $5 and $999) to a nonprofit organization.

Membership drive: a short-term fundraising campaign to encourage existing members to give again and renew their membership and/or to bring on new members; some of the most visible of these campaigns are those run by public radio and television stations.

Mission statement: a brief description of the primary purpose of a nonprofit organization.

Major donor: an individual who makes a substantial donation to a nonprofit organization; each organization defines a major donor differently, but the most common definition is someone who gives $1,000 or more.

Major gift: a substantial donation made by an individual, usually over $1,000.

Major gifts officer: a fundraising professional charged with obtaining large gifts (usually $1,000 or more) from individuals to support a nonprofit organization.

Nonprofit organization: entities with some formal structure that do not distribute any profits to its owners or leadership, but rather devote all resources toward a cause; in the United States, most nonprofit organizations register as nonprofit corporations as defined by the Internal Revenue Service, with a board of directors charged with oversight of the organization's direction and financial health.

Philanthropic giving: the act or process of distributing money to charitable causes.

Philanthropic giving professional: a general term for someone involved in philanthropic giving, including donor advisors, foundation officers and social entrepreneurs.

Philanthropy: derived from Greek and Roman concepts of *philanthropos/ philanthropia* (love of fellow man), any activity to improve society.

Planned gift: a formal and structured arrangement to give assets (such as stocks, property, art, jewelry, etc.) to a charitable organization over time; examples of planned gifts include bequests, charitable remainder trusts and charitable gift annuities.

Planned giving specialist: a fundraising professional charged with educating donors about planned giving and providing assistance in making planned giving arrangements.

Private foundation: a foundation with a single source of assets, usually from a wealthy individual or family.

Program specialist: a general term referring to a staff person at a nonprofit organization engaged in designing and implementing programs or projects that further the mission of the organization; a distinction is made between a fundraiser, who raises money to support activities that further a nonprofit mission and a program specialist who undertakes those activities.

Prospect: a donor or funder that has not yet donated to an organization but has the potential and desire to do so.

Visit Vault at **www.vault.com** for insider company profiles, expert advice, career message boards, expert resume reviews, the Vault Job Board and more.

V∧ULT CAREER LIBRARY   **205**

Prospect researcher: a fundraising professional charged with identifying and gathering information on individuals or organizations with the means and the interest to donate to a nonprofit.

Public foundation: a foundation with multiple sources of assets; the most common form is a community foundation.

Renewal appeal: a written request sent to those who have already given to a nonprofit organization asking that they renew their commitment with another donation.

Site visit: a meeting arranged by a foundation officer to visit the offices of a nonprofit organization, usually to observe the nonprofit's operations and to discuss future funding opportunities.

Social financing: strategies and mechanisms to provide nonprofit organizations with greater access to capital beyond funds given through fundraising activities; examples include low-interest loans and lines of credit, diversified loan pools, and investment partnerships between nonprofit organizations.

Social venture fund: a relatively new kind of grant-making entity made popular by the dot-com entrepreneurs of the late 1990s; with a social venture fund, philanthropic giving professionals make a long-term investment in a handful of nonprofit organizations, and also provide intensive support in building and strengthening these organizations' operations.

Social venture enterprise: organizations or businesses that develop services and products to generate an income but that also seek to address social issues and causes; a social venture enterprise can be a small business with a product or service that addresses a social need, or it can be a hybrid of a for-profit and nonprofit organization, generating income with services and products, as well as through fundraising.

Social entrepreneur: an amorphous term that refers to nonprofit professionals and philanthropic giving specialists that believe in enhancing traditional philanthropic giving and fundraising by applying a variety of business practices used in the for-profit world—including rigorous business planning to generate earned income and the creation of new capital markets.

Special event: in the fundraising world, any kind of public event intended to generate money for and interest in a nonprofit organization or a cause.

Special event coordinator: a fundraising professional charged with running special events for a nonprofit organization.

Strategic planning: a formal process through which a nonprofit organization or foundation reviews past activities and their impact, identifies new opportunities and challenges, and revises its approach, strategies and activities for the future.

Key Associations, Web Sites and Resources

For your job search

With the growth of the nonprofit sector and the advent of the Internet as a job search tool, there are a plethora of resources for finding that perfect job in fundraising and/or philanthropic giving. Here are some sources that Vault recommends:

Web sites

- Craig's List (www.craigslist.org), a free online forum with classified ads for 450 cities worldwide; most nonprofits will post job openings, especially the smaller ones.

- *Chronicle of Philanthropy's* online career center (www.philanthropy.com/jobs), the resource from the fundraising community's primary trade publication; job postings focus exclusively on fundraising and philanthropic giving.

- Idealist's Nonprofit Career Center (www.idealist.org), with easy-to-search job postings for thousands of nonprofit organizations around the world; the site also includes postings for internships and fellowships.

- *Nonprofit Times* (www.nptimes.com), an online trade publication for nonprofit organizations with a comprehensive list of job postings; *Nonprofit Times* also publishes an annual salary survey.

- *Opportunity Knocks* (www.opportunitynocs.org/jobseekerx), a web site focused exclusively on finding jobs in the nonprofit sector.

Print publications

- *Chronicle of Philanthropy*, the print version of the trade publication, which includes extensive job listings from all over the country.

- *Opportunity Knocks*, the print version of the job seeker's resource focused exclusively on the nonprofit sector; they also publish an annual salary survey.

- *The New York Times, The Washington Post, The Chicago Tribune, The Los Angeles Times*, and other major newspapers in most cities include job listings for nonprofit organizations, both in print editions and on web sites.

Visit Vault at **www.vault.com** for insider company profiles, expert advice, career message boards, expert resume reviews, the Vault Job Board and more.

VAULT CAREER LIBRARY 207

Free online guides

- *Grassroots Fundraising Journal* is one of the best sites for practical information on fundraising, with a focus on major gifts (www.grassrootsfundraising.org).

- Idealist.org maintains a site with answers to frequently asked questions related to fundraising and other nonprofit management issues (www.nonprofits.org).

- The Foundation Center's web site (www.foundationcenter.org) houses an extensive library on nonprofit management and fundraising with a focus on foundation relations and writing grant proposals.

- Compasspoint Nonprofit Services maintains a useful web site called the Nonprofit Genie (www.genie.org) with frequently asked questions about fundraising and other nonprofit issues.

- The Free Management Library is a comprehensive online clearinghouse of information on nonprofit management, including fundraising (www.managementhelp.org).

For Fundraising/Philanthropic Giving Professionals

American Association of Grant Professionals (www.grantprofessionals.org): a relatively new membership organization with a mission to foster a community for grant-writing professionals. The association holds an annual conference and is drafting a code of ethics for grant writers. They are also spearheading an effort to develop a certification program for grant writing.

Ashoka Innovators for the Public (www.ashoka.org): one of the first of the social venture funds, Ashoka provides financial support and advice to social entrepreneurs around the world. It's worth reading about their model to better understand how social venture funds operate.

Association for Fundraising Professionals (www.afpnet.org): the primary association for fundraising professionals offering workshops, roundtable discussions and online resources for fundraisers of all levels. While informational materials and training opportunities are focused on all of the fundraising activities, a special focus is placed on educating newly minted fundraisers on acquiring major donors.

Center for the Advancement of Social Entrepreneurship (www.fuqua.duke.edu): An arm of Duke University's Fuqua School of Business, the Center for the Advancement of Social Entrepreneurship

(CASE) disseminates research on social entrepreneurship. An extensive overview of the field is provided on the website, as well as numerous case studies.

Committee for Encouraging Corporate Philanthropy (www.corporatephilanthropy.org): an international forum of business executives focused on expanding corporate philanthropy. In addition to celebrating effective giving programs through conferences, awards and other awareness activities, the committee publishes numerous studies and case profiles that can be found on the web site. Most publications can be downloaded free of charge.

Corporate Responsibility Officer (www.thecro.com): a membership organization for executives involved in all aspects of corporate responsibility, including philanthropy. CRO publishes a magazine and reports on trends in corporate responsibility, as well as hosts conferences and web seminars. Many materials on the web site are available without paying the membership fee. The web site also hosts a job board.

Council for the Advancement and Support of Education (CASE) (www.case.org): the international association for professionals involved in fundraising for educational institutions, including independent schools and universities. CASE provides workshops and online resources focused on building relationships with alumni and students, as well as code of ethics that they ask educational institutions to adopt. CASE also outlines standards and best practices in fundraising for educational institutions.

Council on Foundations (www.cof.org): a membership organization of more than 2,000 foundations across the world that provides training, resources and networking opportunities for foundation officers and CEOs. Along with an annual conference, the Council of Foundations hosts workshops across the country for foundation executives. The web site offers a range of informational materials, as well as a career center. You need to be a member to access most resources.

Direct Marketing Association (www.the-dma.org): the primary association for all direct marketing professionals in both the for-profit and nonprofit sectors. DMA hosts classes, workshops and conferences, and maintains an extensive library or white papers, news articles and case studies on its web site.

Financial Planning (www.financial-planning.com): a site providing resources and continuing education credits for financial planners. There are a number of articles on career advancement, including a description of the skills and education that a successful donor advisor should have and an evaluation of various certification programs.

Visit Vault at **www.vault.com** for insider company profiles, expert advice, career message boards, expert resume reviews, the Vault Job Board and more.

V/\ULT CAREER LIBRARY   209

Foundation Center (www.fdncenter.org): comprehensive resource on foundation giving trends and grant-making. There are offices located throughout the country, as well as a web site. The Foundation Center offers several workshops and online courses on fundamentals of grant writing and developing project budgets. The center also maintains an extensive database that is considered one of the primary resources for information on individual grant makers.

The Grantsmanship Center (www.tcgi.com): resource for training and information for grant writers. In addition to offering workshops with established curriculum on grant writing and program planning all over the world, the center will also customize training for individual nonprofits. The center also publishes a magazine and a comprehensive guide for program planning and proposal development. In addition, they produce a CD-ROM of successfully funded proposals and maintain a database of information on federal and private grant giving. Membership is required to access all information on the web site.

Leave a Legacy (www.leavealegacy.org): public education campaign sponsored by the National Committee on Planned Giving aimed at providing more information to donors on planned giving options, primarily on how to establish bequests. The web site provides boilerplate language for bequests, as well as stories of donors.

National Center for Family Philanthropy (www.ncfp.org): a nonprofit organization focused on providing information to donor advisors and their families about philanthropic giving. The web site hosts an online reference library with articles and case studies describing family philanthropy.

National Committee on Planned Giving (www.ncpg.org): national association for fundraisers involved in planned giving that provides educational workshops and DVDs, hosts a national conference and manages a network of local councils for planned giving professionals. The committee also establishes and educates members on ethical practices in planned giving and serves as the primary liaison to Congress on policies and incentives to encourage and facilitate planned giving. The web site offers online tutorials on planned giving and houses an electronic library for members.

Opportunity Finance Network (www.opportunityfinance.net): A network of financing institutions engaged in providing capital for community development. The network hosts conferences and trainings on social financing, as well as provides information and statistics on various models for social financing. The web site also hosts a job bank.

Planned Giving Design Center (www.pgdc.com): an online resource primarily geared towards planned giving advisors with a treasure trove of articles on various aspects of planned giving and philanthropic giving more generally. Most articles are quite technical, describing the legal and tax ramifications of various planned giving tools.

Social Enterprise Alliance (www.se-alliance.org): a network of nonprofit organizations involved in projects that generate earned income. The alliance provides consulting services and tools for business planning. The web site's Knowledge Center lists numerous blogs, case studies, and other publications describing various aspects of social entrepreneurship.

Social Venture Network (www.svn.org): a nonprofit organization that promotes models of socially conscious businesses and social entrepreneurship. In addition to hosting an online library on tools and best practices, the web site profiles successful businesses and nonprofits engaged in venture philanthropy or that have adopted socially responsible practices.

Selected Bibliography

Books

Friedman, Lawrence J. and Mark D. McGarvie (Eds). (2003). Charity, Philanthropy, and Civility in American History. Cambridge: Cambridge University Press.

Ilchman, Warren F., Stanley N. Katz, and Edward L Queen II (Eds). (1998). Philanthropy in the World's Traditions. Bloomington: Indiana University Press.

Salamon, Lester M. (Ed). (2002). The State of Nonprofit America. Washington, DC: Brookings Institution Press.

Wason, Sara D. (2004). Webster's New World Grant Writing Handbook. Hoboken: Webster's New World.

Articles

Billitteri, Thomas J. "Donors Big and Small Propelled into Philanthropy in the 20th Century." The Chronicle of Philanthropy 13 January 2000. Gifts and Grants section <http://philanthropy.com/free/articles/ v12/i06/06002901 .htm>

Caumont, Andrea. "Giving Funds Provide Flexibility: Foundations, Circles Redefine Ways to Donate to Charity." Washington Post 6 November 2005. section F, p.7. <http://www.washingtonpost.com/wp-dyn/content /article/2005/11/05/AR2005110500289>

Visit Vault at **www.vault.com** for insider company profiles, expert advice, career message boards, expert resume reviews, the Vault Job Board and more.

VAULT CAREER LIBRARY   211

Hall, Jeremiah. "Too Many Way to Divide Donations?" The Christian Science Monitor 20 June 2005. Work and Money section. <http:/www.csmonitor.com/2005/0620/p13s01-wmgn.html>

Jones, Jeff. "Special Report: Nonprofit Times 2005 Salary Survey." The Nonprofit Times 1 February 2005. <http://nptimes/Feb05/sr1.html>

Mullins, Brody. "Government Steps Up Charity Crackdown." The Wall Street Journal 22 June 2005. section D, p. 1.

Salamon, Lester M. and S. Wojciech Sokolowski. (2005). "Nonprofit organizations: new insights from QCEW data." Monthly Labor Review, September 2005, p. 19-26.

Reports

Blackbaud. 2004 State of the Nonprofit Industry Survey. Charleston: Blackbaud, Inc., 2004.

Blackbaud. 2006 State of the Nonprofit Industry Survey. Charleston: Blackbaud, Inc., 2006.

The James Irvine Foundation, Public Policy Incorporated, Williams Group. Community Catalyst: How Community Foundations Are Acting as Agents for Local Change. San Francisco: The James Irvine Foundation, 2003.

Cutler, Ira. The Double Bottom Line: Lessons on Social Enterprise from Seedco's Nonprofit Venture Network 2001-2004. New York: Seedco, 2005.

Fulton, Katherine and Andrew Blau. Looking Out for the Future: An Orientation for 21st Century Philanthropists. Cambridge: Monitor Company Group, LLP, 2005.

Irons, John S. and Gary Bass. Recent Trends in Nonprofit Employment and Earnings: 1990-2004. Washington, DC: OMB Watch, 2004.

Lunder, Erika. Tax-Exempt Organizations: Political Activity Restrictions and Disclosure Requirements. Washington, DC: Congressional Research Service, 2006.

Matthews, Melange. Fellowships in Philanthropy. San Francisco: Ascent Associates, 2005.

McCormick, Kristen J. and Sarah M. Eisinger. Profiting from Purpose: Profiles of Successes and Challenges in Eight Social Purpose Businesses. New York: Seedco, 2005.

Visit Vault at **www.vault.com** for insider company profiles, expert advice, career message boards, expert resume reviews, the Vault Job Board and more.

VAULT CAREER LIBRARY   **212**

Renz, Lawrence and Steven Lawrence. <u>Foundation Growth and Giving Estimates: 2004</u> Preview. New York: The Foundation Center, 2005.

Tierney, Thomas J. <u>The Nonprofit Sector's Leadership Deficit.</u> Boston: The Bridgespan Group, 2006.

Internet sources

<u>Code of Ethics.</u> American Association of Grant Professionals. 2008. 21 February 2008. <http://go-aagp.org/AboutAAGP/Ethics/CodeofEthics/tabid/2573/Default.aspx>

<u>Brief History of Philanthropy in America.</u> Arizona Grantmakers Forum. 2008. 21 February 2008. <http://www.arizonagrantmakersforum.org/resources/HistoryPhilanthropy.aspx>

<u>Accountability – Building Value Together.</u> Independent Sector. 2003. 1 September 2006. <http://independentsector.org/issues/buildingvalue/opsupport.html>

<u>Consulting Fees For Grant Proposal Writing: An Exchange of Ideas and Information from TGCI-Forum.</u> The Grantmanship Center. 1998. 28 October 2005. <http://tgci.com/magazine/98winter/fees2.asp.

Visit Vault at **www.vault.com** for insider company profiles, expert advice, career message boards, expert resume reviews, the Vault Job Board and more.

V**A**ULT CAREER LIBRARY   **213**

About the Author

Anne M. McCaw is a seasoned fundraiser with more than 11 years experience building the capacity of nonprofit organizations of various shapes and sizes, from small arts agencies to national environmental groups. She has engaged in nearly every other aspect of fundraising, from coordinating annual appeals to obtaining corporate sponsorships for events to leading a team of grant writers that produced more than 100 proposals a year. She currently heads her own fundraising practice, One Bright Bird Consulting, LLC (www.onebrightbird.com), that provides guidance and support to help progressive nonprofit organizations in building smart and sustainable fundraising partnerships. Prior to becoming a consultant, she co-led the foundation relations team at The Wilderness Society, one of the oldest and most respected land protection organizations in the U.S., raising between $4 and $7 million annually from foundations and corporations.

Visit Vault at **www.vault.com** for insider company profiles, expert advice, career message boards, expert resume reviews, the Vault Job Board and more.

VAULT CAREER LIBRARY   215